GANDHIAN SARVODAYA:
REALIZING A REALISTIC UTOPIA

GANDHIAN SARVODAYA: REALIZING A REALISTIC UTOPIA

THOMAS VETTICKAL

National Gandhi Museum
Rajghat, New Delhi-110002

in association with

GYAN

GYAN PUBLISHING HOUSE
New Delhi-110002

GANDHIAN SARVODAYA: REALIZING A REALISTIC UTOPIA
[*Gandhian Philosophy, Political Economy*]

ISBN: 81-212-0798-3 (HB)

Published in 2015 *in India by*
National Gandhi Museum
Rajghat, New Delhi - 110002.
Phones: 011-3310168, 3311793, Fax: 3311793
e-mail: gandhimk@nda.vsnl.net.in
web-site: www.gandhimuseum.org
in association with
Gyan Publishing House
23 Ansari Road
New Delhi 110 002
Phones: 011-47034999,9811692060
e-mail: gyanbook@del2.vsnl.net.in
visit our website: http://www.gyanbooks.com

Laser Typeset at Alphabet, Delhi
Printed at Mehra Offset Printers, New Delhi.

To my mother, my father and to my good friends

who entered and enriched my life in some form and

who allowed me to enter into their lives in some way,

co-pilgrims to bringing liberation and harmony in the world,

co-travellers in dreaming sarvodaya:

total cosmic liberation.

Contents

Publisher's Note

This book is based on the Doctoral Thesis of Dr. Thomas Vettickal.

Mahatma Gandhi's concept of Sarvodaya ('Welfare of All') is expressed in numerous references spread over his Collected Works. Even more than his writings and speeches, it is in his life, his struggles against all forms of exploitation, racial, colonial, social and economic, that we get a true picture of the ideal human society which he envisioned and worked for nearly fifty three years of his public life.

One may, however, start with his paraphrase of John Ruskin's 'Unto This Last', which he named as 'Sarvodaya' in Gujarati. Thus, Gandhian Sarvodaya is founded on the assurance of meeting basic essential needs and freedoms, physical and moral, of the humblest individual ('Antyodaya'). At the time of India's independence, he had repeatedly warned that that was only political freedom, and economic, social and moral freedoms were yet to come; also that these would be much harder to achieve.

Even while fighting for India's freedom, Gandhiji had worked on so many economic and social fronts—his campaign for Khadi, his multi-point Constructive Programme particularly for rural upliftment, his untiring struggle for communal harmony, removal of untouchability and equality of women, and his campaigns for universal basic education, basic sanitation and hygiene, Swadeshi and Bread Labour and economic equality are well-known.

'Sarvodaya' was Gandhiji's ideal for human social order in which the individual was supreme but as a unit of the society. Sarvodaya envisages a non-violent, egalitarian, decentralised, people-oriented, sustainable and a flourishing social order.

Dr. Vettickal has drawn a faithful and comprehensive picture of the Gandhian Sarvodaya. He shows that it is inclusive, experimental, experiential, holistic, ever-evolving, and based on fundamental Gandhian premises of Truth & Non-violence (love). It is suffused with the spirit of optimism, participation and creativity. It includes Gandhi's 'Talisman' and his 'India of My Dreams', his Ramrajya or the Kingdom of God on Earth, and his Swaraj. It is a utopia in the sense that it is the eternal goal of human society; like the Euclidean definition of a straight line or a point, it is a realizable utopia since there is ever a scope for betterment.

The author discusses the nature of 'utopia' and certain well-known pre-Gandhian conceptions of utopia, and describes the theory and practice of Gandhian Sarvodaya, including the reasons for its being a 'realizable' utopia. He also refers to the post-Gandhian attempts, by Acharya Vinoba Bhave and Jayaprakash Narayan and Sarvodaya organisations, to realize specific aspects of Gandhian Sarvodaya. These efforts produced partial results. It is an ongoing process, a movement at various levels, which must continue.

The author carries the Gandhian concept still further on to the international plane, setting it up as a goal for the Liberation Theology which arose from Latin America, and for Ecology which is increasingly becoming an universal concern of humankind.

Finally, Gandhian Sarvodaya is not a mechanistic or deterministic manual but an ideal for humankind, for individual and social relationships and for human-ecological relationships in varied and changing circumstances. It enunciates principles and sets the direction, approaches and guidelines. Above all it encourages us to be ever hopeful for building up a better human being, a better society and a better world.

On behalf of National Gandhi Museum, New Delhi, I am grateful to Dr. Vettickal for having offered us the opportunity to publish the book and to Professor Joseph T. O'Connel, University of Toronto, for having written the Foreword. I do hope that the readers will welcome this addition to the serious literature on Gandhian thought.

August 1, 2002

Dr. Y.P. Anand
Director

National Gandhi Museum
Rajghat, New Delhi - 110002

Foreword

Gandhi the Mahatma was very much a realist: as lawyer, negotiator, organizer, politician. He was a realist in motion, a realist with conviction that things could be and should be made better than we find them. He was a 'great soul', a Mahatma, a soul striving to make things better than they are. As a realist impelled to motion by the greatness of the soul that he was, Gandhi knew the value of hope. He knew that we humans need vision, a goal, a conviction of possibility, if we are to break out of the depression and despair of the impoverished and the complacency of the well-to-do. That vision must show us that there really is an alternative, a better way for things to be. It must break the false claim to finality of the status quo—both for those who have and those have not.

That vision of a better way, or a 'good place' (i.e., a utopia), if it is to be effective, must be a vision of a special sort. It must be a vision of a good place : good, for one thing, in terms of the way of life such a place would foster. It should be good also in being so attractive or desirable that people will want to make it happen, will exert themselves and take risks to make it happen. It should be good in the sense of being feasible, as within reach, if only we would exert and extend ourselves to reach it.

Gandhi, we should notice, adds yet another stipulation for what constitutes a genuinely 'good place' or 'utopia', namely good moral means by which to get there. Hence his distinctive emphasis upon *ahimsa* (non-violence) and *satya* (truth), which he welded together in the concept and practice of *satyagraha* (holding fast to truth: in the sense of non-violent but active resistance to evil). The conceptual focus of Thomas Vettickal's book, 'Gandhian Sarvodaya: Realizing a Realistic Utopia', is not, however, directed toward *ahimsa* or *satyagraha* as such. Rather it is toward Gandhi's pervasive, though often enough implicit, strategy for realizing fundamental changes to the socio-economic and political status quo. This is a strategy of appealing to a reasonable and realistic vision of an alternative (and humanly superior) pattern of life: a pattern in which *sarvodaya* (uplift/welfare of all, especially of the poorest) would be the guiding principle. It is what Vettickal aptly calls a 'realistic utopian' strategy.

One great merit of Vettickal's book is precisely that it addresses head-on the issue of whether and in what sense it is accurate and constructive to understand Gandhi's way of striving for the welfare of all as utopian. It does so in part by analyzing just what it is about a realistic utopia that distinguishes it from a fantastic/illusionary utopia (an 'opiate'), and this is indeed crucial. Even more importantly, it argues strongly that it is just as crucial for there to be a vision of a utopia (provided it is realistic enough to be effective) if people are to summon up the hope, the imagination and the motivation to challenge and change an oppressive status quo.

Vettickal draws judiciously from Karl Mannheim and other interpreters of legitimation vs. critique of dominant interests and ideologies to construct a conceptual focus for his historical account of Gandhi's approach to the welfare of all (*sarvodaya*). He uses this combination of conceptual and historical knowledge to argue plausibly that any vision of utopia must be realistic (in a special sense) if it is to be effective. Too ambitious, too removed, too fanciful a utopian vision (if not simply ignored as irrelevant) becomes a mere fantasy, a distraction—in effect a reinforcement of the status quo. Unfortunately, the popular connotation of utopia tends to reinforce this sense of being unrealistic and unrealizable.

The 'special sense' of realistic alluded to above is the visionary face of the utopia. It is realistic, not in the sense of a photographic copy of the here and now, nor in the mechanical sense of a detailed blueprint, nor in any reductionist sense that would constrict the scope for imagination, spirit, faith, hope. It is realistic in a metaphoric sense, as an image or pattern that is close enough to reality as we know it to be recognizable, plausible and credible as an effective critique and potential alternative to the status quo. It hovers just far enough above or at the horizon of the here-and-now to free up our imagination, to stimulate our hope, to be flexibly applicable to all sorts of variations in the historical contexts in which it might be implemented.

It is good that Vettickal takes up that challenge head-on because there clearly is a visionary, a utopian, character to much of what Gandhi said and did in his constructive program and in his overall critique of prevailing economic and political structures. Some may shy away from Gandhi's critique and his advocacy of welfare for all (*sarvodaya*) precisely because they suspect that all imaginative visions of a utopia are but illusions that distract from the real issues. If, however, Vettickal's thoroughly researched and multifaced exposition of Gandhi's utopian vision of *sarvodaya* is as well-founded as it appears to be, such skeptics may find reasons to reassess the merits of Gandhian *sarvodaya*.

It is important, on the other hand, that those who would share Gandhi's realistic utopian commitment to the welfare of all appreciate that he was not supplying a rigid blueprint wedded to the historical conditions of the 1920s and 1930s. He was presenting flexible heuristic principles for designing a good place for humans to live: a simpler, more egalitarian place where the welfare of all would have priority. The task for those who would be guided by Gandhi's vision is to continually reapply its principles to the ever changing historical circumstances in which we live. As Vettickal shows us so clearly—and as the Mahatma himself was so eager to tell us—Gandhi was an inveterate experimenter, ever testing his principles and readjusting their application.

In sum, Thomas Vettickal invites us to reassess the enduring potential for Gandhi's distinctive way of realizing his utopian vision. His gracefully written, carefully articulated study embraces the history and content of Gandhi's utopian vision, theoretical analyses of utopian and ideological thought, applications of *sarvodaya* to 'people-oriented' economics and village life, post-Gandhian versions of *sarvodaya* as epitomized by Vinoba Bhave and Jayaprakash Narayan. It concludes with challenging proposals for imbuing liberation theology and ecology with the realistic utopian spirit and method of Gandhian *sarvodaya*.

'Gandhian Sarvodaya: Realizing a Realistic Utopia' is a serious and hopeful book. It expressess the experience of and aspirations of decades of Thomas Vettickal's involvement in and critical reflection upon the challenges of overcoming massive poverty and inequality. A great deal of careful reading and observation are distilled into an informative, interesting and gracefully written book. It is valuable for the issues it raises and for the conscientious and lucid way it deals with them. It is also valuable as a primer for those who would delve further into the theoretical and practical implications of realizing or making effective any realistic utopian vision of fundamental social, economic and political change. It was a pleasure and an inspiration to be associated with Thomas Vettickal during his doctoral studies in the University of Toronto. I am confident that others will derive pleasure and inspiration—and much food for thought—from his book.

Joseph T. O'Connell

Professor Emeritus in the Study of Religion
Saint Michael's College in the University of Toronto
Canada

Preface

Life as an on-going journey to freedom is liberation from all that make us less human to what make us fully human. Gandhi's sarvodaya world view—vision, ideal—functions as a sign post, on this journey, journey of self-liberation and of freeing others to authentic existence. Every human being, for that matter every reality, participates in this process in some form. This book is the outcome of my in-depth search into Gandhi's struggle, dream, utopia to make cosmic liberation a living reality: realized and yet to be realized.

I am indebted to a number of people for the completion of this study. I like to place on record the gratitude and appreciation I owe to my mentor and friend, Professor Joseph T. O'Connell of the University of Toronto who with great efficiency, insight and kindness has encouraged and directed me through the entire course of this work. I thank him specially for writing the Foreword to my book.

With gratitude I remember all my professors at the Center for the Study of Religion, University of Toronto, especially Profs. John H. Simpson, Douglas Campbell, Roger O'Toole for their encouragement, critical comments and helpful discussions.

During my visits and research at various Gandhian centers in India, I was greatly assisted in many ways. I like to acknowledge the insights shared and hospitality offered by Radhakrishna Menon at Navodya Danagram, Puthukode, Kerala, Fr. Jesudasan at Gansoville, Tamil Nadu, Devendra Kumar at Center of Science for Villages, Wardha, B. Pandey at Samanvay Ashram, Bodhgaya and Devendra Kumar at Gandhigram, Dindigul, Tamil Nadu.

I extend my gratitude to Missionswissenchftiches Institute Missio (Institute of Missiology, Missio) for awarding me scholarship and to the Fellowship and Loans Office, School of Graduate Studies, University of Toronto, for the Travel Grant Fund allotted to me.

My thanks are due to my many friends in Canada and India whose generosity, encouragement and friendship were a source of continuous support throughout this undertaking.

I am thankful to National Gandhi Museum for its editorial assistance and publication.

March 2002 **Thomas Vettickal**

Note on Transliteration and Spelling of non-English Words

Non-English words are italicized in the text with the exception of those which have passed into English usage — as given in *Webster's Ninth New Collegiate Dictionary*—such as ahimsa, satyagraha, or those which are repeatedly used because they were part of Gandhi's own peculiar language (e.g., sarvodaya). The transliterations (without diacritics) found in the text are according to frequently used renderings, not necessarily according to formal linguistic criteria. Transliterated spellings found in quoted material are retained as written.

Proper names, especially of persons and institutions, are given (without diacritics) according to the Roman spelling commonly used for the person or institution concerned. Other Hindi words (or Malayalam proper names in bibliography) are transliterated.

A glossary — explaining the meaning of the non-English words used in the text — is also given.

Introduction

Sarvodaya as an ideal, a vision and a movement is Gandhian in its origin; dynamic in outlook it is solidly based on a philosophy of praxis that demands the commitment of its follower to the care and the uplift of humanity, especially of the last and the least in any society. Gandhi's dream of sarvodaya society is an ideal or vision towards which he worked and expected a continuity till it is realized. Strictly speaking, sarvodaya cannot be seen in isolation from other views of Gandhi. Its significance becomes all the more clear when it is viewed in the whole spectrum of Gandhi's vision. Though Gandhi's immediate concern as he made his entry into India's mainstream of life was the independence of India from foreign domination, his final goal was way beyond the "freedom at midnight". His dream was sarvodaya — the rising of all — welfare of each and every human being, total liberation of all from all that make one not fully human.

The dynamics of sarvodaya entail a process that begins with the least and the last in the society and moves on into the dawn of a *Moksha* on earth or *Ramrajya* or the kingdom (rule) of God. This dynamic nature of sarvodaya essentially projects a vision for the future and opens up a vast spectrum of potentials. From a historical perspective, sarvodaya has a humble beginning in Gandhi. Gandhi initiated a momentum that is heading towards its fulfilment. It was humanly impossible for Gandhi to design the details of a future sarvodaya society; neither was he able to see the full flowering of a sarvodaya society in his life time. Gandhi has sown the seeds of a revolution that is on-going. The guidelines he suggested and the means he proposed towards establishing ideal sarvodaya society have stood the test of history and offer great potential for the future. Sarvodaya vision of Gandhi leaves the door of future possibilities open.

Viewed from the entirety of Gandhi's ideology, praxis and philosophy of life, sarvodaya may be considered the goal he envisioned for humanity in general and for India in particular. The real unfolding of the sarvodaya ideal takes place in the period following the attainment of freedom as a principle of reorganizing and changing the institutions of society, determining the modes and priorities of development and creating conditions of well-being for all sections of society and all parts of the country.

This book is an attempt to explore the areas of new possibilities sarvodaya offers for the well-being and harmony of humanity and the universe. The scope of sarvodaya appears infinite because of the sublime vision Gandhi projected through it. Gandhi was a man of lofty ideals and high visions. He never lost sight of his goal for India and tirelessly worked towards attaining the same. It was not a short-range project but a life-long effort for India and for all Indians. He may not have achieved all that he wanted to achieve for India in his lifetime because his visions were larger than life and they could never be achieved within a short life-span. Maybe they will never be realized in their entirety, but then that is the nature of any vision. It has to remain as an ideal and hence it has an "already and not yet" character which transcends the present reality and leads one into the eternity of possibilities. Gandhi was ever willing to admit this future orientedness or eternal possibilities of his vision. In fact, as he was experimenting with truth all his life, he would be the first to admit the limits to realizability of any vision.

As a preamble, the first chapter studies sarvodaya of Gandhi from a historical perspective, namely an ongoing process. Sarvodaya cannot be seen in isolation from other views of Gandhi. The thrust here is to understand sarvodaya as a movement which is Gandhian in its origin, which is solidly based on a philosophy that demands the commitment of its follower to the care and the uplift of humanity, especially of the last and the least in any society. Gandhi's dream of sarvodaya society is an ideal or vision towards which he worked and expected a continuity till it is realized. Did he ever achieve any considerable realisation of his dream in his life time? His greatest achievement probably is that even today many think that sarvodaya society can still be realized and that many work towards a liberated society. Gandhi's concern was to find a way in which all persons can live together as full human beings, in mutual acceptance and respect, orienting the economic, political, social, cultural and other activities to the benefit of as many members of society as possible. Gandhi's life, in fact, is an excellent illustration of the theory-praxis relationship, of an ideal and its realization, a vision and its actualization. His own leadership and participation in the struggles of his countrymen were guided by one motive: removal of the evils in the society and striving for the emergence of a new society. He called it by a familiar name *Ramrajya*, the society or nation governed by Lord Rama (the kingdom of Rama, the ideal monarch, an incarnation of Vishnu, during whose reign the people enjoyed all-round prosperity). Gandhi in his own way envisioned his programme for establishing a sarvodaya society, which was basically service to humanity. Thus action for social justice and participation in national struggle for political, economic, cultural and religious freedom becomes a new kind of *sadhana* (spiritual discipline). The strategy invented and employed by Gandhi to bring about awakening among the masses, to organise them and to lead them, was what is known as the Constructive Programme. Sarvodaya, as envisioned by Gandhi's liberation of the whole human being and of the society as a whole, has socio-economical, religio-cultural, and political aspects to it.

Chapter 2 will analyze and assess sarvodaya as an utopian model for stimulating and guiding socio-historical change. For this, we will scan rapidly through the history of utopian thought in the West and review some of the theoretical conceptions of utopia and select from this historical and theoretical review a few pertinent principles that are crucial to understanding utopia as a model for stimulating socio-historical change. We will then demonstrate in brief how these principles may apply to Gandhi's sarvodaya. This chapter will, thus, serve as a theoretical base for proposing (suggesting) Gandhi's sarvodaya as utopian model for socio-historical change.

Just as non-violence was the basis of Gandhi's social order as well as his economic order, the problem of poverty that confronted India during British Raj was the immediate background of his economic thought. Primarily, therefore, Gandhian economics was an engaged response rather than academic analysis (even the language is of the market place which common man uses and understands). In his "meta-economics" Gandhi did soul-searching and came out with the insight of "people-oriented economy" ("economics as if people mattered", in the words of E.F. Schumacher) as opposed to money-, machine- or competition-oriented economy. Social wealth consisted in men and women, Gandhi contended, and not in gold and silver, and that human element was the prime factor in economic efficiency. Some critics of Gandhi's economics argue that he was totally opposed to the use of machine and technology and that he considered industrialization as a curse; and others point out that Gandhi's idea of more or less self-sufficient village economy was unrealistic in the sense that no such local self-sufficiency was possible any more in a world of monetary and globally interpenetrating economy, nor was there ever one at any point in history anywhere. It has also been said that Gandhi's economic order was based on the assumption of minimal standards of life and living of people, which ran counter to human nature itself. Nonetheless, Gandhi's philosophy of economics and his methods have become relevant and urgent. Chapter 3 will present the challenge Gandhi's economics offers to India and to the world and its application for our times and for the future.

In the sarvodaya social order that Gandhi envisaged, village undoubtedly occupied the central attention. He strongly believed that, "if India is to attain freedom and through India the world also... the fact has to be recognised that the people have to live in the village, not in towns, in huts and not in palaces."[1] Gandhi's "village mindedness" and "ashramic life" were closely linked as his experiments with village-ashram life were the locus of his praxis. Thus for Gandhi ashram life was an opportunity to rejuvenate the spirit and cleanse the soul through self-reliance, constructive work and a simple life in harmony with nature. Ashram being the centre of action (service and experiment), village work is just an extension of ashram life. Gandhi was not very satisfied with the success of ashram experiments in general, though he strongly believed that village reconstruction and reorganization are the beginning of all changes in the society. In spite of the apparent failures to achieve the goal in its entirety, ashram experiments continue to flourish in India, where Gandhian vision of a liberated society is pursued in one way or other. The chapter on "Ashram to Village: an Experiment in Realization" deals with Gandhi's experiments with ashrams and villages and speculates on the scope of such a model for India.

After Gandhi's death, it fell upon his protege, Vinoba Bhave to provide leadership within the Gandhian circle. With him sarvodaya began to be identified as a movement to push forward Gandhian programmes of social, political and economic reconstruction through, for instance, his *Bhoodan-Gramdan* movement. The village was finally getting the attention that Gandhi wanted to give it, through *Bhoodan-Gramdan*, and sarvodaya was succeeding and the people of India were responding to Vinoba. But eventually (from 1969 onward) the *Bhoodan-Gramdan* movement began to lose its momentum. Vinoba's retreat to his ashram started a new chapter in the development of the sarvodaya movement with Jayaprakash Narayan (JP). The Total Revolution JP called for, he thought, was in line with Gandhian holistic vision and in keeping with the sarvodaya ideals, and it caught the imagination of many sarvodaya leaders as well as the public. By total revolution, JP meant the work of sarvodaya had to be launched on all levels and on all fronts. It is true that sarvodaya movement has been faced with many crises since its beginning and that Gandhian values have been neglected. But the far reaching vision of Gandhi continues to inspire the Gandhians to work without losing hope for a sarvodaya society. Sarvodaya after the death of Gandhi is summarised in chapter five.

Two promising areas of current issues where sarvodaya vision of Gandhi inspires scholars and activists a great deal are suggested in the final chapter. Sarvodaya viewed as a process of liberation from any inhuman situation of oppression has close links with theology of liberation. Gandhi gives us a theology as well as a methodology of liberation which is universal in its scope and meaning and can be applied to the theory and practice of the liberation theology movement. As a man who incarnates the anguish and hope of those who are struggling for national liberation and development in the Third World, Gandhi provides us with a good model for theologizing in the Indian context today.

Sarvodaya implies an all-round — material as well as spiritual — development of each and every individual. But sarvodaya (*sarva*=all; *udaya*=rising) cannot stop at the mere welfare of human beings. Environmental insights can be seen hidden in Gandhi's ideal and life style which make him an environmentalist and human ecologist. He stood for a life-affirming ecology. Gandhi's life, life philosophy, and praxis continue to inspire and guide many who are committed to sustainable development, balanced eco-system, and harmonious living.

The realizability of the Gandhian ideal is problematic to many. And they think Gandhi is too idealistic and therefore impractical; that therefore he has little or nothing to offer for India or for the world of today. From an analysis of sarvodaya — an ideal and a movement — I argue that it has immense potential to establishing a liberated society, i.e., sarvodaya society. Gandhian vision, the sarvodaya ideal especially, which I think is Gandhian utopia, is an ongoing dream realised and yet to be realised with immense possibilities of actualization in the India of today.

Reference

1. Pyarelal, *Towards New Horizons* (Ahmedabad:Navajivan Publishing House, 1959), 4.

One

Mission of Total Liberation: Gandhi's Sarvodaya Vision

Sarvodaya as a vision and movement is Gandhi's in its origin; dynamic in outlook, it is solidly based on a philosophy of praxis that demands the commitment of its follower to the care and the uplift of humanity, especially of the last and the least in any society. Gandhi's dream of sarvodaya society is an ideal or vision towards which he worked and for which he expected a continuity of commitment till it is realized. Total openness to the realizability of the possibilities and ideals of his vision makes Gandhi a prophet of our time; Gandhi's readiness to experiment with "truth" (i.e., reality taken in a comprehensive sense: God, philosophy of life and worldview)[1] makes him an experimental scientist of a special sort: a Prisoner of Hope (Brown 1989), as Gandhi envisions a future society. Though Gandhi's immediate concern, as he made his entry into the mainstream of Indian public life, was the independence of India from foreign domination, his final goal was beyond the "Freedom at Midnight". His dream was sarvodaya — the rising of all — welfare of each and every human being, liberation from all that make one not fully human. Strictly speaking, sarvodaya cannot be seen in isolation from other views of Gandhi; rather its significance becomes all the more clear when it is viewed in the whole spectrum of Gandhi's vision, his world-view.

World View

The dynamics of sarvodaya are deeply rooted in the worldview of Gandhi, within which he thought and acted and from the perspective of which he viewed other realities, and which gave him the inner direction for his search for and experiments with truth. It has been suggested that Gandhi can be captured in three words: satyagraha, sarvodaya and *anasakti* (Tandon 1965:1). His life and work reveal that he made sarvodaya his life's goal, satyagraha a means, and *anasakti* a method of training in self-discipline to gain power. Behind sarvodaya was his concern with justice and ethical behaviour based on a theological assumption that all men and women are created equal. Gandhi's struggle in South Africa and subsequently in India was basically a concern for justice; he "wanted to move towards a 'just civilization', a just society."(Bakker 1993:7) However, in Gandhi we find an expanded notion of justice. It is not to be demanded by force, but reached through self-suffering in pursuit of truth. As society evolves toward a higher plane, the oppressed and the oppressors both participate in the creation of a just social order. The just social order cannot be sustained without a just economic and political order, and a just religious order. Consequently, Gandhi's vision embraced a holistic approach to life. In order to bring about this utopian ideal, he formulated varieties of "constructive programmes."[2] The goal of sarvodaya became *Ramrajya* (Kingdom of God). This kingdom was to be attained on earth and had to be created and nurtured with sarvodaya beliefs and practices. As he put it, he wanted to create equality among all people in order that they may be held together in the "silken net of love." Though he did not claim its discovery, he sought ways to make it a living reality. He wanted to make sarvodaya a way of life for all humanity as it was for him.

Sarvodaya occupies the central place in Gandhi's worldview or philosophy of life. The dynamics of sarvodaya assumes a process that begins with the last and the least in the society and moves on toward the dawn of a *moksha* on earth or *Ramrajya*. This dynamic nature of sarvodaya essentially projects a vision for the future and opens up a vast spectrum of potentials. Gandhi initiated a momentum toward an ideal sarvodaya society. It was humanly impossible for Gandhi to design the details of a future sarvodaya society; neither was he able to see the full flowering of sarvodaya society in his lifetime. He has sown the seeds of a revolution that is on-going. Though the guidelines he suggested and the means he proposed toward establishing ideal sarvodaya society have a checkered history, the sarvodaya ideal keeps its appeal afresh to many by its degree of realizability and its openness to future possibilities. Thus, viewed in the context of Gandhi's world-view, sarvodaya may be considered the goal he envisioned for humanity in general and for India in particular. The real unfolding of the sarvodaya ideal takes place in the period following the attainment of independence of India. It then becomes a principle of reorganizing and changing the institutions of society, determining the modes and priorities of development and creating conditions of well-being for all sections of society and all parts of the country.

Through sarvodaya, Gandhi attempted to recapture the spiritual heritage of India, which had thrived in the villages, and used it to build the nation. He criticized Western civilization, not because it was totally corrupt, but because it was contrary to the needs of India. In Western values he saw a craze for comfort, multiplication of wants, and self-indulgence, which could lead to greed, conflict, suppression of the weak by the strong, and social disparity. Swaraj for him was not mere independence from Britain, but an independence from everything that is oppressive in the society. Gandhi was convinced that decentralization of power is the key to just and equitable society. He developed the concept of satyagraha, which involved a search for truth, nonviolence, and self-suffering. With his satyagraha, he not only challenged the conventional notion of power, but showed that the weaker section of society was as powerful in crucial respects as the strong. Gandhi had a concrete agenda for implementing decentralization of power. On a political level, it meant taking power from the centre and bringing it to the village. On an economic level, decentralization of power meant discouraging big industries and encouraging village cottage industry. "Small is beautiful" (Schumacher 1973) thus would become the economic slogan. On a social level, the Harijans, tribals, and members of the lower castes would be given all the rights of equality.

Being a man of lofty ideals and high visions, Gandhi offered a vision through sarvodaya that is open-ended and not limited to space and time. He never lost sight of his goal for India and tirelessly worked towards attaining the same. It surely was not a short-range project but a life-long effort for India and for all Indians. He may not have achieved all that he wanted to achieve for India in his lifetime because his visions were larger than life and they could never be achieved within a short life-span. Maybe they will never be realized in their entirety, but that is the nature of any vision. It has to remain as an ideal, but an ideal that can modify the here and now. It has an "already and not yet" character which transcends while influencing the present reality and leads one into ever new possibilities. Gandhi was willing to admit this future-orientedness of his vision. As he was experimenting with truth all his life, he would be the first to admit the gradual realizability of any vision. Being fully aware of the fact that "... the ideal is never fully realized in life", he stood for the apparently impossible, with great hope that the impossible can become possible.

The questions asked and the issues discussed in this book may be posed here at the beginning. How did Gandhi construct his ideal of sarvodaya over time and how did he modify it to meet changing circumstances? In what precise sense does Gandhi's ideal of sarvodaya vision become utopia? How does the sarvodaya vision of Gandhi envisage and help to inaugurate a new Indian society? How effective has Gandhi's utopia for India been in his time and after? Has the utopian ideal of sarvodaya potential for realization beyond India?

The Origin

Sarvodaya owes its origin to Gandhi. The concept sarvodaya was first used by Gandhi to express an idea which he found very captivating in Ruskin's *Unto This Last*. In order to understand the full meaning and implications of sarvodaya, one has to situate it in the broader perspective of Gandhi's thinking. Gandhi never attempted to build a systematic thought pattern or sat down to write a whole book containing a systematic exposition of his ideas. Instead, he wrote in bits and pieces, usually for the journals put out by his organizations. He never hesitated to admit inconsistencies in his thinking and writings.[3] There is, however, close relationship among his ideas and thus it is possible to construct a fairly coherent and systematic account of his philosophical view. This is true of his sarvodaya in particular.

Sarvodaya is closely related to other issues of Gandhi's thinking. His speeches and writings are integral parts of a composite and consistent whole sarvodaya social order. Strictly speaking, sarvodaya cannot be seen in isolation from other views of Gandhi, but an attempt is made in this chapter to isolate sarvodaya of Gandhi in order to see its significance in the whole spectrum of Gandhi's vision. His vision of a new social order is closely linked to a just economic and political and a just religious order. Gandhi's vision thus embraced a holistic approach to life. In order to bring this utopian ideal, he formulated various "constructive programmes." For Gandhi, sarvodaya was a concrete manifestation of many spiritual ideas found in many religious traditions.[4] The entire vision of Gandhi is derived from the principle of spiritual unity. As he put it,

> I do not believe that spiritual law works on a field of its own. On the contrary, it expresses itself only through the ordinary activities of life. It thus affects the economic, the social and the political fields.[5]

Gandhi did not claim its discovery, but sought ways to make it a living reality. He wanted to make sarvodaya a way of life for all humanity as it was for him.

Like many other great concepts, the evolving and expanding concept of sarvodaya had a small and humble beginning. Gandhi seems to have borrowed the concept sarvodaya from a Jain scripture written by Acarya Samantabhadra who lived about two thousand years ago. The Acarya, while praising the godly spiritual leader of Jains observed: "*sarvapadam antakaram nirantam sarvodayam tithamidam tavaiva*" ("Your's are the sacred waters of the *well-being of all* that end the miseries for all times").[6] It was merely by chance that Gandhi's friend Polak gave him a small book, *Unto This Last,* by Ruskin while Gandhi was on a railway journey in South Africa in 1904. He was deeply impressed by the book. In Gandhi's words:

> The book was impossible to lay aside, once I had begun it. It gripped me...I determined to change my life in accordance with the ideals of the book...I believe that I discovered some of my deepest convictions reflected in this great book of Ruskin, and that is why it so captured me and made me transform my life (*Autobiography*, 249-50).

He was so impressed by the book that he paraphrased the book into Gujarati and entitled it *Sarvodaya* (the welfare of all). Gandhi understood the teaching of *Unto This Last* to be:

1. That the good of the individual is contained in the good of all.
2. That the lawyer's work has the same value as the barber's, in as much as all have the same right of earning their livelihood from their work.
3. That a life of labour, i.e., the life of tiller of the soil and the handicraftsman, is the life worth living. The first of these I knew. The second I had dimly realized. The third had never occurred to me. *Unto This Last* made it as clear as daylight for me that the second and the third were contained in the first. I rose with the dawn, ready to reduce these principles to practice (*Autobiography*, 250).

What is presented by Gandhi under the title *Sarvodaya* is the substance of Ruskin's book. The "Preface" to *Sarvodaya* gives the rationale behind Gandhi's paraphrasing of *Unto This Last*:

> In order that Indians may profit by his ideas, we have decided to present extracts from his book, in a manner intelligible to Indians who do not know English...The summary of his work which we offer here is not really a translation. If we translated it, the common reader might be unable to follow some of the Biblical allusions, etc... We do not even explain what the title of the book means, for it can be understood only by a person who has read the Bible in English. But since the object which the book work towards is the welfare of all—that is, the advancement of all and not merely of the greatest number—we entitled these articles "Sarvodaya" (CW 8: 240-41).

The appropriate rendering of *Unto This Last* would be *antyodaya* (uplift of the last and the least)[7] rather than sarvodaya (uplift of all). The term *antyodaya* does not appear to have been used by Gandhi,[8] the reason being that sarvodaya implies *antyodaya* and that sarvodaya is more comprehensive. Sarvodaya would very much begin by giving priority to the welfare and emancipation of the lowest of the low and the poorest of the poor. It is sometimes averred that *antyodaya* is the very soul of sarvodaya (*Gandhi Marg*

1985: 201). Just as in a human family, the youngest and the most helpless child commands prior attention, so, too, sarvodaya gives priority of service to the most deprived in the society. Thus, since the last one's uplift or welfare is included in that of all, and also because Gandhi envisaged an integrated universal development of all — the rich and the poor, the strong and the weak, the haves and the have nots — a holistic human approach, he preferred to use sarvodaya rather than *antyodaya*.

Gandhi borrowed the idea as well as the term from Ruskin, and Ruskin borrowed this idea from the Bible. Well aware of the prevailing degradation among the workmen and the ever increasing mechanization of the day, John Ruskin advocated the welfare of all human beings, the good of all, in his book, *Unto This Last*. The very title of the book is biblical in the sense that he has borrowed the term from the parable of the labourers in the vineyard (St. Matthew 22:14). On the basis of the study of the Bible, Ruskin preached three cardinal truths: first, the universality of objects; second the freedom of the individuals; and third the rendering of dignity to the individuality of the poor. In so far as Gandhi admits that Ruskin's book was one of the main sources of inspiration in the formation of sarvodaya, sarvodaya implies biblical origin.

Ruskin was critical of the treatment of economics as the science of wealth because it omitted all religious, cultural, human and moral considerations. As K.M. Prasad observes, "Ruskin's book crystallized his amorphous conceptions of the economic and ethical foundations of Sarvodaya social order" (Prasad, K.M., 1971:3). Gandhi believed, like Ruskin, that the socio-economic organization that ensures the well-being of all is the only one worth striving for. Besides the fundamental principle of *Unto This Last*, that "the good of the individual is contained in the good of all," Gandhi also understood its teaching to be that all labour, manual or intellectual, is of equal value in so far as all persons have the same right of earning their livelihood from their work.

No doubt, for Gandhi, Ruskin's book was one of the main sources of inspiration for the formation of sarvodaya; even so, Gandhi disagreed with Ruskin on several issues. Ruskin did not believe in the possibility of equality between people; he hoped to overcome inequality by an appeal to the conscience of the upper classes. But Gandhi's idea of society was based on a theory of thorough equality. Gandhi derived his ethico-economic theory of trusteeship and inheritance from a deep feeling of spirituality and divinity of the human being expressed in the maxim "*jiva* is always *shiva*": a man is, by and large, divine (Biswas 1969: 185). He considered economic equality the "master-key" to nonviolent independence. Gandhi did not share Ruskin's authoritarian and aristocratic views that refused to give any political control to the masses on grounds of incompetence. Sarvodaya democracy of Gandhi had to be worked out from below by the people of every village and not by few people sitting at the top of the apex. However, Gandhi accepted Ruskin's critique of the dehumanizing effects of modern economic and highly industrial systems. Moreover, Ruskin's principles of the dignity of manual labour, simplicity of life, workers' ownership of the means of production and ownership of property within limits, his belief in the supremacy of moral and spiritual life over intelligence, in the goodness of human nature and in the moral basis of politics and economics were shared by Gandhi.

Other Influences

Ruskin's book may have sparked and given form to the ideas of sarvodaya, but Gandhi admits his debt to certain other sources, like the Gospels (especially The Sermon on the Mount), Tolstoy and Thoreau,[9] besides the traditional Indian influences on his thought. Jain influences were a major factor in his early years. Seen from the viewpoint of his hereditary position in society, Gandhi was a Kathiawadi Hindu of the Modh Bania sub-caste. Seen from the viewpoint of sectarian traditions, he was a Vaishnava, raised in the Vallabhacharya tradition dominant among Hindu Banias (businessmen) in nineteenth century Gujarat. But non-Hindu influences also shaped his mental and spiritual development. Gandhi's mother, for instance, who exercised the greatest influence on his religious development, was herself raised in the Pranami sect, noted for its broad mindedness toward Islamic ideas and social contacts with Muslims. In high school Gandhi's strict headmaster was a Zoroastrian and then as a young barrister in South Africa, he was much impressed with Christian friends and their ideas. Gandhi obviously drew a lot of inspiration from Jainism: the ideas and the living examples of the members of the Jain faith especially of Jaina monks. Gandhi recollected in his *Autobiography* thus:

> Jain monks also would pay frequent visits to my father, and would even go out of their way to accept food from us- non-jains. They would have talks with my father on subjects religious and mundane (*Autobiography*, 28).

Gandhi's liking for the Jain doctrine of *anekantavada* (many-sidedness of reality)[10], his acceptance of the Jain ideal of *moksha* as the complete self-sufficiency of the soul (*svatantrata*) through its detachment from all passion and ignorance, and his ideals of *brahmacharya* (chastity), ahimsa and satyagraha seem to have their roots in Jainism. For Gandhi the problem of Jainism as distinct from, or an alternative to, Hinduism simply did not exist. "I do not regard Jainism or Buddhism as separate from Hinduism", Gandhi observed in 1927 (*Young India*, October 1927).

Besides Jainism, Gandhi's thought owes much to the scriptures of Hinduism, Islam, Christianity and Buddhism. His acquaintance with world religions in England and South Africa strengthened in him the consciousness of the spiritual aspect of the well-being of human being. Gandhi understood the central message of the *Gita* to be *nishkama karma* (action without desiring the fruits of action) as the way to self-realization. The *Gita* was his favourite text and his "spiritual dictionary". Gandhi wrote,

> the book struck me as one of priceless worth, and I regard it today as the book par excellence for the knowledge of truth (*Autobiography*, 57).

He recognized in the *Gita* a "grammar of action" (Erikson 1970: 162). The service of all created beings is the service of the gods, and the same is sacrifice. As Gandhi wrote in another connection,

> *Yajna* means an act directed to the welfare of others... others embraces not only humanity but all life. This body, therefore, has been given to us only in order that we may serve all creation with it" (CW 44: 241-42).

Thus service to the whole world and the entire creation is the message Gandhi took from the *Gita*.

Gandhi's first acquaintance with the New Testament was of great influence to him while he was still a student in England. "The Sermon on the Mount" left an indelible impression on his mind. Gandhi's detachment from worldly possession, non-violence and universal love owe much to the influence of the New Testament. He acknowledged his indebtedness to the Bible in the following words:

> Though I cannot claim to be a Christian in the sectarian sense, the example of Jesus' suffering is a factor in the composition of my undying faith in non-violence which rules all my actions worldly and temporal (*Harijan* 1939: 417).

According to Raghavan Iyer, "no Hindu since Ram Mohan Roy was as eager as Gandhi to respond to the Koran" (Iyer 1973: 20). For Gandhi, the point of brotherhood is manifested in no other religion as clearly as in Islam. He was impressed by the bravery and austere living of the Prophet. "My reading of Koran", Gandhi wrote, "has convinced me that the basis of Islam is not violence". Gandhi regarded Christianity, Buddhism, Islam and Hinduism as religions of peace. He practised the essential principles of world religions in his daily life and showed the path of humanity at large. Though Gandhi called himself a *Sanatana* Hindu (*Young India* October 1939), his neo-Hinduism includes a synthetic unity of other world religions. He wrote, "my Hinduism is not sectarian. It includes all that I know to be best in Islam, Christianity, Buddhism and Zoroastrianism". He further said: "My young mind tried to unify the teachings of *Gita, the Light of Asia* and Sermon on the Mount...I read the chapter on the Hero as a prophet (Mohammed) and learnt of the prophet's greatness and bravery and austere living" (*Harijan* April and November 1938).

Gandhi's life was greatly influenced by his contacts with Leo Tolstoy, especially through reading Tolstoy's *The Kingdom of God is within You*. Tolstoy accepted love to be the law of life. Besides being impressed by Tolstoy's simplicity of life, his ideas of love, peace and equality, Gandhi shared with Tolstoy the vision of a new social order. Tolstoy's philosophical anarchism inspired Gandhi very much. Tolstoy denounced the state and private property because both are inconsistent with the supreme principle of love. The ideal social order envisaged by Tolstoy and Gandhi is one in which there would be no state, no private property, no police, no military, no law courts and no organized religion. The pure ideal of Gandhi is an ideal of philosophical anarchism, a stateless, classless society marked by voluntary cooperation. Yet, "Gandhi is not a thoroughgoing Tolstoyan", remarks T. S. Devadoss. (Devadoss 1974: 71). He was far more practical than Tolstoy. Gandhi championed all his life the freedom of his country and moral uplift, whereas Tolstoy in his later life became more or less "a recluse far removed from the social and political struggles of his country". The observation made by Ernest J. Simmons is significant in this context:

> Though Tolstoy's beliefs, derived primarily from the teachings of Christianity, have so often been dismissed as of no consequence precisely by the Christian West, they are much alive in the non-Christian East, especially in India, where the mass movement of Sarvodaya aims at the creation of a social order based on the Tolstoyan principle of love inspired by non resistance or non-violence (Devadoss 1974: 72).

Tolstoy used the expression "bread labour" for physical labour. Here labour has been taken in two senses: mental and physical. Gandhi made "no distinction between intellectual labour and physical labour". He acknowledged, "obedience to law of Bread Labour will bring about a silent revolution in the structure of society".

Gandhi read Thoreau's "Civil Disobedience", in South Africa; he found in it ample support for his convictions. Though Gandhi was profoundly impressed by Thoreau's essay in civil disobedience, he did not read it until he was himself jailed for that offence (Brown 1989: 55, 80). Thoreau was of the view that the immoral institution of the state supported by coercive authority hampered the individual's moral and spiritual freedom. He, therefore, visualized a society in which government will disappear. Gandhi often quoted Thoreau, who said "(T) that the best government was the one which governed least" (Thoreau 1968: 385; see also Brown 1989: 298). Like Thoreau, Gandhi held the view that democracy can be realized only in a stateless society. Any individual can have full liberties and enjoy utmost freedom in such a society. Such a society can be organized on the basis of truth, love and nonviolence.

From the above brief expose, it is evident that Gandhi was greatly influenced by the Indian cultural heritage, religious scriptures, leaders of religions and authors like Ruskin, Tolstoy and Thoreau, in the formation of his vision, specifically the sarvodaya ideal and action programme.[11] We shall now move on to sarvodaya ideal as such.

Ideal Society

The ideal of sarvodaya is implied in the word itself: *sarva* and *udaya*. *Sarva* means "all" and *udaya* means "uplift". The key to this uplift, for Gandhi, is dedicated service to humanity. As he says: "I claim to be a humble servant of India and humanity and would like to die in the discharge of such service..."(*Harijan* February 1946). When Gandhi used the word sarvodaya, it was completely his own and he was clear in his mind about the meaning of the term and the ideal. As T. S. Devadoss observes,

> the word Sarvodaya epitomises his (Gandhi's) whole social philosophy, which aims at the attainment of mental prosperity (*Abhyudaya*) and spiritual realization (*Nishreyasa*) (Devadoss 1974: 115).

Early in his life and career, Gandhi coined this new term, sarvodaya, in order to articulate his vision of Indian society and the way he wanted to transform it in accordance with his vision and imagination. Though sarvodaya called forth a series of other terms (such as swaraj, Ramrajya, ahimsa, satyagraha, and similar other terms), all suggesting a total reconstruction and transformation of Indian society, "the over-all and all-comprehensive term for all other terms and concepts was sarvodaya" (Biswas ed. 1969: 4; see also Diwakar June 1986:173-76). Sarvodaya had indeed been the very basic idea of the Gandhian way of life even from the days he wrote *Hind Swaraj*, long before he made his appearance on the Indian public scene as the great leader of the Indian people. Sarvodaya is a total view of life and human society comprising individual as well as collective life as much as social, economic, political, moral, religious and spiritual.

The culmination of sarvodaya vision, which was the life-mission of Gandhi, is nothing but a liberated society, a sarvodaya *samaj*. He devoted his entire life for the achievement of this goal. Since sarvodaya stood for the welfare of all, commitment to all kinds of sacrifices, even unto death, for the welfare of others was at the core of sarvodaya. This spirituality of commitment to service (sacrifice), implies absolute adherence to truth and ahimsa, supremacy of renunciation and sacrifice, cultivation of absolute fearlessness, and recognition and practice of bread-labour. It is on the basis of these moral values that Gandhi sought to evolve a social, economic and political order for the poor.

Sarvodaya for Gandhi was an altruistic ethic of self-realization. Satya (truth) and swaraj (freedom) as the ultimate aim of one's self-realization can only grow in an atmosphere of ahimsa (non-violence). Such an atmosphere will prevail only in a society where equal share is given "even unto this last" (for details see Kantowsky 1980: 3-15 and Patil ed. 1989: 475-87). Gandhi's understanding of equality has its roots in his faith that "all are created by God and therefore entitled to an equal share of food, clothing and housing" (Iyer 1991:408). Gandhi indeed considered economic equality a "master-key" to non-violent independence. In speaking of equality, if Gandhi gave prominence to economic equality, it is because he considered that, "true economics...stands for social justice, it promotes the good of all equally, including the weakest, and is indispensable for decent life" (*Harijan* October 1937). Still another aspect of equality is equal opportunity for all. For he says: "My idea of society is that while we are born equal, meaning that we have a right to equal opportunity, we have not the same capacity" (*Harijan* August 1940).

Nonetheless, he admits that some will have ability to earn more and others less because of the varieties of talents and capabilities that exist in the nature of things. Therefore, he proposed equal distribution. Even here, he realised the tremendous difficulties involved to have equal distribution of national wealth. Therefore, he wrote, "My ideal is equal distribution, but so far as I can see, it is not to be realised. I, therefore, work for equitable distribution" (*Young India* March 1927). After having explained what independence means to him, namely, "In concrete terms, then, the independence should be political, economic and moral", he elaborated the notion of "economic independence",

> "Economic" means entire freedom from British capitalist and capital, as also their counterpart. In other words, the humblest feel equal to the tallest. This can take place only by capital or capitalists sharing their skill and capital with the lowliest and the least (*Harijan* May 1946).

One may be tempted to conclude at this point that for Gandhi equality meant only economic equality or equitable distribution of wealth. This is not true, though Gandhi considered economic equality the key to all other areas of equality. This seems to stay unchanged in any society because the power of wealth seems to compromise and overpower other differences of culture, colour and caste.

Sarvodaya being nonviolent socialism, "all members of society are equal—none low, none high...In it the prince and the peasant, the wealthy and the poor, the employer and the employee are all on the same level." (Ramana Murti 1970: 322-23). A nonviolent society of Gandhi's vision is non-exploitative and egalitarian, not only equal in rights and opportunities but in the sense that no part shall exploit the other. No exchange relation should be much more beneficial to one part than to the other. To Gandhi such a horizontal structure is a necessary condition for self-realization in liberating both exploiter and exploited from the shackles of an exploitative structure. It applies at all levels: between individuals, between villages, and between larger units. Gandhi, for instance, wanted to purify the caste system by abolishing the vertical component or the hierarchical structure out of it. He wanted to retain the division of labour implicit in the *varna*, but no caste, no occupation should rank above any other caste or occupation. Gandhi was not opposed to the caste system altogether; instead he maintained that the four divisions of caste as complementary to one another, and none inferior or superior to any other. The caste system should be horizontal, and Gandhi claimed that this was the original system, that what had developed later was an aberration.

Gandhi accepted *varnasrama dharma* because it was based on the teaching of the *Gita*. Gandhi says,

> The law of Varna teaches us that we have each one of us to earn our bread by following the ancestral calling. It defines not our rights, but our duties. It necessarily has reference to callings that are conducive to the welfare of humanity and to no other. It also follows that there is no calling too low and none too high. All are good, lawful and absolutely equal in status. The callings of Brahmana—the spiritual teacher—and a scavenger are equal, and their due performance carries equal merit before God and at one time seems to have carried identical reward before man. Both were entitled to their livelihood and no more (Gandhi 1959: 33, ed. B. Kumarappa).

Varnasrama dharma is different from the present-day caste system. The former is a "rational scientific fact", whereas the latter is "an excrescence, an unmitigated evil" (Gandhi 1959: 44). The caste system as practised is evil; for it sanctions inequality based on birth, between man and man, which negates the fundamental principle of equality, presupposed by *varnasrama dharma*. It thus offends against the "rock-bottom doctrine of Advaita" in which Gandhi believed. "My interpretation of Advaita", says he, "excludes totally any idea of superiority at any stage whatsoever. I believe implicitly that all men are born equal" (Gandhi 1959: 51). Gandhi would thus advocate the division of labour implied in *varnasrama dharma* but would reject a caste system that promotes inequality and class divison on any basis such as birth and occupation. Gandhi's dispproval of the caste system was based on his awareness of division created in the society on a false basis of heredity and on his deep belief in the ideal of equality.

The rejection (disapproval) of caste system involves the rejection (disapproval) of untouchability which is the extreme manifestation of inequality that the caste system seeks to preserve and which is incompatible with Hinduism understood in the light of the teachings of the *Bhagavadgita*. In other words, untouchability is contrary to the *varnasrama dharma*.

> Arrogation of a superior status by any of the Varnas over another is a denial of the law. And there is nothing in the

law of Varna to warrant a belief in untouchability (Gandhi 1959: 41).

Gandhi attacked untouchability vehemently on the ground that there was no sanction for it in the Hindu religion.[12] But the fact of the matter is that Hindu society is legitimately regarded as one of the best examples of a hierarchical stratification of a social order intended to perpetuate inequalities. Gandhi realized the injustice perpetuated on account of the practice of caste and hence took up the question of Harijans (literallly, God's people). One would, at this point, agree with Indira Rothermund that "Gandhi, by using the term *Harijan*, emphasises equality of all Indians both before law and before God... The use of the term *Harijan* thus implies the acceptance of not only the assertive secular power to *Harijans* but, more importantly their claim to human dignity. All persons are created equal by God (as *Harijans*),..." (Patil ed. 1989: 430).

Gandhi was, in fact struggling with two mutually inconsistent and conflicting views: he was deeply moved by the conditions of the untouchables and he struggled for their betterment, yet he accepted and defended *varnasrama* law — a principle of hereditary determinism. The point at issue is that whatever the importance of this law maybe as a principle of social stability, you cannot at the same time accept the principle and reject the natural and logical consequences which are its outcome. Nonetheless, as Sharda Jain observes, "Gandhiji's utopian approach envisaged far-reaching and sweeping changes in human nature and society and an attempt to recast the society as a whole" (Biswas 1969: 309).

The ideal society of Gandhi's vision is not a perfect society, but "one in which all its citizens work toward perfection, knowing that they can always do better..." (Iyer 1985: 410). In its process of growth, swaraj is a step to *Ramrajya*.

Swaraj and Ramrajya

Gandhi for the first time enunciated his ideal of swaraj in *Hind Swaraj*, which contains his "seminal" ideas and basic approach to the problems of contemporary civilization.[13] Swaraj has different perspectives: personal, moral, social, economic and national; and it has gone through "a necessary evolution", during Gandhi's own life and thereafter, but Gandhi is categorical and emphatic on the substance of swaraj. To quote him:

> Let there be no mistake about my conception of swaraj. It is complete independence of alien control and complete economic independence. So at one end we have political independence, at other end the economic. It has two other ends. One of them is moral and social, the corresponding end is *Dharma*, i.e., religion in the highest sense of the term... Let us call this square of Swaraj, which will be out of shape if any angle is untrue (*Harijan* January 1937).

Swaraj is sarvodaya democracy, the democracy of the masses and for the masses. Since the vast masses of India lived in the villages, the pivot of the sarvodaya democratic state of his vision was the villages of India, conceived in an ever-widening oceanic circle. The individual was to be the centre of this circle, and should always be prepared "to perish for the village", and the village in its turn "ready to perish for the circle of villages", till at last the whole became one life organized in the shape and form of a state consisting of widening circles and decentralized in its functions and activities. Such sarvodaya democracy had to be worked out decidedly from below by the people of every village and not by a few people at the top of the pyramid.

In 1924 he wrote: "Swaraj for me means freedom for the meanest of our countrymen. I am not interested in freeing India merely from the English yoke. I am bent upon freeing India from any yoke whatsoever..." (*Young India* June 1924:195). The mere form of political self-government cannot satisfy the essentially democratic concept of swaraj. Hence Gandhi clarifies:

> By swaraj I mean the government of India by the consent of the people as ascertained by the largest number of the adult population, male or female, native-born or domiciled, who have contributed by manual labour to the service of the State and who have taken the trouble of having registered their name as voters... Real swaraj will come not by the acquisition of authority by a few but by the acquisition of the capacity by all to resist authority when it is abused. In other words: Swaraj is to be obtained by educating the masses to a sense of their capacity to regulate and control authority (*Young India* 1925: 40-41).

As the years go by in the history of the national movement of India, Gandhi gives clearer definitions of swaraj:

> The Swaraj of my...our...dream recognises no race or religious distinctions. Nor is it to be the monopoly of the lettered persons nor yet of moneyed men. Swaraj is to be for all, including the former, but emphatically including the maimed, the blind, the starving toiling millions.(*Young India* May 1930: 149).

He wrote on another occasion:

> The Swaraj of my dream is the poor man's Swaraj. The necessaries of life should be enjoyed by you in common with those enjoyed by the princes and the moneyed men. But that does not mean that they should have palaces like theirs... But you ought to get all the ordinary amenities of life that a rich man enjoys. I have not the slightest doubt that Swaraj is not *Poorna* Swaraj until these amenities are guaranteed to you under it (*Young India* March 1931: 78-79).

Then he goes on to clarify what he means by *Poorna* Swaraj as follows:

> *Poorna* Swaraj-"Poorna" complete because it is as much for the prince as for the peasant, as much for the rich landowner as for the landless tiller of the soil, as much for the Hindus as for the Musalmans, as much for the Parsis and Christians as for the Jains, Jews, and Sikhs, irrespective of any distinction of caste or creed or status in life. The very connotation of the word and the means of its attainment to which we are pledged—truth and non-violence—precludes all possibility of the Swaraj being more for some one than for the other, being partial to some or prejudicial to others (*Young India* March 1931: 1).

Gandhi's swaraj was egalitarian and secular. For him "*Hind Swaraj* is the rule of all the people, is the rule of justice".

As was cited above, swaraj for Gandhi was quite a comprehensive vision. Though his politics was not power-oriented, he was well aware of power-politics. Gandhi's goal was to empower the people. Power, that is, sovereignty and supreme power, must belong to the people. The people, for

Gandhi, was not an abstract concept but the toiling people in the fields and factories, the suffering humanity, the dumb millions.[14] His realistic mind could see through the inadequacy of elite swaraj — swaraj of the rich and the educated. He therefore always insisted on poor man's or people's swaraj. One sees a necessary link between sarvodaya and swaraj for the obvious reason that swaraj could only be established by awakening the masses into a sense of their dignity and power. The only way to achieve swaraj is the way of nonviolence, which is the weapon of the poor and the exploited. The literal meaning of swaraj (mastery over self, or self control)[15] becomes all the more relevant at this point. Because swaraj at the social or national level means a societal set-up designed to encourage its citizens to practice self-control. It is not easy for individuals to opt for self-control: all our "natural instincts" tend to drive us in the opposite direction. The social set-up can either further inflame these instincts, or provide an atmosphere where they can be overcome more easily. To the extent that it goes in the latter direction, there is swaraj at the social or national level.

With a keen sense of realism and practicality, Gandhi had to make compromises. For instance, he supported swaraj not as the immediate political support, but as an ideal to strive for. He pinned his faith in *Hind Swaraj*, on the rule of all the people, or rule of justice as he called it. There was a gulf between India of his dream and the immediate objective of the nation. Being fully aware of this gap, in a letter to Jawaharlal Nehru as early as April 1928, he wrote, "I am quite aware of your opinion that someday we shall have to start an intensive movement without the rich people and without the vocal educated class. But the time is not yet" (Tendulkar vol. 8 1960-1963:291).

Ramrajya embodied Gandhi's dream of the perfectibility of man and society. He gave to his ideal society the name *Ramrajya.* The term *Ramrajya* derives from the *Ramayana*'s classic depiction of the victory of Rama, symbolizing the forces of good, over Ravana symbolizing the forces of evil (CW 90: 18) and the consequent establishment of a reign of righteousness and justice in the land. Gandhi's reference to *Ramrajya* aroused fear and suspicion in the minds of many, especially Muslims, and provoked his critics to allege that he wanted to go back to the mythical Golden Age. But his explanation is that,

> By abandoning the kingdom and living in the forest for the sake of truth Rama gave to all kings of the world an object-lesson in noble conduct...He lent splendour to his throne by popular administration and proved that *Ramrajya* was the acme of Swaraj... The subjects of Rama were supremely happy. Such *Ramrajya* is possible even today. The race of Rama is not extinct. In modern times the first Caliphs may be said to have established *Ramrajya*. Abubaker and Hazrat Umar collected revenue running into crores and yet personally they were as good as fakirs (CW 25: 558-59).

But later Gandhi modified his position. In 1927 he said that, "I assure you you will find nothing there (in Gandhi's heart) but love for Rama, whom I see face to face in the starving millions of India" (*Young India* March 1927: 93). This is an instance of his utilising a mythical symbol in the interest of public service.[16]

The picture of *Ramrajya* that Gandhi visualised was an expression of the yearning for a just and perfect society — the kingdom of righteousness on earth. It was a broad vision of perfect society, a kingdom of God on earth which even transcended the narrow boundaries of religion or politics. He explains:

> I warn my Mussalman friends against misunderstanding me in my use of the words "Ramaraj". By Ramaraj I do not mean Hindu Raj. I mean by Ramaraj divine Raj, the Kingdom of God. For Rama and Rahim are one and the same deity. I acknowledge no other God but the one of truth and rightness. Whether Rama of my imagination ever lived or not on this earth, the ancient ideal of Ramaraj is undoubtedly one of true democracy in which the meanest citizen could be sure of swift justice without an elaborate and costly procedure (*Young India* September 1929: 305).

Referring to the criticism of the employment of the term *Ramrajya* for his ideal society, he said:

> It is a convenient and expressive phrase, the meaning of which no alternative can so fully express to millions. When

> I visit the Frontier province or address predominantly Muslim audiences I would express my meaning to them by calling it Khudai Raj, while to a Christian audience I would describe it as the Kingdom of God on earth.[17]

A gradual growth in the understanding of *Ramrajya* can thus be seen in Gandhi's writings. In 1937 he described it as sovereignty of the people based on pure moral authority (*Harijan* January 1937). In 1946 he wrote, "...that independence of my dream is Ramarajya, i.e., the Kingdom of God on earth...In concrete terms, then, the independence should be political, economic and moral...."[18] Again in 1947 he wrote that "there can be no Ramarajya in the present state of iniquitous inequalities in which a few roll in riches and the masses do not get even enough to eat" (*Harijan* June 1947). All these may sound negative in their tone, but the best positive statement was made by Gandhi in June 1945, when he described it as the Kingdom of God on earth. In such a kingdom

> inequalities based on possession and non-possession, colour, race or creed or sex vanish. In it, land and state belong to the people, justice is prompt, perfect and cheap and therefore, there is freedom of worship, speech and the press... Such a state must be based on Truth and Non-violence, and must consist of prosperous, happy and self-contained villages and village communities. It is a dream that may never be realized. I find happiness in living in that dreamland, ever trying to realise it in the quickest way.[19]

Gandhian Alternative

In one of his essays, published posthumously, Gandhi equated the village panchayat (governing committee of five) with *Ramrajya* (*Harijan* October 1949). Gandhi's conception of the state is democratic (sarvodaya democracy) where sovereignty is given to the people who entrust it for the time being to those whom they may choose as their representatives. Even the parliament has no power or existence independent of the people. The State for Gandhi is one of the means for the service of people. Gandhi regarded the State as a "soulless machine", a symbol of "violence in a concentrated and organized form".[20] He viewed with apprehension the powers of the State and subscribed to Thoreau's belief that that government is best which governs the least (*Young India* July 1931: 162; see also *Harijan* July 1940: 211, September 1946: 309). He would prefer a society of "enlightened anarchy"[21], where everyone is his/her own ruler, to a coercive State. In this ideal State, therefore, there is no political power because there is no State. But being aware of the fact that "the ideal is never fully realised in life", Gandhi's thought was moving in the direction of the evolution of a predominantly non-violent State (Dhawan 1990: 279-336). The word "non-violent State" was used by Gandhi himself in *The Harijan* (25 August 1940), where he wrote, "the ideal non-violent State will be an ordered anarchy". A non-violent State is a contradiction in terms because the State "represents violence in a concentrated and organized form". What is at issue for us here is the substance of the concept: Gandhi wanted to establish genuine democracy, where liberty and equality are of topmost priority and exploitation is minimized, and replace the master-servant and the capitalist-labour relationships by a new co-operative order based on rural culture.

Gandhi found the soul (life and spirit) of India in Indian villages. The seat of India's consensual and organic social order is in the village community. "We are inheritors of a rural civilization," Gandhi said. He believed that "if the village perishes, India will perish, too. It will no more be India. Her own mission in the world will get lost" (*Harijan* August 1936). The village being the source of spiritual values, social order, and material production, as it is said to have been throughout Indian history, " a future perfected India must build on her villages" (Fox 1989: 56). Therefore village regeneration becomes a major aspect of Gandhi's vision of India. Gandhi's vision of India was to make it economically viable, educationally self-sufficient, and socially and culturally a well-knit unit which should be able to meet its day-to-day needs and wants independently. He believed that the village is a basic unit and is a strong link in the chain of society. "... the unit of society should be a village or call it a manageable small group of people who would, in the ideal, be self-sufficient (in the matter of their vital requirements) as a unit and bound together in bonds of mutual co-operation and interdependence" (Pyarelal 1959: 8).

Gandhi was attracted by the ancient virtues of Indian villages, such as corporate community life, smallness of size, autonomous character and self-sufficiency. Nonetheless, he was well aware of their limitation too, such as forced widowhood, caste system, untouchability and so on. It is true that, "villages today as well as in Gandhi's day are tragic reminders for them of how much Indian civilization has lost" (Fox 1989: 57). What Gandhi genuinely wanted was a real clean-up: the removal of untouchability, corruption and unsanitary health conditions, and thus to initiate a village regeneration process whose final goal will be *poorna* swaraj and *Ramrajya*.

Panchayat Raj is a plan to reinstate autonomous rule to the Indian village. Every village was to be a republic, having power not only to administer its internal affairs but also "capable of managing its affairs even to the extent of defending itself against the whole world". About the *panchayati* system he said:

> The government of the village will be conducted by a panchayat of five persons annually elected by the adult villagers, male and female, possessing the minimum prescribed qualifications. They will have all the authority and jurisdiction required. Since there will be no system of punishments in the accepted sense, this panchayat will be the legislature, judiciary and executive combined to operate for its year in office (*Harijan* August 1946).

Autonomous and more or less self-contained villages were, for Gandhi, the basic units of his vision of decentralized polity. These primary communities would be federated into larger units in such a way that the possibility and temptation to abuse power do not arise. "These larger units would not be in the ascending order but in the form of concentric circles, the widest circle encompassing the entire world community". The primary unit's (village community) concern would be to see that the real needs of all the members are fulfilled—health, education, agriculture and industry—and that disputes are amicably settled. As far as possible, every primary community would produce at least the essentials of its life. This would ensure freedom and at the same time make co-operation between wider circles of villages easy. The *gram sabha*[22] (village assembly) is formed for the running of the villages. The *gram sabha* would elect a *panchayat* annually to conduct the government of the village.

As for the functions of the *panchayat*, its most important function would be to initiate plans of development and, after their approval by the *gram sabha*, execute them. It is important to bear in mind that the *gram sabha* is the basic unit of the edifice of decentralized democracy, not *gram panchayat*. This *gram sabha* would be completely autonomous, self-regulating and self-determining in its internal matters and self-sufficient in respect to its essential requirements. The *panchayat* will be completely subservient to it.

In order to deal with issues like higher education, bigger industries, transport, bigger hospitals, communication etc., a group of villages may come together and pool their resources. This leads to the formation of the *panchayat* of a second order which is made up of elected representatives of each *gram sabha*. The second tier (order) may elect one representative each and these representatives would form the *panchayat* of the third order. Units of further orders can be formed so as to create the national *panchayat* or a "world *panchayat*". In this kind of democratic structure, actual power would be exercised from below upwards. In such a decentralized sarvodaya democracy of Gandhi's understanding, people would have the fullest opportunity and therefore they would take active interest in the management of its affairs. Since *gram sabha* and *gram panchayat* have close watch over representatives, an effective check upon the inefficiency and corruption of the representatives is possible.

Panchayati Raj is a village regeneration process, where village has to become the seat of India's greatness. As an ideal, it stands for fully decentralized development, which safeguards the political autonomy, economic independence, and social integrity of the village community. The key to such reconstruction of a new social system based on villages was the revolution of personal dedication. Because in Gandhi's words:

> Life will not be a pyramid with apex sustained at the bottom. But it will be an oceanic circle whose centre will be the individual always ready to perish for the circle of villages, till at last the whole becomes one life composed

> of individuals never aggressive in their arrogance but ever humble, sharing the majority of the oceanic circle of which they are integral units (*Harijan* July 1946).

Constructive Programme

Gandhi's genius as a social reformer lay in his uncommon ability to fuse timeless principles with evolving strategies. This is best seen in the order of activities he initiated under the umbrella of constructive programme. From the nineteen twenties until his death in 1948, Gandhi gradually shifted the emphasis of his work from nonviolent resistance to constructive schemes for the welfare of all. For Gandhi, nonviolent resistance (satyagraha) and constructive programme —"an embodiment of sarvodaya"— were corollaries of the same philosophical perspective (Iyer 1985:404). The constructive programme focused upon constructive ways of rebuilding a demoralized society. It sought to re-orient a servile nation habituated to sectional loyalties and social apathy towards a fearless community of mutual service and sacrifice in which every individual identified with others, especially the poor. Gandhi wrote,

> ... the constructive programme is the truthful and non-violent way of winning Poorna Swaraj...(and) is designed to build up the nation from the very bottom upward (Gandhi 1941 (1991): 3).

It may "otherwise and more fittingly be called construction of poorna swaraj or complete independence by truthful and non-violent means". Gandhi used "constructive programme" to express his method of rebuilding India according to his vision of a non-violent, non-exploitative social order. By this he wanted "to bring out the full implication of the revolutionary approach of this non-violent method of individual and social transformation leading to Sarvodaya social order... (and) is therefore central to the understanding of Gandhiji's concept of Swaraj, which was for him a step towards the ultimate goal of '*Ramrajya*'" (Bharathi 1991: 11-12).

The constructive programme consists of several apparently unconnected independent activities. But they are connected within the context of a creative evolution of new social order. Within the

Indian context, this meant nurturing communal unity, abolishing untouchability, fostering adult education and systematic improvement of village. It meant uplifting the peasant and developing nonviolent labour unions, working toward economic and social equality, promoting cottage and small-scale industries as a means for decentralizing economic production and distribution, and eradicating a wide variety of social evils. The constructive programme drew its inspiration from the neglected concept of trusteeship. And since each aspect of the constructive programme is related directly to trusteeship, the various programmes are coherently, if loosely, associated with one another. Also, since it is based on trusteeship as an ideal, it can proceed even when there is varying resistance to the effective realization of the ideal. The scope and simplicity of the constructive programme frustrated socialists, who preferred detailed plans and quantifiable criteria of accomplishment. Gandhi, however, thought that its virtue lay in its generality, both because it avoided the psychological defeatism which readily emerges when rigid objectives are not met, and because it gave ample recognition to the intangible and unquantifiable elements of human progress.

The constructive programme, with its almost unlimited plasticity, embodies the realistic perspective required for social revolution as well as criteria by which to measure what is in fact possible. By fusing means and ends in the constructive programme so that the means cannot contain any element which would be unacceptable in the ends, one could guarantee that the ends would be right when realized. Rather than imposing preconceived ends upon people, Gandhi sought to uphold the highest ideals while making full use of what was possible in respect to specific situations. The mere desire to improve depressing conditions was not sufficient to effect changes in the society. He wrote to a village worker in 1925:

> It is only recently that we thought of going into the village. At first, we wanted things from the village people. It is only now that we are going to the villages in order to give the people something... We have to win back our honoured place among the village people and will get nothing through impatience. Some persons serve their own

> interests under the guise of service... Public workers, therefore must cultivate patience, forbearance, selflessness and such other virtues...[23]

Gandhi's vision of construction or reconstruction of a new social system gave the utmost importance to village communities. He remained sceptical of imposing any social reformation from the top. With all due respect to intelligence and scholarship, he felt that intellectuals could be useful as leaders in social reform only when they identified with and merged themselves with the masses. They could inspire people for nonviolent revolution from within only by moving into the villages and working like villagers to improve their lot. He sounded categorical when he spoke about genuine service for he believed that personal dedication (prophetic witnessing) and identification with the masses (incarnational theology) were the most powerful forces of any social change.[24] He spoke plainly to a gathering of socialists on the eve of Indian independence.

> No doubt the transfer of power will remove many obstacles. But we shall have to do solid work among the people. Since you look upon me as an adviser and seek my advice of your own free will, I have only one advice to give, and that is that, if you wish to establish socialism, there is only one way in which it can be done: go and live among the poor in the villages, live as they live, be one with the village people, work eight hours daily, use only village-made goods and articles even in your personal lives, remove illiteracy among village people, eradicate untouchability and uplift the women. I will even go so far as to suggest that you should establish such a living bond with the village people that, if anyone amongst you is unmarried and wishes to marry, he or she should choose a partner from among the village girls or boys. If any one else seeks your advice on this subject, give him or her, too, the same advice. Make your life an ideal one in this way; when the people see your transparent lives every minute of the day as clearly as we see pictures on a screen, their influence will be felt through the country and reform its life (Iyer 1985: 407-8).

This is a bold and far-reaching vision, but one which Gandhi believed could be adapted according to the changing village contexts in India and one which would remain an index of progress in the establishment of sarvodaya social order. Gandhi's constructive programme for regenerating village communities depended on voluntary service and it functioned independently of the state and other institutions. Speaking of the constructive programme of Gandhi, Gene Sharp has this to say "...(it) is an attempt to build the beginning of the new social order while the old society still exists... (it) has been described as the scaffolding upon which the structure of the new society will be built (Sharp 1979: 81).

Gandhi devised his eighteenfold constructive programme and set up a number of constructive work organizations to work it out in order to knit together in a common bond of fellowship the millions and weave the pattern of non-violent conduct into their lives. The programme included the following steps: communal unity, removal of untouchability, prohibition of alcohol, khadi and other rural industries, village sanitation, *nai talim* (basic education), adult education, uplift of women, education in health and hygiene, propagation of *rashtra bhasha* (national language), *swabhasha-prem* (love of one's language), economic equality, uplift of *kisans* (peasants), uplift of labour, uplift of students, service of backward tribes, and treatment of lepers.[25]

According to Joan Bondurant, the constructive programme is "a positive aspect of Satyagraha in action, and is the concomitant of resistance action" (Bondurant 1958: 36). Gandhi described it as the permanent part of the non-violent effort. From this effort is created the capacity to offer non-violent resistance called non-cooperation and civil disobedience. Gandhi insisted that the constructive programme work was to be undertaken for its own sake and not with the aim of exploiting the people by gaining their sympathies and thus control them. This work would establish living contact with people, because it is "people's participation". The work would raise the status of the people and bring home to them the power of non-violent social change for the ending of exploitation (Sharp 1979: 85).

The constructive programme of Gandhi was basically

"village-oriented", for village uplift. In 1936 Gandhi settled in Sevagram village, to live among the poor and to "show them how to live", by personal example and service rather than by preaching. The constructive programme, if carried out in the right direction, Gandhi believed, would result in the ideal sarvodaya *samaj*. Constructive works as planned by Gandhi are something that everyone can participate in. If all kinds of people (young and old, the unemployed, the middle class, the intellectuals, the rich, leaders and followers, city dwellers and country people...) actively participate in the constructive programme, then it will provide a common experience and be a symbol of democratic common endeavour; it will bridge the gap between the classes and the masses (CW 63: 347,417).

In fact, the items (eighteen steps) selected by Gandhi for the constructive programme are merely illustrative, not exhaustive. Therefore, they can be changed according to the varying needs, contexts, traditions and the socio-economic and political background of the people concerned. The essential aspect to be kept in mind is that they should be basically non-violent and should provide an answer to some keenly felt need of the time and should be simple and universal so as to embrace the largest number of people in their fold (Prasad 1971: 166). Gandhi was deeply convinced that only genuine participation of the people especially the peasants can bring about fundamental economic and social changes which are vital for national development. He outlined the constructive programme in such a way that it enables "the peasant slowly but steadily to develop his own capacity for growth and increasingly to use for his own benefit and the benefit of his family, community and society at large" (Devadoss 1974: 516). The core of rural development thus, lies in making people active participants in their own development. This developmental process is liberating for the people and for the nation.

Sarvodaya: Vision and Movement

Sarvodaya vision is Gandhi's contribution to India, a vision that looks forward to the creation of an ideal society, a sarvodaya society. Gandhi argued that by reforming Indian society, colonial rule would automatically cease to exist. Therefore, on the one hand Gandhi tried to resist oppressions of all kinds and on the other he tried to reconstruct Indian society. Such a society was obviously to be nonviolent and peaceful, non-exploitative and equalitarian in structure. "It was to be the next step in human civilization, what Gandhi called the 'swaraj' society of the future" (Dasgupta 1970: 336).

Gandhi's plan for national social reconstruction based on the principles of truth and nonviolence would have brought about a radical transformation of Indian society. His economic programme, village oriented constructive programme, plan for the establishment of a village republic with democratic decentralization of power, his measures for amelioration of the condition of women, Harijans, *adivasis* and other backward sections of the society and his insistence on self-sufficiency and *swadeshi* were all intended to bring about a revolutionary change in Indian social structure. But somehow the political independence of India and the leadership thereafter seem to have put a damper on Gandhi's vision of Indian society, though "Gandhi repeatedly maintained that political independence did not mean freedom unless India attained economic and social freedom" (Unnithan 1987: 62).

Despite the apparent lack of interest in Gandhi's sarvodaya ideal on an official national level in post-independent India, sarvodaya vision took the form of a movement. After Gandhi's death, Vinoba Bhave provided leadership within the Gandhian circle and gave sarvodaya an organizational structure.[26] A new chapter was started in the development of the sarvodaya movement by Jayaprakash Narayan, who followed Vinoba's lead in shaping the movement's constructive work programme.

Sarvodaya as a movement is facing many crises, and must confront them if it is to survive. In the midst of crises, sarvodaya has not lost sight of its goal. As Iswar C.Harris observes, "The leaders of different groups within it are convinced that Gandhi's dream of Gram Swaraj is the goal of the movement. It is committed to the 'uplift' of the weaker section of Indian society as reflected in the constructive work programs" (Harris 1987: 1046). Gandhi's dream of sarvodaya society has great potential and continues to offer challenges to those who are committed to the coming of the kingdom of God, *Ramrajya*, non-violent society.

References

1. The very title of his autobiography is indicative of Gandhi's basic approach to life. M. K. Gandhi, *An Autobiography or The Story of My Experiments with Truth*, (Ahmedabad: Navajivan Publishing House, 1983; first edition, 1927).
2. Gandhi originally instituted eighteen constructive programmes under sarvodaya. For details see Chapter Two.
3. Gandhi wrote, "I make no hobgoblin of consistency. If I am true to myself from moment to moment, I do not mind all the inconsistencies that may be flung in my face." (CWMG V.59: 308) Elsewhere he wrote, "I want to tell the story of my numerous experiments with truth... my life consists of nothing but those experiments....I claim for them nothing more than does a scientist who, though he conducts his experiment with utmost accuracy, forethought and minuteness, never claims any finality about his conclusions..." M.K. Gandhi, *An Autobiography* (Ahmedabad: Navajivan Publishing House, 1927), See also, *The Collected Works of Mahatma Gandhi*, vol. 59 (New Delhi: The Publications Division, Ministry of Information and Broadcasting, Government of India, 1962), 306; hereafter referred to as *CW*.
4. Archana Sinha, *The Social Philosophy of Sarvodaya* (Patna: Janaki Prakashan, 1978). She tries to show in this book how sarvodaya ideals are found in many religious traditions.
5. M.K. Gandhi, *Young India* (3 September 1925): 304.
6. T.S. Devadoss, *Sarvodaya and the Problem of Political Sovereignty* (Madras: University of Madras, 1974), 109; quoted by the author from Sankara Rao Deo, *Sarvodaya Sastra* (in Hindi), 3.
7. Tarlok Singh, "Sarvodaya and Antyodaya as Social Concepts: Implications for India's Future," *Gandhi Marg* 8 (October 1986): 407-414; and S. Arokiasamy, S.J., "Sarvodaya through Antyodaya-The Liberation of the Poor in the Contextualisation of Morals," *Vidyajyothi* 51 (November 1987): 545-564.
8. "Perhaps it was Vinoba who used it (*Antyodaya*) first when he wrote on *The Sarvodaya Ideal* in the *Harijan* in April 1949", says Tarlok Singh. Tarlok Singh, "Sarvodaya and Antyodaya as Social Concepts...", *Gandhi Marg* 8 (October 1986): 408.
9. Speaking on Gandhi's understanding of truth (*satya*), A. L. Basham remarks that the fundamental concept of Gandhi's philosophy owes nothing to Western sources. It was developed from the Hindu tradition in which he was brought up. Nonetheless, Basham concludes that, "Several of Gandhi's concepts are fully in keeping

with Indian tradition and were probably developed from ideas which he absorbed in his childhood and youth, fertilized and brought to fruition by his contact with the West. Only two major planks in his platform—the dignity of manual labour and the emancipation of women — seem to have had no prototypes in India's past. He was no doubt a great innovator, but he built firmly on the foundation of his own tradition..." See A. L. Basham, "Traditional Influences on the Thoughts of Mahatma Gandhi", in R. Kumar, ed., *Essays on Gandhian Politics* (Oxford: Clarendon Press, 1971), 17, 25.

10. "...I very much like the doctrine of the manyness of reality. It is this doctrine that has taught me to judge a Mussulman from his standpoint and a Christian from his... My *Anekantavada* is the result of the two doctrines of satya and ahimsa." See the "Editorial" in *Young India* (26 January 1926); see also Raghavan N. Iyer, *The Moral and Political Thought of Mahatma Gandhi* (New York: Oxford University Press, 1973), 247.
11. It would be interesting to pursue elsewhere the question in what sense and to what extent Gandhi and his basic ideas may be considered syncretist. Suffice it to say at this point that Gandhi was influenced by Indian and Western thinking.
12. Gandhi observes, "untouchability in its extreme form has always caused me so much pain because I consider myself to be a Hindu of Hindus saturated with the spirit of Hinduism. I have failed to find a single warrant for the existence of untouchability as we believe and practice it today in all those books which we call Hindu Shastras. But as I repeatedly said in other places, if I found that Hinduism really countenanced untouchability I should have no hesitation in renouncing Hinduism itself". M. K. Gandhi, *The Removal of Untouchability*, 18.
13. *Hind Swaraj* was originally written by Gandhi in Gujarati in 1909 on his return voyage from London to South Africa. It was serialized in two instalments in December 1909 in the Gujarati edition of *Indian Opinion*, the weekly published by Gandhi in South Africa. In January 1910, it was issued as a booklet in Gujarati and on 24 March 1910, the Government of India proscribed it along with other publications because they "contain matter declared to be seditious." (*CW*, 10, 245) *Hind Swaraj* as a "whole theory of life," as Gandhi characterized it, has aroused varying reactions among different sections, both Western and Indian. It indeed is the quintessence of all that Gandhi had read, thought and experienced by the age of forty. It may sound at times too reactionary against

modern technology ("it represents a great sin"). It declared parliament to be a "prostitute and a sterile woman". It was very idealistic at other times (speaking of perfect society, "enlightened anarchy", "stateless society"). What is to be kept in mind is the fact that the rudimentary model presented in *Hind Swaraj* is not static. On the contrary, it is dynamic in so far as it assumes a more sharply defined shape as Gandhi's thinking becomes global in character through time. In the words of Mahadev Desai, "the views expressed in the first edition of *Hind Swaraj* have remained in substance unchanged, they have gone through a necessary evolution." ("Preface to the New edition", *Hind Swaraj* (Ahmedabad: Navajivan Publishing House, 1962), 5.

14. Gandhi spoke more in terms of the Indian peasants. It is true indeed that he represented peasant India, the real India as Gandhi used to call it. "Gandhi is the representative of the peasant". S. Radhakrishnan, *Mahatma Gandhi: Essays and Reflections on his Life and Work* (London: Allen & Unwin, 1940), 23.
15. T.S. Ananthu, "Gandhi's 'Hind Swaraj': its appeal to me," a document prepared for seminar organised by Kerala Gandhi Smarak Nidhi, Trivandrum, India, 11 and 12 August 1982, 4. In his presentation, the author attempts to view *Hind Swaraj* giving prime importance to the concept of self-control.
16. He said in 1947: "Rama, Krishna etc., are called incarnations of God because we attribute divine qualities to them. In truth they are creations of men's imagination. Whether they actually lived or not does not affect the picture of them in men's minds. The Rama and Krishna of history often present difficulties which have to be overcome by all manner of arguments" *Harijan*, 22 June 1947. And "My Rama, the Rama of our prayers, is not the historical Rama, the son of Dasratha, the king of Ayodhya. He is the eternal, the unborn, the one without a second". *Harijan*, 28 April 1946, 111.
17. *Harijan*, 18 August 1946, 266. "My Rama is another name for Khuda or God. I want the Khudai Raj, which is the same thing as the Kingdom of God on Earth". - Quoted in Pyarelal, *Mahatma Gandhi: The Last Phase*, vol.1 (Ahmedabad: Navajivan Publishing House, 1965), 549.
18. "'Political' necessarily means the removal of the control of the British army in every shape and form. 'Economic' means entire freedom from British capitalists and capital, as also their Indian counterparts. In other words, the humblest must feel equal to the tallest. This can take place only by capital or capitalists sharing their skill and capital with the lowliest and the least. 'Moral' means

freedom from armed defence forces. My conception of *Ramarajya* excludes replacement of the British army by a national army of occupation. A country that is governed by even its national army can never be morally free and, therefore, its so-called weakest member can never rise to his full moral height". (*CW*, 84, 80).

19. M.K. Gandhi, *Towards Lasting Peace*, 216.
20. Nirmal Kumar Bose, *Selections from Gandhi*, 37.
21. Gandhi's occasional reference to "enlightened anarchy" has given rise to varying interpretations. Some call him a "philosophical anarchist" while some hold the view that though some of the elements of Gandhian political thought bear resemblance to some of the anarchist thinkers, he cannot be categorised as an anarchist thinker. For a detailed discussion on this point, see G. N. Dhawan, *The Political Philosophy of Mahatma Gandhi* (New Delhi: The Gandhi Peace Foundation, 1990); Adi H. Doctor, *Anarchist Thought in India*, (Bombay: Asia Publishing House, 1964) 36-54; George Woodcock, *Anarchism*, (Pelican Edition, 1963), 18; Joan V. Bondurant, *Conquest of Violence, the Gandhian Philosophy of Conflict* (Berkeley: University of California Press, 1965), 172-78; Geoffrey Ostergaard, "Indian Anarchism: The Sarvodaya Movement", in *Anarchism Today*, edited by David E. Apter & James Joll (London: Macmillon Press LTD., 1971) 145-63.
22. *Gram Sabha* is constituted of all the adult inhabitants of the village, male and female, above the age of eighteen (and below a certain age, e.g., sixty or sixty five), "who have contributed by manual labour to the service of the state and who have taken the trouble of having their names registered as voters." M. K. Gandhi, *Village Swaraj* Compiled by H. M. Vyas (Ahmedabad: Navajivan Publishing House, 1962), 3.
23. "Who Is to Blame?" *Navajivan*, 28 June 1925.
24. "Prophetic witnessing" and "incarnational theology" are usages borrowed by me from Christian theological vocabulary. These are terms used in theology to interpret and explain social involvement and developmental action programmes, institutions and individuals engaged in Christian social milieux. Prophets in history, in general, preached and dedicated their lives to removing evil and injustice in society and bringing social change. Incarnational theology, i.e., God becoming a human person, is the inspiration for any Christian to be of service to humanity. The ideal form of that service is nothing but thinking, feeling and being with those who are to be served. Gandhi's ideal of service seems both prophetic and incarnational in this sense.

25. Gene Sharp 1979: 82-84; see also Archana Sinha, *The Social and Political Philosophy of Sarvodaya* (Patna: Janaki Prakashan, 1978), 167. In 1941 Gandhi had listed thirteen items and in 1945 he added on: *kisans*, labour, adivasis, lepers, and students, and made them eighteen. After Gandhi's death the following items were added on by his followers to strengthen the movement: cow protection, nature cure, bhoodan, gramdan, shanti sena.- K.S. Bharati, *The Social Philosophy of Mahatma Gandhi*, 13-14.
26. After Gandhi's assassination, Vinoba brought some Gandhian organizations together under *Sarva Seva Sangh* to carry out the work of sarvodaya. Today the organizational structure is divided into national, state, and local levels.

Two

Ideal Mission: To Realize Utopia

In this chapter we will analyze and assess sarvodaya as a utopian model for stimulating and directing socio-historical change. This analysis is carried out in three stages: 1. scan rapidly the history of utopian thought in the West and review certain theoretical aspects of utopia, such as literary, social scientific, philosophic and theological; 2. draw out from this historical and theoretical review a number of pertinent principles (definitional, evaluative and functional) that are crucial to understanding utopia as an effective model for stimulating socio-historical change; 3. indicate how these principles may apply to Gandhi's sarvodaya.

Realistic Utopia

In the wider context of Gandhi's worldview, sarvodaya has a special place; the sarvodaya society envisioned and inaugurated by Gandhi is, as already remarked, an ideal, a vision. We will argue in the following pages that the sarvodaya vision of Gandhi is a "realistic utopia". It has an essentially eschatological dimension that makes it a process that is being realized in today's society. The "already and not yet" dimension of sarvodaya ideal allows us to expose its past, explain it as a process of realization and explore the areas of new possibilities it offers for the well-being and harmony of humanity in India and worldwide.

There is need for some conceptual clarification, however, in order to understand Gandhi's sarvodaya vision as utopia. We shall therefore sketch the relevant trends in interpreting the category of utopia and situate Gandhi's sarvodaya vision appropriately in that context.

In ordinary language, the word "utopia" is often used in a pejorative sense; it then refers to unrealizable dreams of the future that in practice lead to passivity and despair. In contrast, the social philosopher Karl Mannheim categorized such unrealizable imaginings as "ideological" rather than "utopian", because such dreams simply reinforce the present social order. Ernst Bloch called such unrealistic visions of the future, which reinforce those interests which tend to propagate such ideological deflections of critique, "abstract utopias". Concrete utopias, by contrast, are images of the future that are grounded in authentic intuitions of the ills and contradictions present in society. Concrete utopias negate the finality and legitimacy of the most oppressive elements of this society and present a vision of human life that, even if in pure form is unrealizable, calls for new ways of thinking and acting that could lead to actual social change. According to Mannheim and Bloch, imagining the future can exercise great power in directing people's action.

Dreams of a better world, free of the imperfections, finiteness and corruptibility of what is present, are as old as history. The construction of imaginary worlds, free from difficulties that beset us in actuality, takes place in one form or another in all cultures. These visions can grow out of despair as well as out of hope; they can be conceived "as the dreams and experiments of a glorious past or as a consummation yet to be achieved in the future" (Kraushaar and Moment, eds. 1980: iv). Utopia, as Ruth Levitas says, "is not just a dream to be enjoyed, but a vision to be pursued" (Levitas 1990: 1). But to most people utopia suggests an impossible dream, an escapist fantasy, at best a pleasant but pointless entertainment.

The point at issue here is whether utopia of a certain kind is escapist nonsense or whether it is a significant and effective element in the making of human culture and human history. The word utopia itself contains deliberate ambiguity, namely, is this Eutopia, the good place, or Outopia, no place; and are these perhaps the same thing? (Levitas 1990: 2). In more general terms, utopia can be "... applied to any speculation in ethical philosophy about the good life; or to any speculation in political theory about political principles or forms of government or to any imaginary society found in a treatise, novel, story or poem; or to any vision or conception of a perfect society" (Kateb 1968: 267).

There is ambiguity in contemporary dictionary definitions too.[1] Granted that "the concept itself is an ideological battleground", we should proceed towards finding what is crucial in the variety of definitions within utopian studies. The existing definitions can be categorized as of three types according to whether they emphasize content, form or function. As to those stressing content, there is a common assumption that "utopia" provides a portrayal of the good society. Content is, for many people, the interesting aspect of utopia, inviting them to consider whether, in fact, this would be a good society, if it could exist. The problem with definitions stressing content is that they tend to be evaluative and normative, specifying what the good society should be, rather than reflecting on how it may be differently perceived. Defining utopia in terms of form — either equating utopia with a description of a good society or equating utopia with an ideal Commonwealth — narrows down its scope to a model society, making it very exclusive. Those who define utopia in terms of function propose a definite goal for utopia, positive or negative. Marx and Engels define utopia negatively in terms of its function, whereas Karl Mannheim defines utopia as that which transforms the status quo, irrespective of its form. It is important to underline the fact that the definitions of utopia in terms of form, function or content are analytic approaches that highlight the complexity implied in arriving at any definition at all. These approaches do put limits on "what may properly be regarded as utopian and thus upon the field of enquiry itself; they also obscure variations in the utopian genre" (Levitas 1990: 7). Therefore, in order to arrive at a "working definition" of utopia one may locate something which remains constant while content, form and function vary. This "constant", as Ruth Levitas argues, is "desire for a better way of being and living". If what is the constant or common factor in utopia is "the expression of the desire for a better way of living", "it will not only vary markedly in content but may be expressed in a variety of forms, and may perform a variety of functions, including compensation, criticism and the catalyzing of change."[2]

One who tries accurately to determine what the term "utopia" means finds different descriptions. Some view utopias as unreal wishful dreams and innocent pastime; others regard them dangerous and tyrannical hallucinations; yet others look at them as catalyzers of human progress. The history of the genre or category of utopia in European thought will show us the main classifications, the essential characteristics of utopia.

The Story of Utopias

Utopia has a history. With its expectation of a better man and a better world, utopia always intends to transcend given reality; it refuses to be satisfied with the existing situation. The utopia strives for the ideal of harmony and reconciliation. Utopian imagination dreams of another and better future than the present. Utopian imagination goes beyond the limited world in the direction of the unlimited; it transcends the imperfect condition of the present and moves toward greater perfection and greater harmony. The utopian story, as a process of transcendence, is a historical phenomenon, whose form and content vary according to the situation from which it arises and which it transcends. It assumes different forms in an era when man thinks that he himself must take charge of his future rather than in a period in which the traditions of the past continue to control strongly man's view of life. A brief historical sketch, therefore, can help us to discern with greater clarity the main thrust of utopian thought through the varying historical forms of utopian writings. What interests us here are the main lines of development and not an encyclopedic exposition about the content of the many utopian books.

It is no exaggeration to say that utopia is as old as human history, simply because looking for a better tomorrow is "a natural propensity of the human mind" (Kumar 1987: 9). On this point, George Orwell wrote of "the dream of a just society which seems to haunt the human imagination ineradicably and in all ages, whether it is called the Kingdom of Heaven or the classless society, or whether it is thought of as a Golden Age which once existed in the past and from which we have degenerated" (Kumar 1987: 3). Though ongoing studies on utopia indicate that it is hard to reach a consensus as to the definition, a consensus seems to emerge in the Occident as to what are the "key" or classic utopias. If we were to identify a few texts as "the agreed core" of utopias, they would include Plato's *Republic*, Thomas More's *Utopia*, Francis Bacon's

New Atlantis, Tomasso Campenella's *City of the Sun.* These are texts seldom excluded from any discussion on utopia, though More's *Utopia* is the only work which is universally discussed.

One of the most recent historical surveys of utopias is Frank and Frizie Manuel's *Utopian Thought in the Western World.* The aim of the book is "to identify historical constellations of utopias with reasonably well marked time-space perimeters and common elements that are striking enough to permit framing generalizations" (Manuel 1979: 13). There is a general agreement among the students of utopia that utopia "proper" (Eliav-Feldon 1982: 4; see also Kumar 1987: X and Levitas 1990: 158) begins with Thomas More. Nonetheless, traces of utopia can be found in Greek thought. Utopian themes reach back to the earliest Greek writings.[3] Lewis Mumford opines that, "the first utopias we know were fabricated in Greece...when one digs deeper into the utopian tradition, one finds that its foundations are buried in a much older past than that of Greece...(Manuel 1973: 3). Krishan Kumar starts his analysis of 'Utopianism ancient and modern', with the question, "Is it not a persuasive view, a commonplace even, that all utopias of the two and a half thousand years have been merely footnotes to Plato's *Republic*? (Kumar 1987: 2).

"Plato supplies the great archetype of utopia", says Chad Walsh (Walsh 1962:40). Nell Eurich describes the *Republic* as "the first full-scale utopia, the forefather and archetype of the literary genre as it is known..." (Eurich 1967: 36). Karl Mannheim is of the view that, "it was Plato who furnished, notably in his *Republic,* the general model to which all later utopian fictions have been heavily indebted" (Kumar 1987: 425). The Manuels in their latest survey say: "In the history of utopian thought Plato's influence is paramount... No utopian ever laid the ghost of Plato" (Manuel 1973: 110). The fact cannot be denied that in later utopias we meet some of the features of Platonic utopia, such as the ideal commonwealth, the elevation of public over private life, the communism of property, wives and children, the eugenic approach to reproduction etc. European utopians were clearly fascinated by alternative possibilities suggested by the two exemplars of the ancient world namely Athenian and Spartan.[4]

The utopists borrowed ideas from everywhere: from Plato,

from Aristotle[5] and from the fragments of the Hellenic utopias; "from the information that was reaching Europe about civilization of other continents (the new world and China): and from existing examples — invariably romanticized — within the boundaries of Europe, such as Venice, Florence, Geneva...and the monasteries".[6]

Historically, the Judeo-Christian contribution to utopia consisted in taking over and absorbing classical utopian themes — assimilation of the Golden age and identification of it with the Garden of Eden.[7] The Christian middle ages, however, are a conspicuously barren period in the history of utopian thought. The reason was mainly the anti-utopian influence of St. Augustine, for whom this world is necessarily and inescapably stained by sin and therefore the real life will be in the life to come, in "The City of God."[8] Though Augustine's theology, which was based on *contemptus mundi* and a life in The City of God, hindered the growth of utopian speculation to some degree, Jewish and Christian interpretations of the prophecies and the Revelation of St. John gave a new momentum to the notion of New Jerusalem here on earth, heaven on earth, new heaven and new earth etc. The chiliastic trends in the Middle Ages, which appealed to the vision of John's book of Revelation, show some utopian aspects[9]. It is interesting to note that, despite repeated tendencies towards worldliness and corruption, the medieval monastery, seemed to reflect, for many thinkers, the ideal society. Therefore, as Kumar sums up,

> It is hardly surprising, given this conception and enormous influence of monasticism on Christian thought and practice, that the early utopias should be so evidently marked by the presence of the monastery.[10]

What we have discussed so far is a "pre-history" of utopia. The features referred to, appear in later utopia. These utopian "pre-echoes", as Kumar notes, cannot be identified with utopia itself. The era of the Renaissance can best be characterized as the classical period of utopian thought. It was Thomas More who with his *Utopia* introduced the literary style of utopian writing. The term utopia was invented by Thomas More.[11] "Utopia is one of those mercurial, jocoserious writings which turn a profile to every advancing generation and respond in a different way to every set of questions which is addressed to them", says Robert

M. Adams in his preface to the new translation of *Utopia* (Adams 1975: vii). There are many interpretations of More's *Utopia*. The questions he posed and the answers he gave are to be studied in the context in which they occur to him. Some see him as a modern man far beyond his era, proposing prophetic remedies for the problems of an outworn social system; others see him as a conservative, medieval minded man whose ideal community was patterned on that of the monastery. Still others deny that he meant anything at all, preferring to describe his book as a joke. Some feel that the book can be understood in terms of its literary form or genre, in terms of predecessors among the imaginary commonwealth. Some even argue that utopia was a real place located in Peru, and Hythloday a real man who had visited it and talked with More.

Despite the debate about what the book "really" meant when it was written, the enormous influence it had on people's minds has to be reckoned with. It had its influence not only on socialist utopians of the nineteenth century, like William Morris and Edward Bellamy, but on men of its own time, the sixteenth century. The book took European readers by storm. Robert M. Adams concludes his preface to the translation of *Utopia* with the following words:

> The power of the book's idealism is a real ingredient of its structure; that fact has been demonstrated, not in a learned article but by the testimony of history. We may interpret it as we will, but the way a book like *Utopia* has been read and lived across the centuries is an authentic part of its nature.[12]

More continues to inspire the students of utopia and often his impact on succeeding utopias is taken for granted. He inspired others to make use of the utopian vehicle for expressing social criticism and to adopt some of his ideas for the reconstruction of society. The history of utopia in Europe clearly indicates the unsurpassed popularity and influence of More's *Utopia* throughout Europe.

The utopias of the Renaissance were, "... a curious mixture of optimism and pessimism, the sense of new vigour, a new vitality, and yet helplessness and impotence to effect real changes" (Eliav-Feldon 1982: 7). The utopian visions of this time were deeply based on a belief in the idea of progress—that progress of knowledge will itself lead mankind to total civilization. This belief in progress, in fact, is a product of rationalism and romanticism. The utopian thinking took a radical turn at this period, namely, a conviction that the realization of the utopian was no longer beyond reach but could be looked forward to because of the firm belief that the world was continually making progress towards its final completion. Thus "Realistic Utopias" of the Renaissance become deeply rooted in actuality. These Utopias were:

> 'Realistic' because they were not dependent on any supernatural conditions or on any divine intervention which would change the cosmos, human nature, or the course of history.'Realistic' also because they were not escapist dreams of fantasy or science fiction- they remained well within the scientific and technological possibilities of their age; they grappled seriously with the major and the minor problems of their own society, offering practical, feasible solutions in minutest details...although imaginary by definition, these utopias were deeply rooted in actuality.[13]

Nevertheless, they remain unrealistic in a different sense, because these utopias did not suggest "programmes of action" to transform the society.

It is probably the lack of an effective revolutionary conception and praxis of Renaissance utopias that made Marxists dismiss them as "mere wishful thinking". The utopian rationalism remained influential deep into the nineteenth century. It exists in various degree in Hegel, Spencer, Engels and Marx, though the term utopia does not appear as an entry in the recent comprehensive *Dictionary of Marxist Thought*. There is, however, doubt among the students of utopia whether Marxism itself is utopian.[14] The term utopia is in fact hardly ever used by Marx or Engels other than as a pejorative adjective "utopian", generally in the terms of 'utopian socialism' and 'utopian communism'.[15] "In one sense", as R. Levitas observes, "the whole of the collaboration project of Marx and Engels can be seen as a critique of utopian socialism..." (Levitas 1990: 36).

In so far as Marxism identifies utopian with unrealistic and uses the term utopia to embrace all pure speculation about future society, and in so far as utopia is understood to mean a counter-revolutionary process, then Marxism clearly is anti-utopian. Class struggle being the predominant characteristic of the communist social order, the construction of a society based on harmony looks to Marxism unrealistic.[16] Lenin rejected utopianism unequivocally, while defending the practice of dreaming about the future. Marx and Engels used the term utopia as a negative description of unrealistic policies; and, as Ruth Levitas concludes,

> ...Marx and Engels would defend themselves against the charge of utopianism; and indeed they are not utopian in the sense in which they use the term, even if they may be so according to other definitions (Levitas 1990: 58)

Even so, in common parlance Marxism continues to be utopian, though the place of utopia in Marxist thought has remained a controversial issue. If utopia can be described as dynamic process of social change that look towards a better future, then utopia becomes compatible with Marxism.

The end of the nineteenth century broke with the spirit of the Enlightenment.[17] The rationalistic optimism and expectation of progress, still manifest in Bellamy's work, *Looking Backward 2000-1887*, disappears around the turn of the century. Through a healthy interaction of science and technology, society acquires the power to assume control over its own future. The utopian writings of this period present an anticipating picture of a future which man himself must plan. Science fiction, which anticipates future developments of science, technology and society begins to flourish in this period.[18]

The Manuels, at the end of their long journey through utopia, suggest that we are living in the "twilight of utopia", and wonder whether we are witnessing "a running down of the utopian-making machine of the West". Northrop Frye notes a "paralysis of utopian thought and imagination" in contemporary literature. Robert Elliot points to the widely accepted reason for the fact that "the uninhibited utopianizing imagination" has largely disappeared.[19]

The neo-Marxist trend occupies a special place in contemporary utopian thinking. Against Marx, neo-Marxist writers, such as Bloch, Adorno, Kolakowski, and Marcuse, defend the critico-dynamic role of utopian thinking. The concrete utopia both negates and transcends with respect to the existing situation.[20] Marcuse, for instance, speaks about "the end of utopia", because the so-called utopian possibilities are no longer utopian but already constitute the historico-social negation of the existing situation. Utopia was dead not because it was impossible, or something to dread, but precisely because the possibilities of its realization were now at hand. The apparent contradiction that may seem to exist between the terms "utopia and end of utopia", begins to disappear when these concepts are understood in the context of utopian dialectics. In such a synthesis realization or the possibility of realization opens into new possibilities of realization.

From the brief sketch of utopian thinking in history, it becomes evident that utopia has always existed and utopia continues to exist as a vision to guide the humankind to a better future. The history of utopia seems to suggest discoveries of new utopias. Sarvodaya, as envisioned by Gandhi, is well situated in the ongoing history of utopia. But before we delve deep into sarvodaya as utopia, it is important to highlight the essential characteristics of utopia.

Utopian Dialects

The critical intention to break through the existing conditions and achieve a better future turns out to be the essence of the realistic utopian phenomenon. This intention was already present, though implicit, in the Renaissance utopias; Marx and bourgeois sociology described this intention as naive and in this sense utopian, but today its importance in producing changes in the society receives great emphasis. Utopia fulfils this critical function by presenting a concrete picture of the ideal and thus exercises a constant moral pressure on society to bring about a better world. Any utopia that wishes to offer new perspectives for society assumes a critical attitude toward the existing situation which it tries to change. There is thus the dialectic: it is both explorative and normative, presenting both facts and possibility, the actual and ideal; it is the "no longer" of the paradise lost and the "not yet" of the future; it is critical of the present and offers a constructive image of the future. It is in fact this dialectic that makes utopia a process, a catalysing agent and a vision for the future.

The dialectic of utopia brings out the potential that is in utopia, namely its spiritual power, the power of a new idea. This spiritual power is revolutionary in the sense that it makes society ripe for fundamental change. Utopian thinkers and writers are well aware of the revolutionary nature of ideas and visions. Gandhi was no exception to this rule as we see when we come to his sarvodaya vision.

Utopia or Ideology

Coming back to Gandhi's sarvodaya vision, we argue that it is a realistic utopia. In order to clarify this assertion we need to examine further the contrast between utopia and ideology, as articulated by Mannheim and others. Though utopia literally means "a place of ideal perfection", it tends to connote an impractical scheme. We are not using the term in that sense. Here realistic utopia is used in the sense of "an ideal which, however elusive it may be, is not necessarily impossible" (Bakker 1993: 11).

The dynamic or transforming nature of utopia is better understood in contrast with ideology. Ideology is perhaps one of the most equivocal and elusive concepts one can find in the social sciences. This is so not only because of the variety of theoretical approaches which assign different meanings and functions to it, but also because it is a concept heavily charged with political connotation and widely used in everyday life with the most diverse signification. Karl Mannheim probably is the most well known theorist of utopia. The merit of Mannheim is that he inter-relates ideology and utopia and at the same time preserves their differences. For Mannheim, ideology is a "mentality"[21] or *Weltanshauung*[22] — world view — which 'fails to take account of the new realities applying to a situation' and which attempts to cancel them by thinking of them in categories which are inappropriate (Mannheim 1936: 87). Mannheim expands the concept of ideology to the point where it encompasses even the person asserting it. The viewpoint of the absolute onlooker, the one uninvolved in the social game, is impossible, according to Mannheim. As Paul Ricoeur puts it, "To call something ideological is never merely a theoretical judgment but rather implies a certain practice and a view on reality that this practice gives to us"

(Ricoeur 1986: xv). Any perspective expressed is in some sense ideological.

Mannheim places ideology and utopia in a common framework. For him, ideology and utopia have both a common feature and a differential feature. The common feature is what he calls non-congruence, a kind of deviation or split. It is difficult to say what the non-congruence is a deviation from; we might say it is deviation from the state of action and reality within which it occurs. He describes ideology and utopia as forms of non-congruence, vantage points in discrepancy with present reality. He observes that there are two ways in which a system of thought may be non-congruent with the general trend of a group or society: either by sticking to the past, thus a certain resistance to change, or by leaping ahead, and thus a type of encouragement of change. The concept of non-congruence provides us with the correlation between ideology and utopia: it either lags behind or stands ahead of a given situation. These two modalities of non-congruence are continually fighting against one another. In either case, says Mannheim, "the reality to be comprehended is distorted and concealed..." (Mannheim 1936: 97). Though there exists no natural transition from utopia to ideology in Mannheim's view, "Antiquated and inapplicable norms, modes of thought, and theories," he says, "are likely to degenerate into ideologies whose function it is to conceal the actual meaning of conduct rather to reveal it" (Mannheim 1936: 95).

The first criterion, which utopia shares in common with ideology, is a certain non-congruence, a non-coincidence, with the state of reality in which it occurs. There are many synonyms of this expression in Karl Mannheim; the emphasis is on ideas and interests that are "situationally transcendent". Transcendence, here, is not taken in its philosophical sense but with respect to the present state of reality. The second criterion of utopia is more decisive. A utopia tends to "shatter, either partially or wholly, the order of things prevailing at the time" (Mannheim 1936: 192). Here ideology may be defined by opposition to utopia because it is what preserves a certain order. The transcendent character of utopia is also revealed by its realizability. This is significant, because it runs against a prejudice that utopia is merely a dream. On the contrary, says Mannheim, a utopia shatters a given order; and it is only when it starts shattering order that it is a utopia. A utopia is then always in the process of being realized. Ideology, in contrast, does not have the problem of being realized, because it is the legitimation of what is. The non-congruence between ideology and reality is due to the fact that reality changes, whereas ideology has a certain inertia. Another differential criterion of ideology and utopia is manifested in two ways. First, ideologies relate mainly to dominant groups. Ideological representations, Mannheim holds, "conceal reality" and thus are in fact never realized. The ruling conservative classes love to resort to transcendent ideas to camouflage reality. But to utopian representation Mannheim ascribes a force capable of "transforming reality." As Plattel comments, "these utopian ideas possess a trail-blazing function and they exist especially among oppressed classes which try to become emancipated" (Plattel 1972: 70). Second, ideologies are directed more toward the past, whereas utopias have a futuristic element.

Thus for Mannheim, both ideology and utopia are non-congruent with reality, but ideology legitimates the existing order while utopia shatters it. The dynamic of utopia, for Mannheim, is that the process of history is leading to a decline of utopia and therefore to the progressive disappearance of any non-congruence with reality. Mannheim sees the victory of a certain matter-of-factness (*Sachlichkeit*). People are more adjusted to reality, and because they are adapted they have no illusions; but with the loss of illusions people also lose any sense of direction. There is no longer the impulse to draw general pictures. Mannheim thinks that the utopias will disappear and "whenever the utopia disappears, history ceases to be a process leading to an ultimate end" (Mannheim 1936: 253). Yet, ironically, nothing is less true than Mannheim's claim that we are "in a world which is no longer in the making". It is strange that in the last paragraph of the utopia chapter, Mannheim identifies where the parallelism between ideology and utopia ends:

> It is possible, therefore, that in the future, in a world in which there is never anything new, in which all is finished and each moment is a repetition of the past, there exist a

> condition in which thought will be utterly devoid of ideological and utopian elements. But the complete elimination of reality-transcending elements from our world would lead us to a "matter-of-factness" which ultimately would mean the decay of human will. Herein lies the most essential difference between these two types of reality-transcendence: whereas the decline of ideology represents a crisis only of certain strata,... the complete disappearance of the utopian element from human thought and action would mean that human nature and human development would take on a totally new character (Mannheim 1936: 262).

Realizability is not a valid criterion to judge utopia and ideology because ideologies are in a sense already realized. They confirm what exists. The essential distinction is that utopias unmask ideologies, which are in fact always realized because they confirm the current, whereas utopias can never fully succeed since they show the "distance" between the current and the hoped-for perfected future (see Ricoeur 1986: 179 and Fox 1989: 33). Though Mannheim envisages the actual loss of utopia in the "gradual descent" and the "closer approximation to real life" (Mannheim 1936: 248) of the utopian forces, the decisive trait of utopia is not realizability but the preservation of opposition. If we could imagine a society where everything is realized, there congruence would exist. This society, however, would be "dead", because there would be no distance, no ideals, no project at all. A non-ideological and non-utopian society would be a dead society. The critical mark of utopia, then, is not realizability but the preservation of distance between itself and reality. It may appear that Mannheim's analysis is circular and that we cannot get out of the circle between ideology and utopia. But Mannheim believes that his approach is dialectical. It is a dialectic that is at the heart of any transformation in every social order: every social order gives rise to utopias that break through existing situations and allow society to evolve to the next order of existence.

In his critique of Mannheim, Paul Ricoeur observes that Mannheim stresses utopia as non-congruence rather than as that which shatters. The reason why Mannheim speaks of the dissolution of utopia, the end of non-congruence, a world no longer in the making, is, he claims, because, "Mannheim cannot incorporate into his model the permanent and positive traits of either ideology or utopia" (Ricoeur 1986: xxiii).

The contribution Ricoeur makes to the understanding of ideology and utopia is to give them a permanent and positive status. If the best function of ideology is integration, the preservation of the identity of a person or group, the best function of utopia is exploration of the possible. The utopia puts in question what presently exists; it is an imaginative alternative on the nature of power, family, religion, and so on. We are forced to experience the contingency of the social order. The utopia is not only a dream, though, for it is a dream that wants to be realized. The purpose of the utopia is to change (shatter) the present order. One of the main reasons why Ricoeur discusses Saint-Simon and Fourier is that they exemplify this perspective; they made strenuous efforts to have their utopias realized. But even while the utopia's intention is to shatter reality, it maintains a distance from any present reality. Utopia is the constant ideal, that toward which we are directed but which we never fully attain. Here Ricoeur builds on an idea of Mannheim that Mannheim was not able to incorporate into his theory, that the death of utopia would mean the death of society. A society without utopia would be dead, because it would no longer have any project, any prospective goals.

In Gandhi's language, ideology and utopia both might be called "experiments in truthful understanding." Ideologies are false or failed experiments because they only confirm the present, whereas utopian visions succeed as truthful experiments because they challenge the present system and confront it so as to transform it. The utopia, if it fails in confrontation, can in turn be taken to legitimate the current order as a new ideology. If it succeeds, a new order appears. Though R. Fox uses ideology-utopia dialetic in the specific context of cultural changes (patterns of domination and authority), this dialectic seems to underlie any change or progress. As this dialectic is at the centre of any progress or development in society, Gandhian utopian experiments work in a dialectic: they are authored by Gandhi, authorized by group struggle, and de-authorized by the opposition they meet — until the next time (Fox 1989: 34). Utopian visions, for Gandhi, motivate a continuing human struggle to achieve them, which in turn requires a confrontation with existing systems and structures. Confrontational of a different nature (i.e., nonviolent confrontation), Gandhi's method and vision offered challenges to the prevailing injustice in any given situation. The relevance of Gandhi's vision, that is realizing utopian hope, lies in the challenge Gandhi continues to offer even today.

Ernst Bloch has extensively dealt with the problem of utopia, particularly its relationship to ideology. Bloch wishes to strip the utopia of its pejorative meaning as the fanciful dreams of people who want to improve the world but are strangers to its reality. He introduces the distinction between concrete and abstract utopias. Abstract utopias are sheer fancies and in no way connected with history or the present. They evaporate into "sheer utopizing" and end up with an "empty possibility." Concrete utopias, on the other hand, aim at realistically possible goal and indicate concrete ways of reaching it. They anticipate the "really possible."

Bloch thinks that the utopian function is the "principle of hope" for a human race which assumes responsibility for its own destiny. By introducing "principle of hope" to utopia, Bloch seems to inspire Christian eschatological hope (we will return later to this question). It is this hope that opens the future horizon wider and makes utopia a way more open and flexible than ideology. In the words of Martin G. Plattel:

> The classical ideologies appear less capable for disclosing this horizon. They are too dogmatic and view the horizon of the future as an existing presence. They say too little about the future as *far* horizon and too much about it as far *horizon*. The ideology is too little vision and too much a system of idea, it changes an open horizon into a closed horizon... The ideological man lives in the illusion that he already knows the future as possibility and knows it exactly... The utopia, on the other hand, discloses the horizon not as pure presence but as an absent presence. The main difference is that the ideological man acts *on the basis of* an ideological system while the utopian man acts *in the light of* a utopian portrayal (Plattel 1972: 75-76).

Through the utopia, thus, society creates for itself a horizon, a vision of the future which is open, flexible and realizable. In the light of this vision society can venture to go forward in an experimental fashion. As Bloch succinctly puts it, the utopia is nothing but "something that is kept open for a reality which is possible in the future but has not yet been decided upon and which could be brought about in that empty space" (Plattel 1972: 76).

Utopia: Realistic Imagination

As M.G. Plattel observes, "the utopia is imagination in action in the realm of human pursuits". And writing on "Varieties of Literary Utopias", Northrop Frye says that utopia "presents an imaginative vision of the telos or end at which social life aims" (Manuel 1973: 25). For Ricoeur, "the very character of utopia is imagination". Ricoeur maintains that the correlation of ideology and utopia typifies what he calls the social and cultural imagination; together they form the social imagination. In social life, imagination functions in two different ways:

> On the one hand, imagination may function to preserve an order... ideology represents the first kind of imagination; it has the function of preservation, of conservation. Utopia, in contrast, represents the second kind of imagination; it is always the glance from nowhere (Ricoeur 1986: xxviii and 15).

If ideology is imagination as picture, utopia is imagination as fiction. "In a sense all ideology repeats what exists by justifying it, and so it gives a picture...of what is. Utopia, on the other hand, has the fictional power of redescribing life." (Ricoeur 1986: 18).

For Ricoeur, the utopian quality of the imagination moves from the constituted to the constituting, from the instituted to the instituting. It offers a vantage point from which to perceive the given, the already constituted, and it offers new possibilities above and beyond the given. Utopia is the view from "nowhere" — the literal meaning of the word — that ensures that we no longer take for granted our present reality. Utopia "has a constitutive role in helping us rethink the nature of social life." It is "the way in which we radically rethink" the nature of the family, consumption, authority, religion, and so on; it is "the fantasy of an alternative society and its exteriorization 'nowhere'" that works "as one of the most formidable contestations of what is." Utopia acts not only to de-reify our present relations but to point to those possibilities that may yet be ours.

At the social level, utopia has a metaphoric quality. As productive imagination, its task is "exploration of the possible." It poses an ideal or model (Ricouer says that "A model may reflect what is, but it also may pave the way for what is not" Ricoeur 1986: 311). Utopia, as noted above, is not simply a dream but one that wants to be actualized. "The utopia's intention is surely to change things, and therefore we can not say with Marx's eleventh thesis on Feurbach that it is a way of interpreting the world and not changing it. On the contrary, the thrust of utopia is to change reality" (Ricoeur 1986: 289).

Utopian thought is imaginative, it portrays the possible future, but it is more concerned with visualizing possibilities than with achieving ends. A scientific sense is needed to complement the imaginative nature of utopia, which extrapolates from the present and calculates the future in terms of the present. Utopia thus presents possibilities and asks science to test the feasibility of their realization. It sketches a picture of the future which science must develop and refine. Although science is inventive, it tries to achieve the possible by strongly relying on the actual facts. But the utopian imagination likes to experiment with the entire complex of actual facts and its forte is to foresee the possibility of different complexes of facts. "Utopian imagination", in the words of Gregory Baum, "makes people sensitive to the breaking points of the present system and nourishes in them a longing for a new society, and as such exercises a significant role in social change" (Baum 1975: 171). Gandhi's vision of the future — a model and ideal he proposed through his sarvodaya ideal and longing for a new society — was very imaginative. Nonetheless it was not a pure fantasy because, like a scientist, he experimented with the visions he proposed. Even more, such experiments are being carried out to this day and there is all likelihood that these experiments would go on for years though with adaptations to changing contexts of the Indian and of the global scenario.

Utopia and Vision

Utopia, when operating as such, is always in the process of being realized and thus it has a futuristic element in it.[23] The object (goal) of this realization process is an alternative to the existing situation (status quo). This is because utopia opens the possible, and it does so on the basis of a "metaphoric transformation of the existing" (Ricoeur 1986: xxxii). The futuristic element in utopia is hope in a transformed state of things in general whose details are important in its process of realization. What makes utopia a vision for the future is the sense of future possibilities implied in it and its intent to change things ("shatter the present").

Ernst Bloch explains in his three volume work, *The Principle of Hope*, how utopia is the real anticipation of the new dimension in human history. The designation of utopia as "anticipatory consciousness" is the *"Not yet"* for Bloch. He argues that "the material world is essentially unfinished, the future is undetermined and therefore that the future constitutes a realm of possibility" (Levitas 1990: 87). These possibilities are not *mere formal* possibilities but *real* possibilities. In the context of such "realistically possible goals", Bloch situates utopia as an anticipation of the future, and, through its effects on human purpose and action, as a catalyst of the future. Utopia thus is the expression of hope, a hope construed, "not...only as emotion..., but more essentially as directing act of a cognitive kind" (Bloch 1986: 12).

Bloch's distinction of abstract and concrete utopias explains what he means by real possibilities as opposed to mere wishful thinking. Anticipatory elements are identified with concrete utopia, whereas compensatory elements are identified with abstract utopia. When later he speaks of utopia simply, what he means is concrete utopia, defined by its anticipatory and transformative function and linked to the future. Concrete utopias provide an imagination that actually influences people's thoughts and actions. Concrete utopias are images of the future that are grounded in authentic intuitions of the ills and contradictions present in society. Concrete utopias negate the most oppressive elements of this society and present a vision of human life that, even if as such un-realizable, calls forth new ways of thinking and acting that could lead to actual social change.

To rehabilitate a utopia, Bloch would say, all the abstract elements which clutter up the core have to be removed. Concrete utopia must be winnowed out, stripping wishful thinking of that which is purely fantastic, compensatory and escapist. The process means

> knowledge and removal of the finished *utopist element*, with knowledge and removal of *abstract utopia*. But what then remains: the unfinished forward dream, the docta spes which can only be discredited by the bourgeoisie-this seriously deserves the name utopia in carefully considered and carefully applied contrast to utopianism; in its brevity and new clarity, this expression then means the same as: *a methodical organ for the New, an objective aggregate state of what is coming up* (Bloch 1986: 157).

There seems to be a strong teleological perspective in Bloch's utopia. This teleology is explicit when he says that the true genesis is not at the beginning but at the end and the world is full of propensity towards something, latency of something, and this intended something means fulfilment of the intending.

Not every dream of future happiness is utopian. In modern, capitalist society we are constantly exposed to images of an ideal future based on an ever higher standard of living and the continuing quest for selfish fulfilment of pleasure and comfort. This, to Bloch, is no utopian dream[24] because we can speak of utopia only if the imagination introduces a qualitatively new element in the form of human life. The utopian vision does not prolong the present into the future, but it elevates and recreates the present in keeping with man's unfulfilled potentialities. Bloch elucidates his points by his reference to yearnings for objects that exist in the world and for objects that do not yet exist. The first yearning produces unauthentic feelings such as envy, greed etc., whereas the yearning for objects that do not exist produces strong feelings of expectancy in regard to the future: anxiety, fear, hope, and faith. Of these only hope is authentically human. "In hope alone", as Baum observes, "do people authentically relate their yearning to the future. Only if the day-dream is accompanied by hope does it release the potentialities of matter, direct action and enable people to create the new" (Baum 1975: 282).

Bloch suggests that the idea of the kingdom carries the vision of utopia which Marxism makes a real possibility. This is a complex claim because he is not suggesting that the idea of the kingdom can be reduced to a plan of social utopia; what he is suggesting is the resolution of antagonisms (between humanity and the world) that is represented in the image of the kingdom. The possibility of an "earthly kingdom" or a "godless kingdom" is represented by Bloch because, "the idea of God must be separated from that kingdom, and repossessed as at least a potential embodiment of true humanness..." [25]

Tillich opens with three assertions about the status of utopia. First, utopia "is rooted in the nature of man himself." Secondly, it is not possible to understand history without reference to utopia since human consciousness and action are meaningless without reference to utopia as beginning and end of history. Thirdly, he argues (with clear dependence on Bloch) that "all utopias strive to negate the negative itself in human existence; it is the negative in existence which makes the utopia necessary" (Manuel 1973: 296).

Utopia has both positive and negative characteristics: it contains truth, in so far as it contains telos, the goal and purpose of existence; but it also contains untruth, in that it forgets that estrangement is a condition of human existence. Utopia is fruitful in the sense that it opens possibilities which would have been lost without utopian anticipation; but it is unfruitful in that it is in the nature of the wish to describe impossibilities as real possibilities. Tillich thinks that mere un-realizable goals can make utopias "nothing but a fool's paradise." He continues, "and this is the origin of the fantastic utopias—they conform not to essential possibilities but rather to a fantastically exaggerated wish for existence which itself has to be overcome" (Manuel 1973:300). Utopia contains power, the power of transformation, and "the root of its power is the essential-ontological-discontent of man in every direction of his being"; but utopia is also important because of its negative content, which inevitably leads to failure and disillusion. This contradictory nature of utopia calls for its transcendence (as a consequence utopia is always and necessarily suspended between possibility and impossibility). Tillich sees this transcendence as accomplished by reference to two orders, the horizontal and the vertical. The horizontal is that of the political and social, of immanent utopia. The vertical is that of radical transcendence, the divine, which continually breaks through. In this breaking through the kingdom of God[26] actualises itself in history; but it is always resisted and suppressed, so that fulfilment in the horizontal is only ever potential. Thus, for Tillich, there is a constant tension between utopia and non-utopia in history, and this tension makes utopia a process that is being realized. Of this process Tillich has this to say: "... my own deep feeling is that ours is a period in which the *Kairos*, the right time for utopian realization, lies before us, invisible, while only void, and unfulfilled space, a vacuum, surrounds us" (Manuel 1973: 309).

Following Bloch, Moltmann developed a concept of "creative expectation", which he defined as "hope which sets about criticizing and transforming the present because it is open towards the universal future of the kingdom" (Bentley 1982: 89). What is implied here is that the kingdom of God is, as for Tillich, not merely transcendent but something which demands social transformation. Thus "the social overthrowing of unjust relationship is the immanent reverse-side of the transcendent hope of resurrection" (Bentley 1982: 90). Thus one can find a parallelism in Christian theology because, as Baum comments, "...church's teaching on eternal life is a revealed utopia" (Baum 1975: 283). The message of the kingdom which is partially present among us and yet still to be fully realized, proposes a vision of the future in which people live in justice and peace. This eschatological reign of God, situated at the horizon of history, is being unfolded in the present.

The message of eternal life is of a very special utopia, because Christians hold that it has been divinely revealed and believe in the promises of the prophets and Jesus Christ. The divine promises made known in the Scriptures are utopian because they transcend history and their fulfilment remains open. This openness to the future is the basis of hope that inspires people to work for a just society. German political theologians like to oppose eschatology and utopia and thus refuse to regard the Christian hope for the kingdom as utopian; but not so Latin American theologians of liberation. They believe that this kingdom is no "other worldly reality"; it is not a heavenly dominion above the realms of the earth; "the kingdom was, rather, the divine reign that emerged in history as the longing of the cosmos and the fulfilment of the people's hopes. The Kingdom was preached as the new age" (Baum 1975: 267).

The concept of transcendence, when used in explaining utopia may create problems for some Marxists and those intellectuals who are predominantly positivistic. It involves fundamental questions about the human condition and its future—hope and faith in the possibilities of that future. Utopian thought always relates to the future, whether near or far away, and a future quite different from the present reality. Drastic change, therefore, is somehow part of utopian thinking. As Polak puts it, "the conceptualization and visualization of change (a colossal change in itself) is the precondition of actualized social change" (Manuel 1973: 282). Bloch too stresses the centrality of human vision in social transformation, in support of which he cites a passage about the distinguishing characteristic of the human species:

> We are assuming work in a form in which it belongs exclusively to man. A spider carries out operations which resemble those of a weaver, and a bee puts many human builders to shame with the building of its wax cells. But what distinguishes the worst builder from the best bee from the outset, is that he has built the cell in his head before he builds it in wax, at the end of the work process there is a result which already existed in the imagination of the worker at the beginning of that process, i.e., already existed ideally. Not that he only effects a formal change in the real; he also realizes his purpose in the natural world (Bloch 1986: 76).

The human mind in its imaginative vision emancipates itself from spatio-temporal limits of the existing reality and tries to cross the borders of the unknown. The rationale behind any progress or forward-moving human civilization lies in this forward-thinking. "Images of the future" are imaginatively built as ideals or visions. These ideals in turn direct and inspire man to reach out above and beyond himself to a better future. Being in a process of realization, they are utopian and the basis of any real (revolutionary) transformation in the society. As Bloch rightly says, "The concrete utopia stands at the horizon of all reality" (Bloch 1986: 258). Though horizon circumscribes the reach of man, it opens a perspective for going forward without limit. As Plattel puts it, "without the horizon society and human life would be dying or dead, but the horizon make them pregnant again with new possibilities".[27] Utopia, as forward dreaming,[28] is neither an esoteric byway of culture, nor a distraction from the real business of class struggle, but a central and crucially important element in the production of the future. The transforming function of utopian vision or imagination is well summed up by Geoghegan when he says that "the faculty of imagination enables one to transcend the given by cognitively creating the future which will then serve as spur to its practical realization" (Geoghegan 1981: 28). Speaking of utopian imagination, Martin Buber said that "the utopian imagination incorporated a hard-headed element of rational planning which, far from proposing world-rejecting flight, actually thrust forward thoughtful programmes for social reorganization which were perfectly capable of realization in the not too distant future" (Buber 1949: 11).

The yearning, desire, dreaming, and hoping for a better future is as old as human history; and this "looking forward" to ideal living is the basis of all utopian thinking. This seems to be an inborn propensity of human life. If utopian thinking is a basic striving of human existence, one cannot assume that it is a habit peculiar to the West. Utopian studies and researches are farther advanced in the West than in the East, where one finds very little direct reference to utopia.[29] In comparing and contrasting utopias of the West and Japan, Seiji Nuita observes:

> If we are considering the history of utopian thought from a world view point, we certainly cannot disregard the utopias of the ancient orient, of China and other countries. Strictly speaking, I feel that, outside the West, only in China do you find a tradition of typical utopian thinking that continues from ancient to modern times. Outside of China we find only sporadic examples. Ancient India for instance, created a perfect, spatial image of utopia in Buddhism's pure Land of Eternal Happiness. But typical

> utopias—if we use the West as the type-case—did not arise in later periods of Indian history. In Japan, too, we have several early examples of utopian thinking....Today in Japan there is great interest in futurology....Futurology differs from utopia in that it lacks a thoroughly critical attitude toward society (Plath ed. 1971: 17).

The Exploratory and Normative Value of Utopia

The imaginative nature of utopia makes it a "movement of transcendence", which goes beyond the present into the area of unlimited possibilities. Utopian thinking here has to be complemented by a scientific sense, otherwise it will end up in pure fantasy or utopias of escape. It is only when science and utopia collaborate that man approaches the future in a prospective way. Utopia gains an exploratory value as a result of its collaboration with science. Utopia presents possibilities and asks science to test the feasibility of their realization. It sketches a picture of the future which science must develop and refine. Though imagination plays an important role in scientific research (e.g., in the formulation of hypothesis), its role in science differs from its role in utopia. Although science is inventive, it tries to achieve the possible by strongly relying on the actual facts. But the utopian imagination likes to experiment with the entire complex of actual facts and its purpose is to foresee the possibility of a different complex of facts.

Unlike scientific thinking, utopian thought need not at once be verified or rejected. Yet, scientific thought helps utopian thinking to realize its unlimited possibilities. The utopian sense, thus, corresponds to the creative nature of man, who is "possibility rather than facticity". It is this healthy tension between facticity and possibility in utopian thinking that explains its exploratory nature. Thus, in the words of Plattel, "science without utopia becomes too fossilized, utopia without science becomes sheer fancy. But a...concrete utopia enlarges the field of vision and opens many new perspectives. On the other hand, it guards men's thinking against escaping to empty speculations because of its empirical starting point..." (Plattel 1972:82).

In addition to its inventiveness, utopia also has a critical normative function. It wishes to put the present in the light of a new future, one that functions as ideal or norm. As critique lies at the source of all human progress, man evaluates the present in the light of an ideal or norm. What helps one to think beyond and plan beyond the present is this normative character.

Critical negativity lies at the heart of utopia.[30] Every utopian model of the future is born from a critique of existing evil conditions, a dissatisfaction with the prevailing situation in society. Dissatisfaction with the existing system often takes the form of protest and therefore some form of protest is part of the critical negativity. Protest, in this context is never an end in itself, rather a means toward achieving the utopian goal. Since the critical negation works as a dialectical process, the horizon of meaning or future possibilities posited do not always have the rational exactness of prognosis and planning. Nonetheless the human mind can form a picture of the possible and thus transcend the actual limitations. The utopian horizon projected by the human mind as a possibility, appears to be the impetus to progressive changes and developments in society.

Realizable Utopia

This rather comprehensive historical survey of utopia brings us to the conclusion that utopia has socio-political and philosophico-theological elements in it and it urges people to transcend the present and venture into new possibilities. Common man's usage of utopia for something merely impractical and purely imaginary arises from a misconceived notion and superficial understanding of utopia. It is in order, therefore, to highlight some of the pertinent characteristics of utopia before we go into the application of the varied characteristics of utopia to sarvodaya of Gandhi.

From our survey, it seems beyond any doubt that utopia has always existed and will continue to exist as a vision to guide people to a better future. The dialectical nature of utopia introduces us to the ideology-utopia debate, and explains the process of utopia becoming ideology and at the same time transcending the realm of ideology. Though realizability is not always a valid criterion to judge utopia and ideology, possibility of realization makes utopia a process whose realizability is never exhausted.

Seen as a "principle of hope", utopia is eschatological. Utopia also works as realistic imagination and explores the possible future. Yet, in the words of Paul Tillich, utopia has both positive and negative characteristics: it contains truth and untruth, it offers an ideal yet it has the danger of becoming fantasy.

Critical but creative, utopia is explorative and functions as normative. The normative value of utopia offers a vision, ideal or model for the future.

Beyond "Experiments with Culture"

Richard G. Fox, in his book, *Gandhian Utopia: Experiments with Culture*, portrays Gandhi as a scientist working not within any closed laboratory but within the entire fabric of life. In seeing Gandhi as a scientist, a man given to experimentation, Fox is able to controvert certain stereotypes of Gandhi. Placing him firmly as an advocate of "change", Fox removes Gandhi from the timeless and mystical world of the Hindus to which he is frequently relegated. Unlike Gandhi's detractors, who believe that Gandhi was opposed to the scientific world view and progress, Fox attempts to show how Gandhi was, in fact, a better scientist than most others. Fox argues that "individual experiments make for constant personal becoming". Fox posits the notion of "discontinuous personhoods" to suggest how each of Gandhi's experiments "made him into a somewhat different person", and "he experienced essential transformations" (Fox 1989: 23-25).

It is not just Gandhi's experiments which engage Fox's attention. From the perspective of anthropology, Gandhi is Fox's medium of entry into the various debates taking place within anthropology; and *Gandhian Utopia* is Fox's own experiment with the premises and practices of anthropological inquiry. Fox suggests that if Gandhi still was able to offer effective cultural resistance, he did so by turning Orientalism upside down. Gandhi's Orientalism did not merely look back to the past, to some Golden Age of Hinduism. For, if he was a cultural conservative in some matters, for example in his defence of the village community and *varnashrama dharma*, in most other matters he was a cultural revolutionary, as exemplified in his attempts to improve the position of women and untouchables in Indian society. Gandhi was interested in those cultural elements as propositions for the future, propositions that promised a utopia. Thus, for example, in Gandhi's utopia, which he envisaged as *Ramrajya*, to show the world the way to peace through ahimsa and satyagraha.

Gandhian utopia is exemplary of Fox's notion of "culture in the making," because this utopia, more than fifty years after Gandhi's death, is still in the making and continues to be invoked in experiments with culture and politics conducted in post-independence India, often enough, by defenders of traditional Hinduism and exponents of Hindu supremacy. Hindu fundamentalists and upper-castes have, in Fox's words, "hijacked" Gandhian utopia and converted it into a "justifying ideology" which preserves the status quo (Fox 1989: 162 and 271). Fox quite rightly points to Vinoba's experiments and political practices as a pathological form of Gandhian utopia. Gandhian utopia in Vinoba's hands even came to justify the Emergency, which was proclaimed in the name of keeping law and order. Vinoba resisted any interpretation of satyagraha that would have conserved it as a potent means of revolutionary experiment in India after the demise of Gandhi. Though Fox expresses doubt "whether Jayaprakash Narayan (JP) took his belief in permanent revolution from Gandhi's idea of experiment or from Marx's notion of praxis", in JP's hand, Gandhian utopia seems to take the form of total revolution. But JP was not able to authorize his version of Gandhian utopia independent of certain class and caste interests (Fox 1989: 209, 272). Fox's interest is to analyze Gandhi's experiments with truth as experiments with culture in general. But Gandhi's experiments could never be limited to mere cultural experiments because his utopian vision is larger than life. Its implications are vast and horizons unlimited. Therefore, we will (examine) argue in this book that sarvodaya of Gandhi is a realistic utopia from the perspective of economy, ashramic and village experimentation and from the momentum sarvodaya gathered from its immediate co-authors, such as Vinoba and JP. We shall also explore the hope aspect that lies implicit in Gandhi's utopian vision: theology and ecology.

Experimenting (The) Sarvodaya Vision

Gandhi was not a theoretician or philosopher in the strict sense of the term. He did not produce a theoretical blueprint for the future India. Nonetheless he did propose an alternative for the India of his time, a sarvodaya alternative, wherein he was critical of the present and suggested ways and means for the transformation of the society. In this he was definitely influenced by Western authors. Gandhi was impressed by Leo Tolstoy's simplicity of life, his ideals of love, peace and equality; Gandhi shared with Tolstoy the vision of social order. Tolstoy's philosophical anarchism inspired Gandhi a great deal.[31] Gandhi was profoundly impressed by Thoreau's essay on civil disobedience. Gandhi often quoted Thoreau, who said that the best government was the one which governed least. Gandhi's detachment from worldly possession, nonviolence and universal love owe much to the influence of Christianity and the New Testament.[32]

Gandhi's utopia was not only of his making: it was authored also by European Orientalists, by mid-Victorians, such as John Ruskin and Edward Carpenter, and by Indian nationalists. Richard Fox finds Gandhi's utopian emphasis on India's spirituality pre-figured in Annie Besant's and Sister Nivedita's constructions of India; the idea of selflessness was shared among so many others, notably by Aurobindo; and the call to *swadeshi* had already been made by Tilak, Besant, Tagore and Bengali nationalists. A great deal of what is credited to Gandhi was the result of "group effort". Moreover, "Great Persons are always authorized by little people" (Fox 1989: 13). Gandhi's utopia portrays a cultural renaissance in Indian society that is based on spiritual power, an economic order that is based on small-scale societies living in village republics, and a political system without state. His social utopia has two parts: a vigorous attack on social evils of the present, and an idealized depiction of the imagined society of the future.

The sarvodaya alternative of Gandhi is a realistic utopia. It is an ideal or model that has utopian characteristics in it. These characteristics are typical in the sense that they contain theoretical and practical perspectives, they have an "already and not-yet" element in them and realized and yet to be realized dialectic. The Indian independence struggle, led by Gandhi and which is solidly based on sarvodaya, is an example where total liberation of people from all that make them less human is still a vision (utopia) in the process of being realized, whereas independence from colonial domination or political freedom achieved by India may be seen as a realized vision: ideology.

Sarvodaya as a norm or ideal works in a dialectic, that is to say, all the details cannot be worked out at the start or in the abstract, but are shaped in its process. Also by offering and opening up new possibilities, sarvodaya sustains its hope for the future. Sarvodaya may have become an ideology in the hands of Vinoba Bhave, but it maintained the element of hope under JP's leadership. Gandhi may have been a "prisoner of hope", but his *Ramrajya*, the goal of sarvodaya ideal and movement, is full of hope, hope for a better future.

The dynamic and transforming nature of utopia can be seen reflected in sarvodaya's efforts to bring changes in the society by being critical and radical. Being critical of the many existing evil in the society such as exploitation, poverty, illiteracy etc., sarvodaya offers new alternatives for economy, village reorganization, and political participation. Gandhi's programme of non co-operation was a protest against the existing oppressive British regime. Free-India was a future possibility, the immediate goal of Gandhi's imagination. His critical negativity and dissatisfaction of the then existing situation resulted in a praxis: a sarvodaya vision—future realizable possibilities for India— whose details are being unfolded in the process of history. It indeed was humanly impossible for Gandhi to go into every detail of the sarvodaya action programme, he envisioned for India. He projected a horizon whose possibilities are being discovered and realized. Sarvodaya is radical in its suggestions, especially its potential seems unlimited in the area of indigenous theology and ecology.

Gandhi believed that he was a social experimenter. He correlated his "dream" with his "experiments with truth" that seemed to catalyze scientific research agenda and promote concrete investigations. Gandhi's utopia is an experiment; his very "life-philosophy" was experiments with truth. "I simply want to tell the story of my numerous experiments with truth", wrote Gandhi:

> and as my life consists of nothing but those experiments, it is true that the story will take the shape of an autobiography. But I shall not mind if every page of it speaks of experiments... Far be it from me to claim any degree of perfection for these experiments. I claim for them nothing more than does a scientist who, though he conducts his experiments with accuracy, forethought and minuteness, never claims any finality about his conclusions, but keeps an open mind regarding them... I am far from claiming any finality or infallibility about my conclusions. One claim I do indeed make and it is this. For me they appear to be absolutely correct, and seem for the time being to be final. For if they were not, I should base no action on them (*Autobigraphy*, ix-xi).

Experiments must actively confront the existing cultural beliefs and social systems. For Gandhi the process of experimentation itself is, as Bondurant opines, "essentially creative and inherently constructive" (Bondurant 1958: 192). Such experiments lead to changes in the prevalent social and cultural system. Gandhi confronted Western civilization in his *Hind Swaraj* and developed a utopian resistance to British colonialism. But, for Gandhi, confrontation was only a means to new alternatives. It is these alternatives, such as sarvodaya society, people centred economy, protection and promotion of village life, indigenous thinking and environment, that will be of special interest for us in the following chapters of this book. They were to a great extent Gandhi's individual dreams, but they gradually become one version of India's collective vision.

Though Gandhi's dream drew upon Indian cultural traditions that proved resistant to European colonial domination (Lannoy 1971: 373-412), it has its Western ingredients as well. It is future-oriented, not retrospective or reactionary. It proposes an imaginative vision of the future and suggests practical alternatives for transforming society. It negates the present with its shadows of *Kali Yuga* (Age of Decline), and it strives to usher in an etherealized "utopia" of *Ramrajya* (the Kingdom of God) in an anticipated

Satya Yuga (Age of Truth). Utopia of Gandhi has both individual and social components; it accepts economic ideas which are congruent with its ideal of a stateless society; it prides itself on cultural values.

One may observe trends of "going back to the glorious past" while "looking forward to a promising future", in Gandhi's utopia for there are both conservation and revolution in Gandhi's vision. For instance, "he worked just as hard at cultural conservation—of the Indian village, home spinning, nonpossession, and other Indian traditions he valued—as he did at cultural revolution—against untouchability, suppression of women, caste inequality, and other traditions he disowned" (Fox 1989: 27).

Gandhi's vision of sarvodaya society is based on a realistic (i.e., in the process of being realized) utopia, "future as a possibility" (Plath 1971: 81). But Gandhi was reluctant to take the West as a model for any of his utopias. He was quite explicit in his attempts to disregard modernistic and Western fashion and to build up Indian villages along the lines of harmony, personal relationships, and emotional security—all things he thought were disappearing in the West. There was, as Fox comments, "hijacking of Gandhian utopia" by Hindu Nationalists and other politicians (Fox 1989: 162-68, 182-83, 195-97). Though this so-called "hijacking" has done damage to the utopia of Gandhi, it appears to be only a transitional phase. There is "dying" and "rising" in realistic utopia of sarvodaya as an ideal or vision in the making, just as in his lifetime Gandhi had to adapt himself and his developing vision to immediate circumstances.

The transformation in a society in Gandhi's view can be brought about only through a transformation of persons in that society. Gandhi often noted that his experiments with society required struggles with himself. That is, individuals must struggle with themselves as they attempt to master and change surrounding circumstances and ongoing experiences. These struggles can bring about radical changes in individual attitudes and outlooks which eventually change one's philosophy and social relations. Gandhi's vow of celibacy (*brahmacharya*), vegetarianism, and change to Indian dress are just a few instances of such personal conversion which have revolutionalized his social relations. Gandhi's "utopian dedication" and personal commitment become more evident in his satyagraha experiments, specially in the ashram experiments. We will return to this in Chapter Four. Gandhi never worked in a vacuum, but rather his vision, dream or planning was solidly based on concrete historical events where he was personally involved. This dedication and consequent transformation lie at the heart of Gandhi's praxis and make Gandhi's utopia realistic and realizable. It is no exaggeration to say that Gandhi could never envisage any change without first accomplishing a personal transformation. In the words of Vinay Lal, "Gandhian utopia conceives that change... must ultimately stem from the heart" (Lal 1990: 239). As Gusfield concludes,

> Perhaps the nineteenth-century American communitarians and the contemporary followers of Gandhi or Buber must be taken most seriously in their belief that the transforming capacity of utopias is best conducted outside of political institutions. Alongside the state, as Gandhi believed, it was necessary to have men who sought to change others by the force of their vision and the exemplary life with which they brought that vision into existence on a small scale. Such men do not seek to change laws, or create new institutions, but transform society by transforming attitudes and feelings in an essentially apolitical fashion: by an utopian appeal (Plath 1971: 85).

Sarvodaya: Undying Hope

Another element that makes Gandhi's sarvodaya vision a realistic utopia is hope. Richard Fox's assertion that "Gandhi therefore never rose above his times,... His new dream of a "nowhere" India was opposite to the present, not beyond it. Utopia bounces off, it does not rise above, the current ideological constitution of society" (Fox 1989: 167), seems to underrate Gandhi's utopia and cannot go unchallenged. Fox does not seem to give any place to future possibilities of Gandhian utopia; the hope aspect is entirely missing from his analysis of Gandhian utopia.

If hope is the hallmark of the visionary, then hope indeed was the hallmark of Gandhi's thought and action: he insisted that he had never lost hope and never would, because it was an essential ingredient of his undimmed faith in nonviolence (CW 90: 2-3). Gandhi's life was sustained by a religious vision which created in him an abiding sense of hope and prompted him to speak and act on issues which have proved crucial to mankind in our century. In Gandhi's sarvodaya, there is "creative expectation": "hope which sets about criticizing and transforming the present because it opens towards the universal future of the kingdom" (Bentley 1982: 89). Even when Gandhi sensed old age, and "suffered from bouts of extreme dejection and loss of confidence", and became so dispirited that he talked of totally abandoning a public role, "he remained truly a prisoner of hope, bound by a conviction of the ultimate reality and power of truth" (Brown 1989: 288). Gandhi's optimism in the future is far from illusion, and this optimism rested not only on his belief in the ultimate triumph of truth but more immediately on his sense that individuals could change for the better, because in each there is a spark of truth or goodness. His optimism kept him free from worrying about the long-term future, instead it focused on the present. Gandhi once told Jawaharlal Nehru, "My difficulty is not about the remote future. It is always the present that I concentrate upon and that at times worries me. If the present is well taken care of, the future will take care of itself" (Brown 1989: 288).

Sarvodaya ideal of Gandhi stems from an undying hope in the better future of India: utopian economy that is people-oriented and which promotes appropriate technology, social and communal life that is village-based, theology and spirituality that is indigenous and a sustainable eco-system that is harmony with nature. Gandhi initiated a process that can be realized and is open to immense possibilities. We shall discuss and explore the areas of actual and possible realizability of sarvodaya vision in the coming chapters of this book.

As a visionary, Gandhi never ever worried about the success of his experiments. Gandhi, the "utopian experimentalist forever pursuing elusive truth", has an answer to this enigmatic question:

> I may be taunted with the retort that it is utopian...If Euclid's point, though incapable of being drawn by human agency, has an imperishable value, my picture has its own for mankind to live...Euclid's line is one without breadth,

> but no one has so far been able to draw it and never will. All the same it is only by keeping the ideal line in mind that we have made progress in geometry. What is true here is true of every ideal (CW 85: 297).

Amidst the numerous questions arising about the relevance, practicality, success or failure of Gandhian vision—utopia—one should not fail to see Gandhi as a scientist, as an utopian experimentalist for whom "success lay in the mere fact of opposition" (Maureen 1985: 178). Canonization of Gandhi by the Indian masses made him an icon, a token saint; for many, thus, he is the Mahatma "too good for this world and therefore leaving no useful legacy for ordinary people."

It is true that "there are many people in India today who would argue strongly that Gandhi's ideas represent a romantic ideology and a set of unrealistic and outdated ideas that do not come to grips with the realities of industrialization, military conflict, national integration, the desire for consumer goods and so on" (Bakker 1993: 13); and there are others who argue that "Sarvodaya partakes of the nature of a total ideology" and "is irrelevant today" (Biswas 1969: 105-112). We will argue in the following chapters that Gandhi's sarvodaya, understood as a total development of all that is human and related to humanity, is a realistic utopia, a utopia in the process of being realized.

The following chapters, therefore, will show that Gandhi's sarvodaya has the ingredients of utopia that is being realized; and that it is a vision for the future. Its hope for a better future opens up horizons to new possibilities. The dialectics of already and not yet, a vision that is realized and yet to be realized make sarvodaya a process that has immense possibilities of realization. What makes sarvodaya an utopian process seems to me to be the apparent tension between realizability and unrealizability, and its basic experimental character. As a vision in the process of realization, sarvodaya is never a finished product; it has been consistent, it has a continuity and has a goal yet to be achieved. Since sarvodaya functions as a normative ideal, because, as explained in the present chapter, it has the ingredients of hope, dialectics, future possibilities, new horizons, creative imagination and so on, all the details cannot be worked out. What we are doing in this book is to select some of the essential characteristics of utopia and apply them to Gandhi's sarvodaya vision as concretely visible (reflected) in people-oriented economy, ashram-village experiments, the Vinoba-JP follow-up, indigenous theology and ecology. The reason for the selection of such themes is, that as a realizable ideal, sarvodaya suggests people-based economy, village reconstruction on the basis of communal sharing, self-reliance and service. Also sarvodaya has been experimented with by Vinoba and JP, but from different perspectives. And, as a model, sarvodaya offers insights into indigenous theology and balanced ecology.

What in the last analysis makes Gandhi's sarvodaya a utopian vision is nothing but the untiring hope in the future. There is a dialectic of known and unknown, possible and impossible, actual and potential in this vision. The fact that utopia is in the process of realization and that sarvodaya is being realized today, indicate that there is a continual unfolding: from unknown to known, from impossible to possible and from potential to actual. The known, possible and actual are not stagnant because the vision sarvodaya offers has infinite potential and possibilities for actualization and realization. We will be returning to some actual and possible sarvodaya realizations in our coming chapters, especially in the area of economics, because, while people-centred economy is an ideal Gandhi thought suitable to India, Gandhi's village-oriented communal living experiments were based on sarvodaya vision, which believes in a praxis that starts at grass-root level and grows into total development of every human being. Vinoba carried out Gandhi's sarvodaya vision with some success, JP gave a face-lift to the sarvodaya ideal. Sarvodaya's global appeal and continuing interest the world over can be brought to light by showing its close link to theology and ecology.

The realizability of the Gandhian ideal is problematic to many. They think Gandhi is too ideal and therefore impractical; therefore he has little or nothing to offer for India or for the world of today. From an analysis of sarvodaya as ideal, utopian vision and movement, we argue that it has immense potential for establishing a liberated society i.e., sarvodaya society. It is an ongoing process realised and yet to be realised with immense possibilities of actualization in the India of today.

References

1. *Chambers Twentieth Century Dictionary* gives both a non-evaluative and an evaluative meaning. Utopia is "an imaginary state described in Sir Thomas More's Latin political romance or satire utopia", or "any imaginary state of ideal perfection" - E. M. Kirkpatrick, ed. (1983) *Chambers Twentieth Century Dictionary* (Edinburgh: Chambers, 1983), 1433. The *Shorter Oxford English Dictionary* reflects the same issues. We have both the initial reference to More, and "a place, state, or condition ideally perfect in respect of laws, customs and conditions" or "an impossibly ideal scheme, especially for social improvement". C. T. Onions, ed. *Shorter Oxford English Dictionary*, Vol.2 (Oxford: Book Club Associates and Oxford University Press, 1983), 2444.
2. Levitas concludes from a critical survey of Utopian authors like Moritz Kaufman, Henry Morley, Lewis Munford, Joyce Hertzler, Harry Ross, Marie Beneri, Negley, G. and Patrick, J.M. and A. L. Morton, that "three different functions, not necessarily mutually exclusive, are thus identified: compensation, critique, catalyst" (Levitas 1990: 8, 34).
3. From Hesiod's *Works and Days*, of the early seventh century BC, came the canonical depiction of the Golden Age, when men "lived as if they were gods, their hearts free from all sorrow, and without hard work or pain"; when "the fruitful earth yielded its abundant harvest to them of its own accord, and they lived in ease and peace upon their lands with many good things". Reworked by Virgil and Ovid as the lost age of Saturn (the Roman Kronos), the pastoral perfection of the Golden Age reappeared as the classic Arcadia, a time and place of rustic simplicity and felicity. See Krishan Kumar, *Utopia and Anti-Utopia*, 3.
4. The Athenian model was democratic, tolerant, boisterous, given over to a cultivated hedonism. The Spartan model was authoritarian, ascetic and communistic.
5. "...it is Aristotle who considers more definitely the actual structure of ideal city; in fact one may say that the concept of utopia pervades every page of *Politics*..." Lewis Mumford, "Utopia the city and the machine" in F. E. Manuel, ed., *Utopias and Utopian Thought*, 7.
6. Speaking of the Renaissance utopian authors, the author opines that "one could spend many years of scholarly research tracing the affiliation of their ideas, as well as proving their influence on latter day works." Mariam Eliav-Feldon, *Realistic Utopias*, 11.
7. The Golden Age could stand as the representation of the blissful

condition of mankind before fall. The notion of paradise lost is after all not a paradise that is lost entirely but a paradise to be regained in some future time.

8. Krishan Kumar calls St. Augustine's book, *The City of God*, "great fifth century anti- utopia." The *contemptus mundi* was profoundly discouraging to utopian speculation. Krishan Kumar, *Utopia and Anti-Utopia*, 11.
9. Chiliasm expected an early reign of Christ before the Last judgment. A kingdom lasting a thousand years was to come and it would be characterized by peace and justice. Mannheim argues that the chiliast "is not actually concerned with the millennium that is to come," but a leap over into ecstasy. K. Mannheim, *Ideology and Utopia*, 191-195.
10. *Ibid.*, 19. Thomas More actually lived for four years with the monks of the Charter House, and the monastic ideal is pervasive in his *Utopia*. Carthusian and Benedictine rules underlie much of the highly regulated order of Utopia: the plainness and uniformity of dress; the absence of pomp and the general air of austerity; the devotion to work, study and prayer; the community of property and dwelling; the communal meals... Similarly, with the *City of the Sun*: its author, Tommaso Campanella, was trained as a monk and monastic characteristics feature strongly in his utopia. Even in Francis Bacon's *New Atlantis*, of all the seventeenth century utopias the one least obviously indebted to Christian conceptions, the House of Saloman is modelled fairly clearly on the monastery.
11. The name utopia, is derived from Greek words, *Eutopos* = "good place", *outopos* = "no place". Thomas more did not just invent the *word* utopia, in a typically witty conflation of two Greek words: he invented the *thing*. Part of that new thing was a new literary form or genre; the other, more important, part was a novel and far-reaching conception of the possibilities of human social transformation.
12. Karl Kautsky, "The roots of More's Socialism" in Robert M. Adams, tr. and ed., *Sir Thomas More Utopia: A New Translation, Background Criticism*, 148. Here Kautsky presents More as precursor of Socialism: "We believe that we have disclosed the most essential roots of More's socialism: his amiable character in harmony with primitive communism; the situation of England, which brought into sharp relief the disadvantageous consequences of Capitalism for the working class; the fortunate union of classical philosophy with activity in practical affairs—all these circumstances combined must have induced in a mind so acute, so fearless, so truth-loving as

More's, an ideal which may be regarded as a fore-gleam of Modern Socialism".

13. *Ibid.*, 129.
14. For further reference on this issue, I like to suggest the following readings: "Castles in the air: Marx, Engels, and utopian socialism", in Ruth Levitas, *The Concept of Utopia* (1990), 35-59; "Utopianism and Millennial thought", in Amitava Ray, *Political Utopianism: Some Philosophical Problems* (Calcutta: Minerva Associates Publications Pvt. Ltd., 1979), 27-62; Martin Buber, *Paths in Utopia* (London: Routledge & Kegan Paul, 1949); "The socialist utopia", in K. Kumar, *Utopia and Anti-Utopia in Modern Times* (Oxford: Basil Blackwell, 1987), 50-65.
15. Ruth Levitas, *Concept of Utopia*, 35. "Utopian socialism" refers initially to the ideas and movements inspired by Saint-Simon and Fourier in France and Robert Owen in England. By "utopian communism" Marx and Engels chiefly referred to the followers of Cabet in France and of Wilhelm Weitling in Germany.
16. Lenin unequivocally rejected utopianism while defending the practice of dreaming about the future. On the one hand, he argued that "Marxists... are hostile to any and every utopia", since "utopia is a wish that can never come true..." Further, "there is no trace of utopianism in Marx, in the sense that he made up or invented a 'new' society". V. Geoghgan, *Utopianism and Marxism* (London: Methuen, 1987), 54.
17. The enlightenment in the eighteenth century meant a new bloom of utopian writing. One sees varieties such as: wondrous travel tales, Robinson Crusoe stories, Arcadias, planetary novels, pictures of future, ideal societies, etc. The Enlightenment starts from the assumption that there exists a "natural order", the working of which can be understood by man's reason. The era was characterized by the utopia of reason. See Martin G. Plattel, *Utopian and Critical Thinking* (Pittsburg, Pa.: Duquesne University Press, 1972), 32.
18. H. G. Wells (1866-1946) is considered to be the founder of this type of utopian writing. In America also science fiction began to develop at the end of the nineteenth century. The principal topics are the exploration and conquest of space, the visit or invasion by intelligent beings from other planets, the robot, the city of the future etc. Martin G. Plattel, *Utopian and Critical Thinking*, 35.
19. Frank E. Manuel and Fritzie P. Manuel, *Utopian Thought in the Western World*, 21; Northrop Frye, "Varieties of Literary Utopias", in Frank E. Manuel, ed., *Utopias and Utopian Thought*, 29; Robert C. Elliott, *The Shape of Utopia: Studies in Literary Genre*, x, and 84-8.

20. "The concrete utopia, on the one hand, fosters the active negation or negative dialectics with respect to the existing situation; on the other, it constructively transcends this negation" Martin G. Plattel, *Utopian and Critical Thinking*, 40.
21. See "The utopian mentality" in K. Mannheim, *Ideology and Utopia*, 192-248, where the author analyses four forms of utopian mentality. Paul Ricoeur borrows this terminology from Mannheim in his *Lectures on Ideology and Utopia* (New York: Columbia University Press, 1986), 159-181 and 269-285.
22. Jorge Larrain tackles the development of the historicist tradition in Mannheim and Goldmann, who introduce the sociological analysis of literature and cultural phenomena using the concept *Weltanshauung*. "Ideology acquires a more definite subjective character as the word-view or 'perspective' of a class and is universalized to a point where its usefulness as an analytical and critical notion can be doubted." Jorge Larrain, *The Concept of Ideology* (Athens: The University of Georgia Press, 1979), 15 and 100-129.
23. "Ideology, in contrast, does not have the problem of being realized, because it is the legitimation of what is...Ideologies are directed more toward the past and so are stricken by obsolescence..." Paul Ricoeur, *Lectures...*, 273.
24. Dream is given a positive intellectual role. Bloch made a distinction between day-dreams and night-dreams, claiming that nocturnal dreams feed on the past and are a space in which "very early wishes circulate"; day dreams are subject to direction and therefore contain more anticipation, less compensation. See, E. Bloch, *The Principle of Hope*, 79. Jack Goode makes an important distinction between "the involuntary dream of the night and the willed dream of the day...the fullest possibility of vision is available only to the dream that is beyond the individual will". J. Goode, "William Morris and the dream of revolution" in J. Lucas, ed., *Literature and Politics in the Nineteenth Century* (London: Methuen, 1971), 269-70. Bloch and Goode distinguish between sleeping and waking dreams on the basis of the element of intentionality in the day-dreaming. For Marcuse this dream is an "impossible dream", "something that can nowhere be realized". D. Kellner, *Herbert Marcuse and the Crisis of Marxism* (London: Macmillan, 1984), 93 and 115.
25. Bloch's position is atheistic. There is an act of transcending here, but it "is the act of transcending without any heavenly transcendence but with an understanding of it: as a hypostatized anticipation of being-for itself" (Bloch 1986: 1288).
26. "Kingdom of God" is a socio-political symbol, which religious and

secular utopias have expressed in symbols such as, "kingdom of heaven", "kingdom of justice", and "the consummation" (Manuel 1973: 308).

27. Martin G. Plattel, *Utopian and Critical Thinking*, 95. In his view, "the horizon of visions helps society orient itself within the reality encompassed by it. The horizon is the *Totum*, the overarching whole which integrates all perspectives into a meaningful totality" (Plattel 1972: 94).
28. "The function of the dream form is neither to posit a goal nor to construct a compensatory fantasy, but to emphasize the role of vision and will in the process of social transformation." R. Levitas, *The Concept of Utopia*, 119.
29. Seiji Nuita compares and contrasts utopias in Japan and the West, in an article on "Traditional utopias in Japan and West: A study in contrast", in David W. Plath, ed., *Aware of Utopia* (Urbana: University of Illinois, 1971), 12-32.
30. As one can see in the classical example of Thomas More, the writer begins with a penetrating analysis of the evils afflicting Europe and especially England at that time, and only then he proceeds to paint a picture of the ideal society. More discovered the value of the utopian negation. The negative dialectics is emphasized by writers such as Bloch, Marcuse, Adorno and Kosik. They emphasize that man and society must view the existing situation antithetically, protestingly and dialectically if they wish to become aware of new real possibilities. "The logic of protest (Marcuse), the system of the anti-system (Adorno) constitute the critical negativity which keep alive man's consciousness that he is possibility rather than facticity". M. G. Plattel, *Utopian and Critical Thinking*, 84.
31. Tolstoy denounced the state and private property because both are inconsistent with the supreme principle of love. The ideal social order envisaged by Tolstoy and Gandhi is one in which there would be no state, no private property, no police, no military, no law courts and organized religion. The pure ideal of Gandhi is an ideal of philosophical anarchism, a stateless, classless society marked by voluntary co-operation.
32. "Though I cannot claim to be Christian in the sectarian sense, the example of Jesus' suffering is a factor in the composition of my undying faith in non-violence which rules all my actions worldly and temporal." M. K. Gandhi, *Harijan*, 1 January 1939, 417.

Three

"People-Oriented" Economy: A New Vision

On 22 December 1916, Gandhi spoke before an economic society of Muir College, in Allahabad. His paper was titled, "Does Economic Progress Clash with Real Progress?" He starts with a warning to his audience,

> Frankly and truly, I know very little of economics, as you naturally understand them. Only the other day, sitting at an evening meal, a civilian friend deluged me with a series of questions on my crankisms. As he proceeded in his cross-examination, I being a willing victim, he found no difficulty in discovering my gross ignorance on the matters. I appeared to him to be handling with a coarseness worthy only of a man who knows not that he knows not. To his horror and even indignation, I suppose, he found that I had not even read books on economics by such well-known authorities as Mill, Marshall, Adam Smith, and a host of such other authors. In despair, he ended by advising me to read these works before experimenting in matters economic at the expense of the public. He little knew that I was a sinner past redemption. My experiments continue at the expense of trusting friends. For, there come to us moments in life when about some things we need no proof from without. A little voice within us tells us "you are on the right track, move neither to your left nor right, but keep to the straight and narrow way." With such help we march forward slowly indeed, but steadily. That is my position (CW 13: 310-17).

What Gandhi means by real progress is not merely material progress but integral human progress where moral progress is of high priority. He argued in his address cited above that material advance has a strong tendency to lead to moral decay. For him material advancement and moral progress do not seem to go together. He substantiates his thesis that mere material advancement generates moral degradation by illustrations from Roman history, Egypt, the descendants of divine Krishna, from South Africa of Gandhi's time; and he draws support for his argument from the testimonies of the greatest teachers of the world such as Jesus, Mohammed, Buddha, Nanak, Kabir, Chaitanya, Shankara, Dayanand and Ramakrishna. Then he proposed: " 'You cannot serve God and Mammon' is an economic truth of the highest value. We have to make a choice. Western nations today are groaning under the heel of the monster-god of materialism. Their moral growth has become stunted". As for Gandhi, material progress "add(s) not an atom to our happiness". He was all against aping the British system because, if we copy her because she provides us with rulers, both they and we shall suffer degradation. He therefore pleaded for an ideal economy where there is more truth than gold, and greater charity than love of the self. He concludes his address with an admonition to his audience: "Let us seek first the kingdom of God and His righteousness and the irrevocable promise that everything will be added with us. These are real economics. May you and I treasure them and enforce them in our daily life" (CW 13: 316).

This short lecture, which took place relatively early in Gandhi's long career, marks one of the few instances where he focused directly on the subject of economics. Gandhi is hardly known as a celebrated economic thinker in any real sense of the term. He made it clear that he was not an economist in the professional sense. Malcolm S. Adiseshiah is of the view that it is rather misleading to use the term "Gandhian economics", though the term was coined during his lifetime and is in use even today. He argues that there is no Indian economics or American economics or Communist economics etc., but only general economic principles as applied to India or America or the Communist system. In the same vein, "...it is not economics which is Gandhian, but its application to our time and conditions as declared by Gandhi's perception" (Adiseshiah 1992: 389-403).

In his grand vision of sarvodaya society, economic equality occupies a central place, it "is an essential principle and indispensable condition" (Prasad 1984: 84). Gandhi was not interested in developing a theory, that was not his style. He drew his thoughts on economic affairs from three main sources. The first was his ethical-spiritual convictions, the second was his close involvement with the economic conditions of the people and his deep awareness of the poverty of the "dumb millions", and the third was his reading and reflection on Ruskin's *Unto This Last* and Tolstoy's *The Kingdom of God Is within You* (Jesudasan 1986: 9-22).

Gandhi's attempt to apply the already existing economic principles to the Indian context has opened the door for a fresh look at economics purely from a human perspective, economy with a human face or economy as if people mattered.[1] The total well-being of human beings, i.e., sarvodaya, was the thrust of Gandhi's praxis. This total well-being of humanity can never be wrought by bringing about a change in the material conditions of life alone. Economy gains a human face only in so far as it works towards the fuller and near-perfect development of woman and society. Thus, only in the wider context of Gandhi's vision, which was a praxis for total human development, should one try to understand and assess the meaning, import, relevance and realizability of Gandhi's application of economic principles to the Indian situation. His economic strategies are to be evaluated from the perspective of an ideal social order: non-violent, non-exploitative, humanistic, egalitarian sarvodaya society.

Gandhi was least interested in the scope and method of economic science as economists naturally understand it. Instead, he worked for a whole lifetime on articulating the principles of an alternative and more real human economy centring on the very themes outlined in his lecture: "the lack of correlation between material expansion and genuine process, the need for an economics-cum-ethics that will enable moral growth and dignity for all, the fallacy of seeking happiness in individual acquisitive behaviour, and the need for encouraging people to seek a life rich in self-esteem and genuine meaning" (Diwan and Lutz 1985: 10).

Gandhi's unique way of giving a human face to economics

and making it an integral part of establishing sarvodaya society was to link economics with ethics and see the spiritual depth that is hidden in economic realities. For this he goes in tune with the ethical tradition as pointed out in the ancient Indian way of approaching any human problem, a tradition which includes Kautilya and Valluvar and more recently Vivekananda and Tagore in India, and Mill, Marx, and Marshall outside India. For Gandhi, "True economics stands for social justice and moral values." Gandhi is a promoter of "meta-economics" which is related to metaphysics and other human sciences for he says:

> I must confess that I do not draw a sharp or any distinction between economics and ethics. Ethics that hurt the moral well-being of an individual or nation are immoral and therefore sinful. Thus economics that permit one country to prey upon another are immoral (Tendulkar vol.2 1960: 63-64).

Gandhi's economic strategy was primarily a response to the challenge the poverty-ridden India flung at a particular phase in the process of Indian history. He took the most pressing economic problems and issues into account and offered his own solutions. And from these solutions and experiences, there emerged an economic strategy as articulated via utopian model. That strategy is ethical economics; and some of the key issues and problems he dealt with are: village-mindedness, *swadeshi*, khadi, self-sufficiency, bread-labour, costructive programme, small industry, decentralization, trusteeship and industrialization. As we analyze these and similar themes, special attention will be paid towards the feasibility of such Gandhian suggestions in the present Indian context.

Background and Influence

From a historical perspective, Gandhi's thoughts may appear suited only to a specific time in history; but history itself is a proof that his thoughts have transcended the limits of time and space. This is true of Gandhi's economic insights too, because there is much material rich in insight and relevance for both developed and developing economies as well as for contemporary economic theory. As Romesh Diwan and Mark Lutz observe, "It is our contention that Gandhi's legacy offers a new set of economic theories and policies that may one day come to be seen as a promising rival to the accepted doctrines that have prevailed to this day" (Diwan and Lutz 1985: 10). Such compliments to Gandhian economics and a contemporary revival of interest in the study of Gandhian economics are indicators of the insights Gandhi offers for a re-thinking and re-interpretation of the present economic system, i.e., effectiveness and "durability" of utopian model rather than specific theory.

The problem of poverty that confronted India during the British Raj was the immediate background of Gandhi's economic thought—Gandhi reacted sharply to the crushing effect and demoralizing influence of grinding poverty of the masses of the country. Though this prominent fact is to be constantly kept in mind as one studies his economic thought, there are other influences that shaped the economic thoughts of Gandhi.

Hind Swaraj is the quintessence of all that Gandhi had read, thought and experienced by the age of forty. Gandhi's harsh critique of modern civilization in *Hind Swaraj* has deep roots in his formative phase as a student in England and his active public life in South Africa. While in England he became a member of the Vegetarian Society, which consisted of men who were critical of the urban-industrial society and favoured simple living. Gandhi was introduced to the *Gita* through the Theosophical Society (the *Gita*, as he said later, opened for him a new view of life). The most crucial formative period for crystallizing his ideas, outlook and view of life, however, was in South Africa. It was there that he read extensively, thought deeply and gained first-hand experience of the working of Western civilization. The most distinctive influence came through the works of Tolstoy, Ruskin, Thoreau, all vehement critics of industrial life and advocates of simplicity. It was also from South Africa that he started communicating with Shrimad Rajachandra,[2] who had a very decisive impact on the formation of Gandhi's views on Truth, God, renunciation and personal life. Even though, as Gandhi admits,[3] the immediate context of writing *Hind Swaraj* was his encounter with the Indian anarchists in England and their cult of violence, critique of the entire Western or material civilization forms the very backbone of *Hind Swaraj*.

There are writers who think that Gandhi's critique of modern Western civilization may well be peripheral to his thinking and may not constitute an essential element of his thinking. Even so, "*Hind Swaraj* is preoccupied with an uncompromising critique and rejection of modern Western civilization" (Saran 1980: 681). Gandhi's denunciation of modern civilization and his proposal for reordering it stem from his concern for the destiny of man, which modern society distorts. Therefore what lies behind such harsh condemnation ("forthright, brutal, and shocking", in the words of Ramashray Roy, Roy 1985: 39) of modern civilization is a worldview or vision of a new society. Later in life, *Ramrajya* was to be Gandhi's favourite name for his vision of a new social order where every individual becomes "a full-blooded, fully-developed member of society". But the modern civilization Gandhi came in contact with was violent, selfish and hypocritical. Gandhi's critique of modern civilization has nothing to do with a scientific analysis of social conditions, the institutional structures and individual motivations and their interactions that produce an outcome which he labels "the satanic civilization". As Raghavan Iyer states, Gandhi does not "provide a rigorous social analysis from which his political conclusions could be logically derived" (Iyer 1973: 30). His was a moral response to what he perceived as the evils of modern civilization.

In his critique of modern civilization, Gandhi focuses only on some aspects of it and exposes faults and defects of these aspects to show how they distort and despoil the meaning of life. For Gandhi, first of all, what lies at the core of modern civilization is "the hunger for wealth and the greedy pursuit of worldly pleasures." Secondly, this inordinate desire to amass wealth necessarily leads to violence at the individual and at the collective levels, which is reflected in one nation exploiting other nations and even in wars between nations. Thirdly, Gandhi concludes that the hopelessness, the cruelty, the oppression, the exploitation, the inequality, etc., that prevailed and still prevail in society are the immoral by-products of modern civilization. In the words of Ramashray Roy, "Gandhi's condemnation of modern civilization is, by implication, also the condemnation of the economic system which it has brought into being and which sustains it on its satanic journey" (Roy 1985: 118). Therefore Gandhi comes to suggest an economics with a human face or "ethical-economics".

Ethical Economics

One of the greatest contributions of Gandhi to the domain of economics is constant concern to approach it from an ethical, even spiritual, perspective; with his experience and wisdom he was able to transcend the realm of mere matter and money in order to give economics a theological backing. The spiritual perspective that Gandhi gives to economics is integral to his value system and world-view.[4] Since the entire Gandhian world-view (philosophy of life) is based on two fundamental, interrelated principles, Non-violence and Truth, one cannot understand any of the structural components of this system, economics in particular, without understanding the philosophical foundations of the superstructure. Gandhi formulated his economic ideas and principles in the context of his ideal social order: a non-violent, non-exploitative, humanistic, and egalitarian society, i.e., a sarvodaya social order. He never lost sight of this social order, which was the fundamental philosophy of his life, the dream he cherished and the ideal he pursued. He thus approached every realm of this social order, whether economics, politics, or sociology, from his philosophical premises namely *satya* (truth) and ahimsa (non-violence). Since, "Truth and nonviolence are the foundation in Gandhian thinking of all human life and the whole socio-political system," as A. K. Saran says, Gandhi's "one and only concern was Truth, to which he demanded absolute commitment" (Saran 1980: 705). Gandhi equates truth with God:

> For me, Truth is the sovereign principle, which includes numerous other principles...not only the relative truth of our conception, but the Absolute Truth, the Eternal Principle, that is God...But I worship God as Truth only...Sat or Truth is perhaps the most important name of God. In fact it is more correct to say that God is Truth... (S. Narayan, ed., *Selected Works*, vol. 6, 1968: 95-96).

The ultimate goal of his life, as Gandhi sums up, "is self-realization, to see God face to face, to attain *Moksha*" (*Autobigraphy*, x); and "...the only means for the realization of Truth is ahimsa (nonviolence)..." (*Autobiography*, 419). Gandhi firmly believed that the key, perhaps the only key, to this self-realization, was ahimsa. In his own words: "In its positive form, *Ahimsa* means the largest love, the greatest charity. If I am a follower of *Ahimsa*, I must love my enemy or a stranger as I would my wrong-doing father or son" (Iyer vol.2 1973: 180). Ahimsa, for Gandhi, is love; truth for him, is God-realization and self-realization. This love has a very essential aspect to it: love in action. Gandhi acknowledged his chosen path of *karmayoga*, the path of selfless service and work, as inspired by the Gita. To Gandhi, the Gita taught that total commitment to social action regardless of consequences to oneself was the moral law that was consistent with his principle of Truth-realization through Love. Identification with the whole of mankind and commitment to people can never remain separated from the kind of love Gandhi believed in. Speaking of such commitment, Amartya Sen has some beautiful insights: it is neither sympathy nor benevolence, it is an unselfish act, it implies a willingness to sacrifice in the form of reputation, career, even life, for the sake of an ideal.[5] Commitment, like love, is fundamentally a relation to something other than one's self, a surrender. What makes this idea of commitment outstanding is that one acts irrespective of the consequences arising for oneself. A truly dedicated person is not only dedicated to his work but also detached from the results at the same time.[6] Commitment, being responsible to another, is a life of response and responding. As such it is based on a trust relationship ultimately grounded in faith. Gandhi, when committing his life to Truth, did so in faithful response to a living and self-acting power to which he felt he could turn, and the supremacy of which he was convinced. Even the identification with the poor which he derived from his commitment to living Truth was not to be just an abstract identification in one's mind, rather it was an identification with one's whole being, immersing oneself within concrete situations in living equality.[7]

The idea of love as an act of self-giving commitment may sound so spiritual and demanding as to be a threat to the modern economics of everyday. But this is not necessarily so because, as A. Sen suggests, much of public choice, collective planning, class solidarity, etc., is pregnant with this type of non-maximizing commitment; similarly within such narrower groups as families, local communities, peer groups, and economic and social classes. The ethico-economics of Gandhi is based on ahimsa, non-violence or love, which gives priority to the human person, as opposed to mere material progress. In Buberian terms, the thrust of this economics is I-You relationship rather than I-It relationship. Economics, understood in the typical sense, ignores the former. Concluding his analysis on human nature in Gandhian economics, Mark Lutz says, "...the core of Gandhi's economic thought has to be seen in the wider context of his view of human nature reflecting the whole of psychology, philosophy, and religion. His system represents a radical departure from the mainstream of economic thought. No doubt it becomes remarkably coherent and logical as soon as we accept the axiomatic premises of his world-view" (Diwan and Lutz 1985: 44). In Gandhi's world-view, man is the centre of his economic thought, not the material prosperity or scarcity. Human beings do not only have the need to survive, but they also have the need to exercise their capacity to care for others. A nonviolent economy, one that draws its inspiration from love, commitment and truth has to be non-exploitative. It cannot promote unhealthy competition which in reality ignores the human being and one's basic needs and makes him an object in order to acquire more and to become richer.

It was impossible for Gandhi to think of an economics that would be "ethically neutral". In his own words: "That economics is untrue which ignores or disregards moral values. The extension of the law of nonviolence in the domain of economics means nothing less than the introduction of moral values..."(CW 25:475)

No serious student of economics can ignore the human side or the moral milieu of economics. Many conventional economists rooted either in the neo-classical or the Marxist tradition still take pride in asserting that economics is a positive science, meaning that it observes and describe what IS rather than entering into the area of what OUGHT to be. This view was very strongly held from 1920 to 1960. Today most experts in scientific method have learned to question this traditional doctrine and admit that it is impossible to present any entirely value-free science. Whether we like it or not, values are always present, either in explicit or in implicit form. Good science, therefore, needs to operate with good values.

Believing, as he does, in the essential unity of life, Gandhi sees compartmentalization of life activities as a severe threat to the central vision of self-realization and to the totality of life itself. As he says: "The whole gamut of man's activities today constitute an indivisible whole. You cannot divide social, economic, political and purely religious work into water-tight compartments..." (CW 68: 200). Once the indivisibility of life activities is accepted, it follows that all life activities must be geared to and influenced by the central purpose of life: self-realization, which eventually leads to social transformation (sarvodaya- literally, the rise of all). Life activities such as politics or economics become means of self-transformation. Therefore, there has to be a harmony between man's inner life and social order. Such harmony preserves the essential wholeness of life itself.

It is in this connection that we can appreciate why Gandhi fuses economics with ethics. He firmly rejects the idea that economic activities have their own laws and need not be influenced by moral and spiritual values. If economic activities must reflect ethical values, it follows that the economic system must be such that it does harm to no one. "I must confess", said Gandhi, "that I do not draw a sharp or any distinction between economics and ethics. Economics that hurt the moral well-being of an individual or a nation is immoral and, therefore, sinful" (*Young India* October 1921: 325). He continues to assert that, "that economics is untrue which ignores or disregards moral values. The extension of the law of non-violence into the domain of economics means nothing less than the introduction of moral values as a factor to be considered in regulating international commerce" (*Young India* December 1924: 421). Thus, for Gandhi, there is no opposition between morality and economics. They constitute different facets of the same entity, i.e., spiritual well-being. "True economics never militates against the highest ethical standard, just as all true ethics to be worth its name must at the same time be also good economics" (*Harijan* October 1937: 292). When he proposes that the scriptures of the world are far safer and sounder treatises on laws of economics than many modern textbooks and gives the example of

Jesus as the greatest economist of his time, "He succeeded in economising time and space; he transcended them" (Ramana Murti 1970: 295). Gandhi is laying the foundation for the construction of a new normative economics.

A normative economics of Gandhian style, one that intertwines economics and ethics into one inseparable whole, projects a multidimensional image of man where the traditional Aristotelian or Cartesian dichotomy of body-soul or spirit-matter seems to disappear. Rather, Gandhi has a holistic picture of the human person, especially when he speaks about economics, which is quite in tune with contemporary psychology, which believes in an integrated and holistic approach to personality. This integrated and holistic approach in economics, as R. Diwan and M. Lutz conclude, "boils down to this simple injunction: never advocate actions or policies that lead to ("economic") material advancement at the cost of ("non-economic") social, moral, or spiritual improvement. Instead, the economist, as the holistic economist, should ascertain that his organizational principles and policies enable, possibly even encourage, a higher overall quality of life for all" (Diwan and Lutz 1985: 13).

Gandhi, nonetheless, was not advocating a purely "spiritualistic or saintly economics" by his holistic approach to economics. He had "a hard core of common sense and deep insight into social realities" (Nanda 1985: 144). Gandhi said,"every human being has a right to live and, therefore, to find the wherewithal to feed himself and where necessary to clothe and house himself. But for this simple performance we need no assistance from economists or their laws" (Tendulkar vol.2 1960: 194). To a starving person, the real God is food, for he says, "to a people famishing and idle, the only acceptable form of God that can dare appear is work and promise of food as wages" (Nanda 1985: 127).

His insights about mammon, God and man make him say that "*Daridranarayan* (literally: God of the poor) is one of the millions of names by which humanity knows God who is unnameable and unfathomable by human understanding and it means God of the poor, God appearing in the hearts of the poor" (*Young India* April 1929: 110). Because, "for the poor economic is spiritual. You can not make any other appeal to those starving millions. It will fall flat on them. But you take food to them and they will regard you as their God. They are incapable of any other thought" (*Young India* May 1927: 142). "It is good enough to talk of God", he says, "whilst we are sitting here after a nice breakfast and looking forward to a nicer luncheon, but how am I to talk of God to the millions who have to live without two meals a day? To them God can only appear as bread and butter" (*Young India* October 1931: 310).

Gandhi does not ignore the divinity of man, which is epitomised in the great maxim that "a *jiva* is always *shiva*": a man is divine. And in this respect it is very difficult to distinguish between man and man. It is from this deep feeling of spirituality and divinity of man that later on Gandhi derived his ethico-economic theory of trusteeship and inheritance (more about trusteeship later in this chapter). He wrote, "Everything belongs to God and was from God. Therefore it was for His people as a whole, not for a particular individual. When an individual had more than his proportionate portion he became a trustee of that portion of God's people" (*Harijan* February 1947: 39). That is why Gandhi always talked about the equality of distribution of national wealth.

Gandhi condemns the economics of dead matter for its worship of bodily comfort and its denigration of morality and spirituality. "True economics, on the other hand, stands for social justice, it promotes the good of all equally including the weakest, and is indispensable for a decent life" (Gandhi 1951: 33). The introduction of moral values as a factor in the domain of economics is to humanize it. Thus the economics that is based on ahimsa rejects the principle of self-interest and avarice as the foundation of economic activities and relations and replaces them by "social affections" or concern for others as the true basis of economics. As Ramashray Roy says, "Human economics takes man in the concrete rather than in an abstract category and is concerned with man's total rather than just economic welfare. Since man's total welfare consists in self-development, economic activities and relations must be geared to facilitating the quest for truth... This quest can proceed only on the basis of *sarvodaya*, the welfare of all..." (Roy 1985: 129).

Foundational Premises and Principles

Gandhi's economics is ontologically and epistemologically founded on Truth (*satya*) which is both Absolute, in so far as Gandhi identifies Truth with God, and relative because Truth is in a process of human realization (in fact, the purpose of life is to realize Truth) through ahimsa (non-violence), i.e., self-giving love.[8] From this philosophical principle, which emphasizes self-giving love as the key to the realization of Truth one can come to the following foundational premises related to Gandhi's economic thought. 1. Economics, ethics, politics, and religion constitute an indivisible whole. 2. Economics is the science of human welfare. Its goal is sarvodaya: the welfare of all. 3. The supreme consideration has to be humankind. 4. Economy giving prior consideration to the human element has to be a decentralized social economy. 5. Economics has to respect the law of *swadeshi* (implied meaning is self-reliance).[9]

From the above foundational premises, it is easy to derive the main principles or contents of Gandhi's economic thought. Mark Lutz gives seven principles as basics to Gandhi's economic thought. They are: trusteeship, appropriate technology, non-possession, bread labour, cooperation, equality, and nonviolence in reforming economic systems. J.D. Sethi suggests six concepts as basic to Gandhi's economic thought; namely, truth, satyagraha, nonviolence, equality, *swadeshi*, and bread labour (Sethi 1978: 33). Romesh Diwan and Sushila Gidwani also think that there are six basic concepts that are essential to Gandhi's economics; they are: *swadeshi*, bread labour, *aparigraha* or non-possession, trusteeship, non-exploitation and equality. The authors mentioned above are of the view that the concepts of Gandhi's economics they have referred to are related to each other and sometimes even overlapping. There is no hierarchy among them, that is to say that they are of equal importance. As soon as we accept the axiomatic premises of Gandhi's world-view, his economic thought becomes remarkably coherent and logical. *Moksha* (self-realization or Truth-realization and gradually the total liberation of every human being) being the goal of such a world-view, economy is a powerful means to achieve the end, i.e., sarvodaya. Hence, we deal with a sarvodaya economy, human economy, nonviolent economy and the "economics of love" (Diwan and Lutz 1985: 86-108), when we speak of Gandhi's economics. We will argue that nonviolent economy of Gandhi is a non-exploitative economy for village India in particular, and for whole India in general. For this purpose we shall look into the following areas: trusteeship, industrialization and appropriate technology, bread labour, *Swadeshi* and Khadi, simplicity and limited wants, service and cooperation, distribution and equality.

Nonviolent Ownership: Trusteeship

Economic equality being an essential principle and indispensable condition of the sarvodaya society, trusteeship is a natural corollary of Gandhi's sarvodaya. "It is sarvodaya extended to the firm", in the words of Mark Lutz (Diwan and Lutz 1985: 41). Gandhi suggests trusteeship as a means for correcting the inequalities of assets ownership; it emanates from his overriding belief in nonviolence to bring about a change of the unequal social relationship without violence. He also had profound belief in the goodness of human beings and so appealed to the higher sense of the landlord and the industrialist.[10]

Gandhi propounded the principle of trusteeship largely in the context of the question of ownership of the means of production; it follows from and is based on the principle of non-possession (*aparigraha*), (Non-possession may be considered as a form of nonviolence, if possession involves violence). Non-possession lies at the heart of his trusteeship, though Gandhi formulated the doctrine of non-possession as one of the key philosophical principles underlying satyagraha movement.[11] Gandhi had been gripped by the concepts of *aparigraha* (non-possession) and *samabhava* (equality), which he found in the *Gita* as far back as 1903. He wrote,

> To me the *Gita* became an infallible guide of conduct...Words like *Aparigraha* (non-possession) and *Samabhava* (equality) gripped me. I understood more clearly in the light of the *Gita* teaching the implication of the word "trustee"...I understood the *Gita* teaching of non-possession to mean that those who desired salvation should act like the trustee who, having control over great

> possession, regards not an iota of them as his own. (*Autobiography*, 221).

By trusteeship is meant that beginning with one's body one holds everything one has as a trust and this includes intelligence, talents, powers, possessions and other natural gifts. Non-possession follows from truth and nonviolence. It implies that a person should not possess anything that one does not need. According to Gandhi, the doctrine of non-possession means that everyone should limit one's own possession to what is needed by one and spend the rest for the welfare of others. He considered this as a desirable, nonviolent method of reducing inequality of income distribution and maldistribution of wealth. Non-possession means "possession by all". "I can only possess certain things when I know that others, who also want to possess similar things, are able to do so. But we know—everyone of us can speak from experience—that such a thing that can be possessed by all is no-possession, not to have anything whatsoever. In other words, a willing surrender" (Gandhi 1966: 50). Non-possession, in other words, means voluntary poverty.

The morality behind the idea of non-possession is that all human beings are equal and that one person is not to be exploited by another. Gandhi's concept of theft is based on *aparigraha*. Accordingly, anyone who possesses things and objects not needed by oneself but needed by others is a thief. In the words of Gandhi:

> It is theft to take something from another person even with his permission, if we have no need of it. We should not receive any single thing that we do not need. Theft of this description generally has food for its object. It is theft for me to take any food that I do not need, or to take in a larger quantity than necessary (Gandhi 1966: 47).

The whole idea of private property comes under question here. It may be remarked that non-possession is not compatible with capitalism.[12] Later on, he discovered in *Ishopanishad* the real meaning of property, "God, the Ruler, pervades all there is in the universe. Therefore renounce and dedicate all to Him and then enjoy or use the portion that may fall to thy lot. Never covet anybody's possession". "Since God pervades everything, nothing belongs to you, not even your body. God is the undisputed, unchallengeable Master of everything you possess" (Gandhi 1959: 113). Trusteeship is based on the idea that "what belongs to me is the right to an honourable livelihood, no better than enjoyed by millions of others. The rest of my wealth belongs to the community and must be used for the welfare of the community." "Gandhi himself believed that the concept of Trusteeship was one of the few that he thought would survive the ravages of time and history and even some of his own concepts because it dealt basically with the question of economic structure and organization which other systems, past and present, have failed to answer" (Sethi 1986: ix). The dynamic nature of trusteeship consists in its being a movement as much as an idea with strong moral imperatives towards reforming, and restructuring of the economic system.

Gandhi is very articulate about the moral or spiritual principle underlying the very idea of trusteeship. It is a principle of economic conscience. All those who are concerned with economic decisions (the producers, those who make policies) have to listen to the voice of their conscience before their self-interest. Trusteeship thus is a satyagraha or a movement towards invoking the conscience of those who are involved in the system. It is not enough just to listen to their conscience, but they need a *metanoia*, i.e., a change of heart; for Gandhi said,

> We may not dispossess the zamindars of their thousands of bighas. And among whom shall we distribute them? We need not dispossess them. They need a change of heart. When that is done, and when they learn to melt their tenants' woes, they will hold their lands in trust for them, will give them a major part of the produce keeping only what is sufficient for themselves (*Young India* 1931: 49).

He maintained that, "by the nonviolent method we seek not to destroy the capitalist, we seek to destroy capitalism. We invite the capitalist to regard himself as trustee for those on whom he depends for the making, the retention and increase in his capital (*Young India* March 1931: 49).

In a message to the zamindars, Gandhi seems to warn them in the context of the *kisan* struggles, especially in Uttar Pradesh (India):

> I would like the zamindars to recognize the correctness of the *kisan's* position and make a correspondent change in their own outlook... They should become trustees and trusted friends of their tenants. They should limit their privy purse. Let them forego the questionable perquisites they take from the tenants in the shape of forced gifts...They should give them fixity of tenure, take a lively interest in their welfare...and...make them feel that they, the zamindars, are their true friends, taking only a fixed commission for their manifold services...(*Young India* May 1930).

In its gradual growth, Gandhi links trusteeship with "voluntariness". Gandhi wanted an end to the zamindari system and genuinely hoped for a voluntary trusteeship in its place. When he realized that his appeal to conversion—of capitalists to trustees—went unheeded, he advocated even state intervention to implement trusteeship. About the state intervention, Gandhi has this to say:

> As for the present owners of wealth they would have to make their choice between class war and voluntary converting themselves into trustees of their wealth. They would be allowed to retain the stewardship of their possessions and to use their talent to increase the wealth, not for their sake, but for the sake of the nation and therefore without exploitation. The state would regulate the rate of commission which they would get commensurate with the services rendered and its value to society... (*Harijan* March 1946: 63).

Gandhi's frequent reference during this period to the intervention by the state towards some form of trusteeship make voluntariness recede more and more to the background.[13]

Gandhi realized that the perfect ideal of non-possession is unattainable because it demands total renunciation. Nevertheless, he initiated a movement towards total renunciation through the process of gradual reduction of wants and minimization of consumption. Reduction of wants or simplifying our wants is a central point in Gandhi's concept of non-possession. Simplifying wants in the Gandhian sense means, first to make a concerted effort to reduce the sheer number of encrusted desires and habit patterns that vitiate our altruistic impulses and dreams for others, and to self-consciously check the tendency of the aggressive self to acquire more at the expense of others. Secondly, it means to be more responsive to the needs of fellow human beings. Thus our feeling for what others may attain is gradually enriched, while our fantasies about what we hope to acquire wane. There is a dynamic growth here, from the realm of narrow selfishness to other-centredness.

Trusteeship and ownership appear contradictory because in the words of Dada Dharmadhikari, a close associate of Gandhi, "The way of emancipating ourselves from the concept of ownership is trusteeship" (Sethi 1986: 97). In the words of K. R. Rao,"The concept of trusteeship excludes the notion of property right, as no individual right can override the right of all individuals to minimum needs."[14] In the economic field, ownership or private property is the source of power and inequality. Private property and the social sanction for inheritance lead to the perpetuation and accentuation of inequality. Private ownership of instruments of production leads to exploitation and appropriation of surplus value, leading to the accumulation of capital and wealth, and the concentration of the ownership of the instruments of production in the hands of a few. Capitalism sanctifies the system of concentration and centralization in the name of the liberty of the individual, the right to private property, the right to inheritance, and the right to pursue private profit without concern for the resultant cost of society. Gandhi held that true liberty of the individual was inconsistent with these "rights". The unilateral exercise of these rights without self-restraint or social sanction had only resulted in inequality, injustice, exploitation, suffering and conflicts. Ideally Gandhi would prefer affluent people not to create wealth for its own sake and accept the vow of poverty as long as poverty existed in the world. If people acquire wealth, then he would want them to turn themselves into trustees, managing it for the benefit of the community.

Gandhi did not believe that the solution of the problem of exploitation lay in the violent dispossession of the owning class and the abolition of private property; nor did he believe that the transfer of ownership to the society or the State would automatically lead to the elimination of classes, and the emergence of a non-exploitative society. Nonetheless he proposed trusteeship as a third alternative to private ownership (capitalism) and State ownership (communism). In Gandhi's scheme, trusteeship, being an essential component of *gramswaraj* (village self-rule), is a movement for people's self-rule, people's birthright; village ownership in this sense is his third alternative. Vinoba Bhave called his *gramdan* "trusteeship in action" in which the individual owner surrenders his legal title collectively to the village, and not to the state, retaining his right to till the land.

Gandhi held on to the ideal of trusteeship as a "grand alternative" because of his firm conviction that trusteeship, if followed in all its details, will usher in a nonviolent, non-exploitative sarvodaya society. He was fully aware though that this ideal may never be realized in its entirety. He was also aware of the possibility of his theory being criticised as simplistic, unrealistic and impractical. He made considerable effort to counter such criticism. He realized that a lot of "ridicule" had been poured on it. And yet he stated, "...I adhere to my doctrine of trusteeship" (Gandhi 1941: 21). Gandhi's adherence to trusteeship in spite of its failure to achieve set goals made Acharya Kripalani, one of the closest associates of Gandhi for over thirty years, to say about the fate of the concept of trusteeship that: "Gandhiji was rather disillusioned in the end and held that his capitalist friends could never become the trustees of the people...The capitalists went to him for their own purposes mostly...but Gandhiji could not turn the heart of even one capitalist. They remained what they were..." (Biswas 1969: 220). This frustration of Gandhi's efforts was inevitable according to S. Naqvi, because Gandhi failed to understand "the mechanism and dynamics of the capitalist system and the parasitical and reactionary nature of the *Zamindari* system..." (Biswas 1969: 220). Gandhi could never have expected all the capitalists to give up their property and become trustees, at his appeal. Nonetheless he pleaded for individual landlords and capitalists to be humanitarian, charitable, noble and patriotic, but these appeals fell on deaf ears of the system. Gandhi was not ignorant about the impersonal, competitive, exploitative and violent nature of capitalism though. His ideal alternative was trusteeship.

The principle of trusteeship has been subjected to much misconceived criticism. It has been described as a "makeshift", as an "eyewash", as a shelter for the rich and as "merely appealing to the more fortunate ones to show a little more charity". It has been generally objected to on the ground that, as a means of effecting social transformation, this theory, its ethical content notwithstanding, is ineffective. Prof.M.L. Dantwala in his *Gandhism Reconsidered* quotes a Marxist appraisal of the doctrine:

> The division of the society into the property owning and the property-less classes, which is the characteristic of capitalism, is sought to be retained in Gandhism also. The only difference in Gandhism is that the erstwhile capitalist, property owning class will consider itself trustee on behalf of the proletariat. The change is purely on the subjective sphere. The objective conditions of production will continue by remaining as they were in capitalism...The class appropriation of surplus value, which trust production will continue in a pious guise, will mean larger and larger accumulation of the capital on the one hand and pauperization of the masses on the other...These evils cannot be banished by wishing a change in the hearts and minds of the owners of property (Dantwala 1945: 54-55).

E.M.S. Namboodiripad has attacked not only Gandhi's philosophy but also his very intentions. In his view, Gandhi's ideas were catering to the bourgeoisie, Not only in relation to the rural poor, but also in relation to the working class and other sections of the working people, his was an approach which, in actual practice, helped the bourgeoisie. His theory of trusteeship,...proved in actual practice to be enormous help to the bourgeoisie in a) rousing the masses in action against imperialism and in b) preventing them from resorting to revolutionary mass action. This ability of his to rouse the masses and yet to check them,...made him the undisputed leader of the bourgeoisie (Namboodiripad 1958: 115).

Even a sympathetic reviewer of Gandhian economics, like J. J. Anjaria, doubts the validity of trusteeship as a long-term solution.

"As a short-term measure this is excellent. Coercion is ethically bad; on any large-scale, it is also not expedient. But to run away from the problem by merely appealing to the more fortunate ones to show a little more charity—awful word—is no solution" (Anjaria 1945: 31). As for Gunnar Myrdal, the author of *Asian Drama*,

> the trusteeship idea is fundamentally a concept that fits into paternalistic, feudal, pre-democratic society. Possibly Gandhi realized this, for he demanded a moral revolution, a change of heart among the rich. But in the real world, such a revolution is unlikely and the trusteeship ideal is nought but a vision of society where the rich are charitable so that the poor can remain weak...by his stress on the principle of trusteeship, and his friendliness towards many in exalted economic positions, he established a pattern of radicalism in talk but conservatism in action that is still very much a part of the Indian scene (Myrdal vol. 2 1968: 755).

Jawaharlal Nehru too disagreed with Gandhi's theory of trusteeship. He wrote in his autobiography,

> Again I think of the paradox that is Gandhiji. With all his keen intellect and passion for bettering the downtrodden and oppressed, why does he support a system, and a system which is obviously decaying,... Is it reasonable to believe in the theory of trusteeship—to give unchecked power and wealth to an individual and to expect him to use it entirely for the public good? Are the best of us so perfect as to be trusted in this way?... And is it good for the others to have even these benevolent supermen over them? (Nehru 1982: 528).

The critics cited above seem biased and see only the negative side and totally undermine the positive elements in the theory of trusteeship. Maybe it is an unintentional refusal to understand the implications of the concept. Trusteeship may be considered as another *meta*-category which is meta-legal or meta-economic. It defines a way of exercising responsibility or control over resources whether as owner, official or bureaucrat. Stewardship thus can become an ideal model for any citizen in a sarvodaya society. As ideal or model, trusteeship becomes an effective utopian symbol to inspire people and challenge their conscience and the prevalent sense of justice. If, for instance, the capitalist were to become a genuine steward, he would inevitably reform (and perhaps reform beyond recognition) capitalism. The stewardship ideal does not discard economic issues, it is a meta-ideal needed to get true results out of whatever economic system prevails.

It is true that there is no historical example of trusteeship to go by. Moreover, full trusteeship has not been experimented with anywhere. Experiments with limited trusteeship are few, mainly because of its deep and broad implications. The fact is that generally people are unwilling to limit their wants and part with their wealth. Ganesh D. Gadre explains the real depth of trusteeship by an illustration from the *Panchatantra* story of the four wise men.[15] "The *Mantra* of trusteeship", writes Gadre, "can infuse life into the skeleton of Gandhism, which, if revived, will swallow us along with our comfortable armchairs" (Biswas 1969: 123). It will snatch away from our rulers, leaders, industrialists, bureaucrats, intelligentsia, and other elites their luxuries and comforts and will distribute them to the less privileged. This fear of loosing possession of excess wealth and other luxuries and the very thought of giving up those things make most people shun any experiment with trusteeship. These very people will give all possible reasons to show that trusteeship is illusory and impractical. The theory of trusteeship can transform the docile *Daridranarayana* (God in the form of poor and downtrodden masses) into a vigorous *Narasimha* (God in the form of the mythical man-lion) that will tear to shreds all the subtle system of exploitation of man by man. This fear haunts us. Despite this fear, Gandhi's ideas of trusteeship have been consciously applied in India and abroad.

As to the implementation of trusteeship, Gandhi had this to say, "when the people understand the implications of trusteeship and the atmosphere is ripe for it, the people themselves, beginning with *Gram Panchayats*, will begin to introduce such statutes" (*Harijan* March 1946). The late Dr. Ram Manohar Lohia had given notice of his intention to move an Indian Trusteeship Bill to the *Lok Sabha* in March 1967. This was to provide for the voluntary conversion into trust corporations of concerns owning industries, plantations, banks, trade, transport etc., worth about Rs.10,00,000.

If the share-holders of any such concern offered to become trustees and accepted the workers as their partners, the Government would constitute a *Panchayat* of trustees to manage the affairs of that concern. The bill made detailed provisions for efficient management of trust corporations in the light of Gandhi's views on trusteeship. The President of India withheld sanction to the introduction of this bill in *Lok Sabha* on the ground that it is a Monetary Bill. Dr.Lohia had appealed to the President for reconsideration; but he died before he could pursue the matter.

George Fernandes introduced the same "The Indian Trusteeship Bill" in the *Lok Sabha* in November 1969, but it lapsed without discussion. Atal Bihari Vajpayee introduced the same on 18 April 1975, but it also lapsed with the dissolution of the *Lok Sabha* in 1977. The Janata Trusteeship Bill by Prof. Ramjee Singh on April 20, 1978 also met with the same fate.

Gandhi had hoped that statutory trusteeship would be India's gift to the world (*Harijan* February 1947). To this day it remains an ideal, an objective. Whether the members of parliament will ever make statutory provisions for enabling conscientious trustees to fulfil their moral responsibilities is anyone's guess. One of the most important steps towards the implementation of trusteeship is mass drive for educating the people in the responsibilities of trusteeship and organizing workers behind the demand for co-operativization of large concerns. Shri Shankarao Deo, the veteran sarvodaya leader, had initiated some work on these lines. He suggested that, "the tea plantation industry in India provides an ideal target for intensive experiments in the implementation of trusteeship." The workers' demand should therefore be, not for higher wages, but for ownership of the concerns where they work. If the owners fail to become trustees, workers should resort to non-violent satyagraha, making it impossible for the owners to continue their exploitation. Gandhi had advised the owners that,

> they should willingly regard workers as the real owners of the concerns which they fancy they have created...they should at once offer the strikers full control of the concern which is as much the strikers' as theirs (*Harijan* March 1946).

Writing on "Applied Trusteeship", K. Arunachalam claims

that "Gandhian ideas of trusteeship have been consciously applied here and abroad in a few industrial and commercial units" (Sethi 1986: 154). Arunachalam gives some case studies: *Madras Khadi Gramodya Sangh*: A commercial unit, The Khira Trusteeship Projects (P) Limited (KTP), Cooperative Societies, The Political and Economic experiment of the Raja of Aundh and Segaon experiment- where trusteeship has been experimented with great success. "The idea of *Gramdan*", Arunachalam concludes, "in its broadest sense, is based on the principle of trusteeship".

Trusteeship even has found global relevance, says Shann Turnbull. "Trusteeship offers a way to avoid not just violence between humans but also violence between humans and their environment. If human life is to be indefinitely sustainable on the planet, then irreversible violation of the world's atmosphere, water, soil, flora and fauna will need to be avoided; this could be achieved by adoption of the trusteeship principle at the local level on a global basis" (Sethi 1986: 170). Some of the practical elements of the Gandhian concept of trusteeship are emerging in many parts of the world. Tax incentives have been introduced in leading market economies, such as England, France, Germany and the USA to promote the expanded ownership of enterprises on an evolutionary, voluntary basis.[16] The World Council of Churches generally embraced the stewardship model, which says we are trustees and keepers of creation.

Sethi develops the scope and applicability of trusteeship in the context of workers' participation in management. Participation of workers in management logically leads to co-determination, which necessarily implies consultation. He gives the example of Japan and Germany, where they have developed an intermediate arrangement based on the principle of co-determination.[17]

Gandhi claimed that trusteeship was likely to be his most lasting contribution, whereas the votaries of all the existing systems reject it. Partly it is due to the fact that Gandhi did not elaborate it sufficiently, and partly because we ourselves have not paid adequate attention to it. Gandhi did not leave behind a detailed model for trusteeship; instead he enunciated the basic principle of its organization. Trusteeship has to be understood as part of the scenario of nonviolent revolution, as an instrument in the satyagrahi's struggle for economic equality and the elimination of classes. Trusteeship of Gandhi needs to be looked at both as ideal and as experiment. As ideal, trusteeship may be considered as another *meta*-category which is *meta*-economics. When Gandhi speaks of *aparigraha* and *samabhava* as the basis of trusteeship, voluntarily limiting one's own needs, sharing of wealth for the welfare of others, appealing to the goodwill of capitalist and zamindaris for a *metanoia*, i.e., change of attitudes and even suggesting voluntary poverty, he was laying the spiritual (theological) foundation for trusteeship. Such *meta*-categories may be considered as moral imperative towards reforming and restructuring the existing economic system. This offers challenges to the existing global economic system that is based on competition, profit and accumulation without any limit. The issue that is often ignored is the possibility and extent of limiting one's need. Trusteeship as ideal also reminds every human person of one's responsibility of being a steward of property and wealth. As ideal, trusteeship is based on global sharing of resources. Trusteeship as experiment may have failed in many respects, but even a failed experiment does not defeat the ideals on which such experiments are carried out. A failed experiment prepares the way for a new experiment; and thus keeps the dialectic of the process in focus. This seems to be true with Gandhi's economic insights and trusteeship in particular.

As the grand alternative, "Trusteeship aims at achieving larger social benefits rather than work for a narrow economic objective such as profit;.... As it is more equalitarian than all other systems, it makes participation not merely formal or of unequal economic, political or status weights, but bases it on the principle of all-round equality. Trusteeship cuts across classes in such a way as to produce over a longer period a classless system. Trusteeship is also self-government, not only of workers but of the entire community. Above all, trusteeship, being divorced from the profit motive, introduces the element of fraternity without which neither equality nor freedom can be adequately safe-guarded" (Sethi 1978: 168).

Industrialization and Appropriate Technology

Gandhi in his *Hind Swaraj* made a massive attack on machinery, of which reverberations can still be heard. In fact his severe attack on machinery, started therein, has made the name of Gandhi a synonym for anti-machinery, anti-technology. Gandhi took an extreme position about machinery and industrialization in the book *Hind Swaraj*, in which book he certainly was an uncompromising critic of all machines and declared himself in no uncertain terms against them: "It is machine that has impoverished India. It is difficult to measure the harm that Manchester (home of the British Textile Industry) has done to us". In *Hind Swaraj*, he posits an ideal state of things in which there will be no machine, no railways, no doctors, lawyers and such symbols of modern civilization. The target of Gandhi's attack in *Hind Swaraj* is machinery, that is, technology. (Though Gandhi did not use the word "technology", his entire critique of machinery in effect is the critique of modern technology, Prasad ed. 1985: 151). Through his indictment of machinery, Gandhi made a thorough indictment of this whole machine-based British rule in India and of the machine-based Western civilization. Gandhi was reacting to a machine-oriented civilization or culture.

In Gandhi's human economy, machinery can be enslaving and large-scale industrialization degrading to human beings.[18] From his experience of poverty and unemployment in India, he came to the conclusion that the problem of poverty could not be tackled through the Western method of large-scale industries; instead he was seeking the resuscitation of the village through the revival of its handicrafts and village industries.

He was concerned with the misuse and abuse of machinery because the use of machinery tends more and more to concentrate wealth in the hands of a few in total disregard of millions of men and women whose bread is taken by it out of their mouths. It was this underlying man-machine conflict that bothered him and, while he was prepared to accept machinery of certain type on a limited scale, he was concerned that the machine would one day become the master. He saw in the improper use of machine a dehumanising influence that needed to be countered if man was to retain his individual dignity and freedom.

In almost the last words he wrote on the subject in December 1947, after India became free, he reiterated his faith in the supremacy of man over machine. "Through khadi", he wrote, "we were striving for the equality of all men and women in place of the gross inequality to be witnessed today" (CW 90: 230). He saw in the machine an instrument of that inequality and exploitation of the poor by the rich of his own country now that the foreign master had left.

His opposition against machinery in *Hind Swaraj* was mainly based on moral and religious considerations. *Hind Swaraj* was a moral response to what Gandhi perceived as the evils of modern civilization. He saw violence rooted in modern civilization. For Gandhi, the propelling force of modern civilization is what he calls "the hunger for wealth and the greedy pursuit of worldly pleasures." The desire to amass wealth in a situation marked by resource limitations leads inevitably to violence both at the individual and the collective levels. Also, modern civilization, in Gandhi's opinion, places the pursuit of self-interest at the centre of man's existence. But once the pursuit of self-interest is recognised to be central in life, the pursuit of other things—morality, spirituality etc., — gets crowded out of the individual's life. As a result, morality and spirituality become insignificant and irrelevant. Gandhi considered industrialization and craze for machinery as part of modern civilization. Hence his opposition to machinery is a logical consequence of his opposition to modern civilization. But his later writings on machinery contained arguments based on economic rationale. His opposition was three-fold in nature: sociological, based on the quality of life; economic, the impact it has on rural life and the employment opportunities available in the village; and political, since machinery, he saw allied to the forces fighting Indian freedom.[19]

It is true that the advancement of science and technology has made it possible to produce more and more things on a large scale. But the problem is that technologically induced and sustained economic growth makes centralization of power and decision-making an essential part of modern life. Industrialization has succeeded largely in producing goods and services on a larger scale and at a faster rate. But for Gandhi, it is a curse for man because it "depends entirely on your capacity to exploit, on foreign markets being open to you, and on the absence of competitors" (CW 48: 224).

Colonization (industrialized country colonizing non-industrialized countries), domination (minority dominating a majority), and unhealthy competition ending in violent clashes and world wars have been the natural consequences of such industrialization. There is a kind of tacit approval of such exploitation in the global scenario which is enjoyed by the developed countries. Foreign aid, political control, and manipulation of trade relationship are various methods through which economic exploitation of the weaker nations is done. Industrialization tends to destroy differing national economies and breaks their self-sufficiency and imposes the dominant countries' style of operation on other countries. Gandhi opposed industrialization as a means of solving India's economic problems; he argued that:

> ...a big country, with teeming population, with ancient rural tradition which hitherto answered its purpose need not, must not, copy the Western model. What is good for one nation situated in one condition is not necessarily good for another differently situated (CW 41: 220).

Gandhi admits that abject poverty can and does lead to moral degradation and recognizes that, for a poor man, bread is his god. But he disagrees with the argument that material progress spells moral progress. On the contrary, he asserts that, after a ceratin minimum of physical well-being, it spells moral and spiritual disaster. In Gandhi's view a reconciliation between modernity and spirituality is impossible. An industrial India would mean an exploiting India, because, "...evils are inherent in industrialism and no amount of socialization can eradicate them" (CW 73: 30). An India exploiting other lands was a horror to Gandhi:

> God forbid that India should ever take to industrialism after the manner of the West. The economic imperialism of a single tiny island Kingdom (England) is today keeping the world in chains. If an entire nation of 300 millions took to similar economic exploitation, it would strip the world bare like locusts (CW 38: 243).

Gandhi rejects industrialisation also on the grounds that it fails to offer a better standard of living for all. Inequality and exploitation force the majority of people to live a life of subsistence or even worse. What it does achieve, in reality, is to raise the standard of living for the already rich and widen the gap between the rich and the poor. In this regard, Gandhi's assessment of the West[20] and his prediction about India remain valid.

Industrialism stimulates a multiplication of wants but satisfies the wants of only a few. When unlimited wants and amassing of wealth become the essence of any culture, greed will rule the day; and dehumanization, ruthless exploitation and denigration of morality and spirituality will follow. In his human economy, therefore, Gandhi argued that India still remained primarily an agricultural country. He firmly believed that "India could retrace her advance towards industrialism and reconstruct her economic life and relations in accordance with the principles of human economy" (Roy 1985: 135). It should be pointed out that his suggestions for the reconstruction of economic life and relations undoubtedly emanate from his distaste for industrialism. He firmly believed that a nonviolent society cannot be built on the foundation of industrialism.

The past and current policies of the Indian government involve the furtherance of capitalist method of production and industrialism. Industrialization and introduction of new technologies seem to have created more unemployment and poverty. It has made a few rich people richer. One would agree with R. Diwan that "India cannot, any more, maintain its industrialist structure" (Diwan and Lutz 1985: 184).

Gandhi's struggle against industrialism was nearly neglected after India got political independence. (Already during the mid-thirties the demand for the industrialization of the country arose inside and outside the Congress; liberals like Nehru, nationalists like Subhas Chandra Bose, radicals like M. N. Roy and the emerging forces of socialism inside and outside the anti-imperialist platform stood for industrialisation). Nehru formed the national government and gave up totally Gandhi's struggle against industrialization.

Gandhi's only solution to industrialization is the reconstruction of rural economy with an emphasis on the primacy of agriculture and the supplementary and complementary importance of cottage industries. By the revival and rejuvenation of the village economy, Gandhi wants to emphasize the simplicity of village life, decentralized, self-sufficient, self-reliant and autonomous communities, production by the masses instead of "mass production", and limitation of machinery. Such Gandhian alternative may be qualified as "appropriate technology",[21] "intermediate technology"[22] (self-help technology, or democratic or people's technology), "new technology"[23] or "holistic technology".[24] It is not correct to say that Gandhi was anti-machinery. What he was opposed to was the indiscriminate use of machinery. More specifically, he objected to what he called the "craze for machinery". In his words:

> What I object to, is the *craze* for machinery, not machinery as such. The craze is for what they call labour-saving machinery. Men go on "saving labour" till thousands are without work and thrown on the open streets to die of starvation. I want to save time and labour, not for a fraction of mankind, but for all. I want the concentration of wealth, not in the hands of a few,, but in the hands of all. Today, machinery merely helps a few to ride on the backs of millions... (CW 25: 251).

The Gandhian choice of technology is simple and straightforward. Production for him is a simple function of labour. Labour should produce what it needs. Machinery should be subservient to labour. He maintained that,

> Machinery...must not be allowed to displace necessary human labour. An improved plough is a good thing, but it must not be allowed to displace necessary human labour...I would welcome every improvement in the cottage machine, but I know that it is criminal to displace hand labour by the introduction of power driven spindles, unless one is at the same time ready to give millions of farmers some other occupation in their house (Gandhi 1951: 40).

Machinery may be introduced provided there is healthy alternative to the eliminated occupations of people.

He detests machines if they remain the instrument of the

satisfaction of the greed of a few. "I am aiming," says Gandhi, "not at eradication of all machinery, but limitations" (CW 25: 251). The basic question Gandhi posed was whether "technology would remain controlled and in the service of man to reduce his drudgery and to help solve man's material problems" or "whether man would become so subservient to technology that ultimately he would be forced to sell his soul to Mephistophelian materialism and become alienated both from his fellow beings and nature by plundering it" (Sethi 1979: 49). What he asked for was an "appropriate technology", which can be adapted by the village homes. He said: "My machinery must be of the most elementary type which I can put in the homes of the millions" (*Harijan* November 1934: 301).

E.F. Schumacher takes Gandhi's economic principles seriously as much in dealing with the advanced industrial countries as in discussing the Third World. Being influenced by Gandhi's economic ideas, he has professed his faith "in the evolution of small-scale technology, relatively non-violent technology, technology with a human face..." (Schumacher 1973: 17). Like Gandhi's, Schumacher's ideal is small production resting on small-scale technology. He is, like Gandhi, against "the technology of mass production" (it "is inherently violent, ecologically damaging, self-defeating in terms of non-renewable resources, and stultifying for the human person") and advocates "the technology of production by the masses" (which "making use of the best of modern knowledge and experience, is conducive to decentralisation, compatible with the laws of ecology, gentle in its use of scarce resources, and designed to serve the human person instead of making him the servant of machines") Schumacher named it "intermediate technology".

It was not, however, Gandhi's intention to turn one's back on technology; in the words of Alvin Toffler, such a step would be "not only stupid but immoral...such a step would be to condemn billions to enforced and permanent misery at precisely the moment in history when their liberation is becoming possible. We clearly need not less, but more technology". But such technology needs to be tamed for man's use, to be relevant to his needs and to be responsive to his ideals. Toffler continues, "We desperately need a movement for responsible technology. We need a broad political grouping, rationally committed to further scientific research and technological advance -but on a selective basis...it should formulate a set of positive technological goals for the future" (Toffler 1971: 381-82). Today we are faced with a technological over-choice and society must be careful enough, and wise enough to select its machines, processes and techniques to choose its style.

Gandhi was to some extent, pleading for the same approach; he was not against the upgrading of technology; in fact, he took positive steps, as in the case of spinning, to devise an improved model. But his distinctiveness lies here: he insisted that the new technology should be relevant to rural India and not create more social and economic problems than those it was intended to solve. He wanted production limited to immediate needs and equitable distribution. Gandhi was opposed to an economy or technology where the interest of the masses figured but little. Instead, he posited a new technology which may involve the masses in decisions meant to shape their life. As we have seen earlier, modern technology tends to centralise power—economic and political—in few hands. Gandhi's alternative is decentralisation of power. To him, the solution of concentration of power lies in the small-scale manageable techniques capable of being worked upon by individual producers, the cooperatives in the villages or the region. If such a technology could be evolved and put in the hands of the village, the problem of concentration of power might be easily solved. Such a development in the application of technology will obviously be opposite to the present trend and will be an altogether new dimension of technological growth.

In such decentralised technology as Gandhi visualised, every village is able to own the technology and the economic power will be diffused in the villages. It will be village-oriented technology aiming at perfecting the cottage and village industries. The village will thus emerge in the Gandhian scheme as the nucleus of social life. The emphasis here, is on small-scale technique of production carried to every home and family in the village. When industry of the type Gandhi conceived is carried to the village, the relationship between industry and agriculture is changed. What is called for is a healthy balance between industry and agriculture at the village level because it will be the village which will occupy the place of importance in the social order of Gandhi's conception. Pyarelal has very lucidly described this relationship: "Agriculture in this set up will go hand in hand with industry. Such products of the village as enter into the daily consumption of the villagers or are needed for their cottage crafts will be processed in the village itself; the surplus alone being sent out to the cities in exchange for services and goods on a fair and equitable basis. Cities will serve as emporia for village products instead of the villages being used as a dumping ground for the manufactured goods of the cities. Machines will not be abolished. On the contrary, the people will have many more of them. But these machines will be simple machines which people can themselves operate and own individually or collectively" (Pyarelal vol.2 1958: 585).

When a healthy balance is established between agriculture and industry in any society, production will be regulated by the needs of the village. The needs of the village will assume priority over the need to produce for the market. One factor that makes any technology people-oriented is this capacity to produce goods needed by people. Production for the needs of the village is based on a much misunderstood Gandhian notion: self-sufficiency. In the village the means of production of the elementary necessities of life are to be "freely available to all as God's air and water" and are not to be "a vehicle of traffic for the exploitation of others" (*Young India* November 1928). The village is to be self-sufficient in the matter of its vital requirements as a unit; and inter-dependent with other villages in many other spheres. As Gandhi put it, "My idea of village *Swaraj* is that it is a complete republic, independent of its neighbours for its own vital wants, and yet inter-dependent for many others in which dependence is a necessity..." (*Harijan* July 1924: 238). Self-sufficiency is not to be interpreted as absence of commerce and exchange with other villages. Provided villages manufacture mainly for their own use, "there would be no objection to villagers using even modern machines and tools that they can make and can afford to use. Only they should not be used as means of exploitation" (*Harijan* August 1936).

Interdependence, while maintaining the independence of the village in essential goods, is the keynote of Gandhi's approach to village life. Many observers, especially those who are more conversant with Gandhi's economic thought, think that although Gandhi wanted to make the village self-sufficient and self-reliant with respect to the basic requirements of consumption, Gandhian economics is not entirely based on small farm agriculture and cottage industry. Gandhi recognised the need for some large industries which are basic in character. He wanted a mixed pattern of industrial growth- a broad based network of production units in the villages with a few key industries in the urban areas, preferably under communal or state ownership. He regarded the latter as a necessary evil but looked to the former for supplying most of the wants of the people, whether in towns or cities. Gandhi would reverse the present rural-urban relationship and make the latter a market for the products produced in the former.

Gandhi was hopeful that cottage industries and big industries can be harmonised, provided "they are planned so as to help the villagers". He amplified it later: "I do visualise electricity, ship building, iron works, machine-making and the like existing side by side with village handicrafts. But the order of dependence will be reversed. Hitherto, the industrialization has been so planned as to destroy the villages and village crafts. In the state of the future, it will subserve the village and their crafts" (CW 71: 130).

Gandhi was keen that India should, at any cost, avoid industrialisation of the Western model. Even if the need for industrialization is accepted, there has to be an alternative pattern that can be adopted by the developing countries, because for a developing country like India large-scale industrialization of the Western type may be neither suitable nor desirable. The basic problem in India is adequate food production for the rapidly increasing population. In fact, cottage and large-scale industries were not competing alternatives, but complementary and helpful to each other. Small-scale production and large industries would have to be developed in such a manner that each sector will provide those supplies which cannot be produced by the other. Each sector thus will help the other by supplying certain requirements and by taking in some of its output. The reason is that small farm agriculture and cottage industries based on local resources cannot make the village entirely self-sufficient and self-reliant. The village would require infra-structural support and tools and implements produced through large investment as well as a few consumer goods. Even more, the output of the village industries may not be fully absorbed by local demands. Therefore, it is necessary to combine small-scale rural production with large-scale heavy industries for the growth of rural economy. With the growth of rural economy, a large part of the local demand could be met by local production and the villages could be made much more self-sufficient than they actually were.

In the light of Gandhi's views on economics and technology, P.L. Dhar suggests, "...a fresh appraisal of our concept of technology and development so that a uniform, unbiased perspective of technology—valid for both rural and urban development—could emerge" (Dhar 1988: 756). Dhar prefers to name such technology, "holistic technology", where technology is viewed in the context of general human welfare. Drawing his inspiration from the Maslovian[25] model of man, which forms the basis for the holistic technology, harmonious development of an individual, i.e., integral human welfare, is the goal of holistic technology. Holistic technology logically aims at sarvodaya because "a technology conceived in response to the moral and spiritual needs would be true holistic technology, and would ensure integral human welfare" (Dhar 1988:761).

To many, Gandhi's vision of technology may appear "to be more of a utopia visualized by a saintly person than a practical possibility suited for modern times", as Dhar opines. But, in the same vein, he says that "an alternative technology based on Gandhian vision thus seems to be a dire necessity" (Dhar 1988: 653). What we need, therefore, in the light of sarvodaya economy, is a transformation of strategy based on the development of both low-stream, village-oriented, capital-cheap, rural industries and certain carefully selected, high-stream technologies, with an economy zoned to protect or promote both. "A new balance has now to be struck between" the most advanced science and technology available to the human race and "the Gandhian vision of the idyllic green pastures, the village republics", as Jagdish Kapur writes. Such a practical combination, Kapur declares, requires a "total transformation of the society, its symbols and values, its system of education, its incentives, the flow of its energy resources, its scientific research and a whole lot of other institutions..." (Kapur 1975: 13; see also Toffler 1981: 344). The pre-requisite to such technology is an acceptance of a basic world-view: true welfare of individual and society culminates ultimately in holistic growth (physiological, emotional, intellectual, and spiritual). The most conducive atmosphere to develop and implement such technologies would be small units, like monasteries, ashrams and other similar organizations (the Benedictine monasteries [Mumford 1967: 263] of the middle ages are certainly the most illustrious examples of such holistic technologies). Gandhi's vision of the ideal village could become a reality "if a collaboration of like-minded scientists and technologies with such organizations could be worked out" (Dhar 1988: 655).

Swadeshi, Khadi and Charkha

Gandhi advocated charkha and handlooms with the intention of making "the largest contribution to the economic and the moral regeneration of India...Every revolution of the wheel spins peace, goodwill, and love. And...in as much as the loss of it brought about India's slavery, its voluntary revival with all its implications must mean India's freedom" (Gandhi 1960: 23-24).

In the context of Gandhi's appropriate technology and in the larger context of Gandhi's economics, it seems quite appropriate to discuss *swadeshi*, khadi and charkha or the very philosophy of *swadeshi*. These notions are closely interlinked. *Swadeshi* may have started as the rejection of British goods and the imperial policy of creating a class which willingly allowed itself to be enslaved by Western technology and culture. Gandhi never confined this concept to this limited objective, instead he broadened the definition of *swadeshi*. *Swadeshi* literally means "belonging to one's own country". It was a politico-economic strategy which had been employed against British in India while Gandhi was in South Africa. But for him it had a far deeper and wider meaning than mere boycott of British goods. For Gandhi it was inextricably tied to the values of simplicity and self-reliance, of limiting one's wants, and of manual labour. Writing on the significance of *swadeshi* as early as in 1909 Gandhi says,

> *Swadeshi* carries a great and profound meaning. It does

> not mean merely the use of what is produced in one's own country...there is another meaning implicit in it which is far greater and much more important. *Swadeshi* means reliance on our own strength (CW 9: 118).

The purpose of *swadeshi* movement, according to Gandhi, was to foster village industries, small-scale industries and self-reliance. He defined the concept of *swadeshi* in the following words:

> *Swadeshi* is that spirit in us which restricts us to the use and service of our immediate surroundings to the exclusion of the more remote. Thus, as for religion,...I must restrict myself to my ancestral religion...In the domain of politics, I should make use of the indigenous institutions and serve them by curing them of their proved defects. In that of economics, I should use only things that are produced by my immediate neighbours and serve those industries by making them efficient and complete where they might be found wanting.[26]

Elsewhere he says,

> My definition of *Swadeshi* is well known. I must not serve my distant neighbour at the expense of the nearest. It is never vindictive or punitive. It is in no sense narrow, for I buy from every part of the world what is needed for my growth. I refuse to buy anything however nice or beautiful, if it interferes with my growth or injures those whom nature had made my first care (*Young India* 1925: 88).

He clarified his position from "Yeravda Mandir", (i.e., prison)

> To reject foreign manufactures merely because they are foreign and go on wasting national time and money in the promotion in one's country of manufactures for which it is not suited would be criminal folly and a negation of the *Swadeshi* spirit. A votary of *Swadeshi* will never harbour ill-will towards the foreigners, he will not be activated by the hatred. It is a doctrine of selfless service that has its roots in the purest *ahimsa*, i.e., love.[27]

The spirituality or the theology (Brown 1989: 90) of *swadeshi* lies in one's love for one's own country, culture, people and what they produce. *Swadeshi* does not aim to hurt the foreigner; it only hopes to aid the native and the local. Vowing *swadeshi* means buying from your neighbour, not from afar; it means going to your village barber, even if his skill is less.[28] It means doing without goods that India did not produce. Above all, it means being proud of India and Indian things and resisting the sense of inferiority inculcated by Western domination:

> If we have no regard for our respective vernaculars, if we dislike our clothes, if our dress repels us, if we are ashamed to wear the sacred thread, if our food is distasteful to us, our climate is not good enough, our people uncouth...our civilization faulty...in short, if everything native is bad and everything foreign pleasing...I should not know what *Swaraj* can mean for us (Gandhi 1965: 74).

In its widest sense, *swadeshi,* for Gandhi meant "that spirit in us which restricts us to use and service of our immediate surroundings to the exclusion of the more remote". It was, in short, the humble way of love, of serving in the immediate context in which one found oneself; it excluded ideological or material aggrandizement or violence, and it included matters of religion, politics and economics (CW 13: 219-25). However, it was this last and more narrowly economic aspect on which Gandhi spoke most widely and which became inextricably linked with his name at home in India and abroad. As Judith Brown remarks, *swadeshi* is the basis of the "moral economics" (Brown 1989: 106), Gandhi advocated for India. Gandhi argued passionately that material progress as commonly understood was in fact the enemy of real, moral advancement. Indians should fight materialism by holding fast to their civilization and cherishing a simple lifestyle, where the principles of sufficiency and compassion would overcome the evils of grievous poverty, over-consumption and economic violence.

Swadeshi strategy is closely linked to the economic reconstruction strategy namely, village-oriented, people-oriented economy. However, politically, it is not so much the elimination of domestic poverty which motivates the *swadeshi* programme as the patriotic drive for self-reliance which makes possible the sacrifices (on the part of the elite) which are necessary for the anti-poverty programme. Gandhi noted the fact that an elite accepts sacrifices only under the pressure of national and patriotic motivations. He therefore made the principle of *swadeshi* the major motivational basis of the entire programme and the call for swaraj the political slogan under which his economic reconstruction programme would sweep the country.

Strict adherence to the principles of *swadeshi* will ultimately lead to the abolition of exploitation on the international scale and the restoration of the rights of the peoples of all countries to a stable and equal conditions of material welfare. This comes about through a gradual process of non-cooperation. The cooperation of the exploited is essential to the exploiter, whereas there is no such essential dependence of the exploited on the exploiter. If, therefore, the exploited are willing to pay the price of non-cooperation, their non-cooperation will have a compulsive effect on the exploiters. The result is that the rich economies will no longer have the opportunity to use trade as a weapon to exploit the rest of the world to maintain their own prosperity; they will be forced to change their economic structure in such a way as to reduce and eventually eliminate their dependence on the poor economies for sustaining their own prosperity. When correctly perceived, non-cooperation in the international field does not represent an act of hatred for the rich nations but rather an act of love for the peoples of the rich countries. In Gandhi's own words,"*Swadeshi* is the only doctrine consistent with the law of humanity and love"; and "*Swadeshi* is not a cult of hatred. It is a doctrine of self-less service that has its roots in purest *Ahimsa*, that is love" (Prabhu and Rao eds. 1968: 414-415).

Swaraj follows from *swadeshi*. Gandhi, in answer to the question whether he saw swaraj at the end of a *swadeshi* movement said,"Why not, once I said in spinning wheel lies Swaraj, next I said in Prohibition lies Swaraj. In the same way I would say in cent per cent *Swadeshi* lies Swaraj" (*Harijan* September 1934: 259).

Gandhi's economy is village-oriented and his constructive programme is geared toward village reconstruction. Gandhi considered khadi almost as the lead industry. Emphasis on khadi was moral as well as material, hence he recognized khadi mentality as decentralization of production and distribution of necessities of life and the beginning of economic freedom and equality of all in the country. In khadi Gandhi saw "the revival of the entire economic, social and cultural life of the village which constitute our country" (Gandhi 1955: iii). He realized that by making India economically self-dependent, khadi would help in hastening the achievement of political freedom. Khadi therefore, had for Gandhi, not merely an economic significance, but also great cultural or psychological value. As such, it contained the seeds of true swaraj or self-rule, or democracy in the real sense of the term. Gandhi had a clear rationale behind the choice of khadi. His efforts to revive khadi and to establish khadi movement was not merely "to serve the temporary purpose of wresting power from Britain, but he expected by it to lay the foundations of a non-violent economic and social order which would bring peace and happiness to us and to all mankind" (Gandhi 1955: iv). By introducing khadi and promoting it, Gandhi believed that it could give work to all, especially in the villages, because, he said,"if government could provide full employment to all people without the help of khadi and village industries, I shall be prepared to wind up my constructive programme in this sphere".

Gandhi never looked upon khadi as mere cloth. He has always been emphasizing the spirit behind khadi. In 1927 he wrote,

> The "Khadi spirit" means that we must know the meaning that the wearing of Khadi carries with it. Every time that... we wear Khadi garment, we should remember that we are doing so in the name of *Daridranarayan* and for the sake of the starving millions of India. If we have this "Khadi spirit" in us, we would surround ourselves with simplicity in every walk of life. The "Khadi spirit" means illimitable patience, illimitable faith in truth and non-violence...fellow feeling with every human being on earth (*Young India* September 1927).

The true spirit of khadi, therefore, goes beyond the realms of politics, economics, into the very spirituality (values and attitudes) of the human person. He toured the country, "preaching the gospel of Khadi" (Brown 1989: 203) and he wrote the "The Gospel of *Swadeshi*" (Gandhi 1967) to clarify his views on khadi and to spread the spirit of khadi. Deeply convinced of his philosophy of khadi, he found time for spinning and weaving and he wore khadi. His "prophetic witnessing" to khadi may have made a good impression on his immediate followers. Nehru supported the khadi programme even though he believed it was an outmoded form of production. He saw other benefits from it: it fit in well with the rural production system of India's peasantry, it helped organize that peasantry, and it served to check price-gouging by Indian mill owners.

Gandhi advocated the khadi and village industries for the uplifting of the rural masses. For him, khadi and village industries is not an end in itself but a means for the all-round socio-economic development of rural India. He strongly believed that India has the potential (manpower and material resources) and has the congenial socio-political climate (Indian villages, unemployment and poverty) for a steady progress to be achieved through the promotion of khadi and village industries. Nonetheless, Gandhi himself was disillusioned about the progress khadi and village industries achieved. In his own words,

> ... this grand picture of Khadi as the means of all-round uplift of the villages which I have been putting forward for so long is not being realized. So I feel I must retrace my steps...That is the call of truth. I retrace my steps consciously or intelligently, and not in a mood of defeatism or of cowardice... (Gandhi 1955: 185).

As Hitesranjan Sanyal comments, "Even Khadi textile and the local resource-based village crafts covered by the Khadi and the Village Industries Commission have not been able to grow up as self-supporting rural enterprises. Khadi is now viewed as a commercial enterprise. But it has failed to be commercially viable...At present the survival of Khadi depends on the artificial measure of Government subsidy and on the unethical means of catering to the middle class taste for fashionable piece goods. Khadi enterprises are now pleading government protection" (Prasad ed. 1985: 180). Since Independence, khadi production has passed into the hands of specialists, who spin and weave khadi for their livelihood. Khadi producers depend on long-term government loans and grants. Though khadi is marketed through special shops operated by Gandhian organizations and subsidized by the government, few Indians wear khadi nowadays probably because hand-spinning makes khadi cloth coarse and irregular and also it is more expensive than cloth from Indian mills. Though Richard Fox is correct in concluding that, "Neither as an experiment in bread labour, nor as a major employer of India's rural underemployed, nor as a check on mill owners' greed, but only as a destination for government funds has khadi succeeded" (Fox 1989: 181), the real khadi spirit goes beyond the hand-spun cloth. Khadi production is uneconomical, as Ostergaard and Currell admit (Ostergaard and Currel 1971: 252), but Gandhi elevated the spinning wheel as an ideal of self-reliance and symbol of self-suffering, bread labour and simplicity, "to significance as an economic necessity, religious ritual, and a national symbol" (Erikson 1970: 260; Fox, Mathew 1983: 238). Functioning as appropriate technology for village India, "...the spinning wheel could dramatically activate in hundreds of thousands of localities what was at the time not at all ready for industrialization" (Erikson 1970: 398).

Agriculture

Gandhi wanted khadi and village industries to be linked with agriculture and woven around it, since agriculture was after all the primary occupation of the large bulk of the people. The reason why he "dwelt upon the *Charkha* so much" is because he regarded "it as the centre of village uplift" (Gandhi 1955:161). He suggested other village crafts, like bullock oil-press, hand-made paper, hand-chakki (grinding stone) etc., as means of employment and self-sufficiency. Gandhi admitted that he is "...rather ignorant in this respect (agriculture) for I have no personal experience"; nevertheless, he says that, "In regard to agriculture, we must do our utmost to prevent further fragmentation of land, and to encourage people to take co-operative farming".

Gandhi's approach of linking agriculture and industry by making village industries agro-based is now seen as an effective way for meaningful development of agrarian societies. Unless industries in rural areas are linked with the primary occupation of the vast mass of the people, which is agriculture, they would make little impact on the lives of the people. Though many large undertakings have been established in semi-urban and even rural areas, their impact has been extremely limited because their scale of operation represents a sharp discontinuity with the normal scale of rural occupations and there is little in common between the large undertaking and the local skills so that meaningful linkages have never been built.

Gandhi's contribution to agriculture may be minimal; but he promoted agro-industries and small scale farming for India because agriculture was the mainstay of most people residing in villages. The reason why Gandhi linked village craft with agriculture is because both lead to self-sufficiency that is at the centre of sarvodaya economy.

Small is Possible

There is a great deal of idealism in the meta-economics of Gandhi's vision. This is no reason to bracket Gandhi's economic views as totally unrealisable and impractical as some do. Raj Krishna, for example, is highly critical of the realizability and practicality of the "Gandhian Model of Economics", which he says is basically "a variant of normative economics which proposes an ideal economic order".[29] Nonetheless, Raj Krishna admits that "their realization would require a radical reversal of contemporary historical trends." It is to be emphasized that Gandhi was not a system- or model-builder. He was essentially a pathfinder towards definite social and individual goals. He developed a total approach to man and his problems as he went along. Gandhi's insights on economics are to be seen in the wider context of sarvodaya. Those insights are both a critique of the then existing system and suggestions for an economy where people, and not machine or matter become the centre. Thus, in his attempt to give a human face to economics, he discovered "the Soul of Economics", or the spirituality of economics. His search was based on a simple philosophy that "Small is Beautiful" and "Small is Possible".

The brief analysis of Gandhi's basic conceptions about the ideal economy shows that their realisation would indeed require a radical reversal of contemporary historical trends. We can tabulate the opposition between the two as follows:

	Historical/contemporary trend.	*Gandhi's Suggestions.*
1.	Profit-oriented, money-oriented economics.	Ethical economy, service-oriented.
2.	Machine-centred technology	Holistic technology
3.	Multiplication of wants	Limitation of wants
4.	Mass (large-scale) production	Production by the masses (small-scale production)
5.	Centralization of economic power	Decentralization, limited State ownership, widespread village ownership and trusteeship
6.	Urbanization	Self-governing, self-sufficient villages
7.	Inequality	Equality of wages
8.	Promotion of large-scale industry	Promotion of small-scale industry

In presenting his economic insights, Gandhi was aware that structural, and societal transformations will be slow, hence he spoke in meta-economic terms not in economic terms per se. But he had great faith in the basic goodness of human beings, and he believed in the power and willingness of people to change. If, therefore, personal *metanoia* is the basis and secret of any social and institutional changes, then, Gandhi's economic insights are realizable utopia.

It is true that Indian economic planning failed to give sufficient emphasis and thrust to the realization of Gandhi's vision of economic programme. Programmes like National Rural Employment Programme (NREP), Rural Labour Employment Guarantee Programme (RLEGP), the Integrated Rural Development Programme (IRDP), the Training of Rural Youth for Self-Employment Programme (TRYSEM), and promotion of village and small-scale industries, have made progress towards rural transformation and integral development of the Indian villages.

These programmes are launched by the Government of India as rural anti-poverty initiatives. As Ashwanti Saith observes,

> ...the IRDP launched by the Government of India as a rural anti-poverty programme is massive in scale. It functions in all regions of the country, and commands vast resources. Recent ostensible (though queried) declines in the incidence of rural poverty have been ascribed to the influence of IRDP, though as yet no methodologically satisfactory decomposition of the effects of growth and this policy on rural poverty has become available. IRDP covers a wide range of activities: minor irrigation, dairy development, animal husbandry, animal-powered transport, e.g., carts, petty industry, services and business...IRDP, in its selection of beneficiaries from the rural poor, is expected to follow the "*Antyodaya*" approach, whereby the poorest of the poor are first identified and selected as beneficiaries. Reality, as usual, follows its own predictable course... (Breman 1991: 483).

How far these programmes are effective in reducing the number of people living in poverty is a worrisome question, because the data show that the number of persons whom the programme is able to lift above the poverty line is a little less than the new generation of those born into the poor families. There is urgent need for decentralized planning and execution at village, panchayat, and block level.

It is nearly impossible to prove the realizability of Gandhi's economic insights from a case study because through those insights Gandhi offers a vision that is yet to be realized. Global or even national realization may never be achieved. But small groups of dedicated Gandhians may create and maintain a few model institutions and communities adhering to the economic insights of Gandhi. But the number of such communities will always be small. They will be embodiments of what is possible on a small scale.

The contribution of Gandhi to economics is his linking economics with ethics; by doing this he gives a real face-lift to economics. One can therefore speak of the "spirituality of economics", meaning that economics is not just material progress but human development, sharing of wealth, trusteeship, limiting wants, self reliance, simple living etc. Although the ultimate Gandhian ideal is unrealized and may appear un- realizable in the context of modern society, "its value lies in pointing out the direction" (Ramachandran 1967: 312). "Gandhi would object to the word "utopian" in the sense of something un- realizable", as A.M. Huq observes (Diwan and Lutz 1985: 173). He admitted that many of his thoughts pertain to "the world of tomorrow". At the same time he expressed his conviction that the "world of today" is moving towards "the world of tomorrow" as he visualized it. A global economic and political order, based on non-violence, non-exploitation, and high degree of international cooperation, appeared to him a distant but not an un-realizable or utopian goal. In order to achieve this goal there is urgent need for rediscovering values that go beyond the ordinary understanding of economics. This is precisely what Gandhi did. The Gandhian legacy for economics "is nothing less than a coherent outline of a brand new economics of love waiting to be realized". Gandhi left us a guide to nonviolent economic action:

> I will give you a talisman. Whenever you are in doubt, or when the self becomes too much for you, apply the following test. Recall the face of the poorest and weakest man whom you may have seen, and ask yourself if the step you contemplate is going to be of any use to him. Will he gain anything by it? Will it restore him to a control over his own life and destiny? In other words, will it lead to *Swaraj* for the hungry and spiritually starving millions? Then you will find your doubt and yourself melting away. (CW, 89: 125).

New Economy: An Utopian Vision

The questions that remain to be answered at the end of a somewhat detailed analysis of Gandhi's economics are: In what sense is Gandhi's economics utopian, or what are the characteristics that suggest the utopian character of Gandhi's economy? Can any of the elements of an utopia be detected in or applied to Gandhi's economics?

In dealing with Gandhi's people-oriented economy as

utopian, our focus is on the tension that is the very texture of utopian vision, between the ideal and real, the realized and the realizable, the "already" and the "not yet" and the actual and the potential. We have concluded (in Chapter Two) from the historical analysis of utopia that, "utopia has always existed and utopia will continue to exist as a vision to guide the humankind to a better future". Also we said that "the history of utopia seems to suggest discoveries of new utopia. Sarvodaya of Gandhi is well suited in the ongoing history of utopia". Sarvodaya economics, being part of Gandhi's total vision of welfare of all, people-oriented economic vision fits in well with the ongoing history of utopia.

Speaking about realistic utopia, we also said that as an ideal utopia exposes its past and explains it as a process of realization and explores the areas of new possibilities. Gandhi's economic vision keeps these three functions in focus as it unfolds. *Hind Swaraj*, which in some sense contained Gandhi's ideas in seminal form, is preoccupied with an uncompromising critique and rejection of modern civilization. Gandhi's condemnation of modern civilization is, by implication, also a condemnation of the capitalist economic system. Since "critical negativity lies at the heart of utopia" (Chapter Two) and "every utopian model of the future is born from a critique on existing evil conditions, a dissatisfaction with the prevailing situation in society", Gandhi's critique of modern civilization is utopian critical negativity and his mind constructs a picture of the possible and transcends the actual limitations. Though Gandhi did not use the word "technology", his entire critique of machinery in effect is the critique of modern technology. Through his harsh opposition to large-scale industry, Gandhi was seeking the resuscitation of the village and revival of cottage and village industries. Gandhi did not stop with the mere critique, he explored new possibilities of small-scale technology or human-centred technology, alternative technology based more on renewable resources, like animal, water, oil and solar energies, etc., self-sufficiency in the context of man's vital wants and basic needs, decentralization of economic and political power, and voluntary simplicity and poverty. For thirty-eight years (after he wrote *Hind Swaraj*) Gandhi, in his private life, cultivated fearlessness, non-violence and love and self-reliance and voluntary poverty. He encouraged and inspired, taught and trained thousands of individuals to reorder their private lives according to the prescriptions in *Hind Swaraj*. During these years he also tried to guide scores of organizations and institutions in accordance with the values laid down in *Hind Swaraj*.

Gandhi, by such critique and condemnation of enslaving machinery and heavy industrialization, was advocating concrete utopias that "negate the finality and legitimacy of the most oppressive elements of this society and present a vision of human life"—self-sufficiency, limitation of wants, priority and promotion of local products, simple life style, decentralization of political and economic power, responsible stewardship—"that, even if in pure form is unrealizable, calls for new ways of thinking and acting that could lead to actual social change" (Chapter Two).

Utopian visions are sometimes taken for "the dreams and experiments of a glorious past or as a consummation yet to be achieved". It is "not just a dream to be enjoyed, but a vision to be pursued", and it is a vision of a perfect society. This seems to be true of Gandhi's utopia because his economic visions come from his conception of a society, a perfect society in its full sense. Such perfect society may never come into existence as visualized, yet it is a vision to be pursued. Gandhi's simple people-oriented economy is his way of pursuing that very vision of perfect society.

In the light of utopia's function to "transform the status quo" and tendency to "transcend given reality", and "refusing to be satisfied with existing situation", Gandhian economics has made some contribution. Gandhi spoke of an economics of truth and charity; for him economics stands for social justice and moral values (Chapter Three). Gandhi's reactions to machinery and heavy industrialization can be seen as dissatisfaction with the situation prevalent in his time. By suggesting appropriate technology, man before machine, limitation of wants and distribution of power and wealth, Gandhi transcends the given reality of economics and "offers a new set of economic theories and policies that may... be seen as promising rival to the accepted doctrines that have prevailed to this day" (Chapter Three).

What makes utopia realistic or unrealistic (from a historical perspective) is its potential programme of action for social transformation and for a better future: "the critical intention to break through the existing conditions and achieve a better future is the essence of the realistic utopian phenomenon" (Chapter Two). Gandhi's sarvodaya economics is more of an action programme than abstract theory and principles. The purpose of its being critical of the existing condition is to offer alternatives towards achieving a better future. This is beyond any dispute because Gandhi visualized and worked for self-sufficient villages, economics with a human face, priority for the human person as opposed to mere material progress. Since the ethico-economics of Gandhi is based on ahimsa (non-violence or love) and since it draws inspiration from love, commitment and truth, it has to be non-exploitative. A non-exploitative economics may sound paradoxical because exploitation of nature, other resources and the powerless workers and consumers seem to go hand in hand with so-called economic progress. This apparent contradiction in Gandhi's economic vision may make many think that it is a mere fantasy. Also the idea of love as an act of self-giving commitment may sound so spiritual and demanding as to be a threat to modern economics. It is here that Gandhi's "system represents a radical departure from the mainstream of economic thought" (Chapter Three). The economy that draws inspiration from love, commitment and truth can never promote unhealthy competition. Instead it stands for human beings and their basic needs. In the context of Gandhi's ethical economics, we have said that Gandhi has a holistic picture of the human person, especially when he speaks about economics. Accordingly, Gandhi advocates a holistic economics which rejects the principles of self-interest and avarice as the foundation of economic activities and relations and replaces them by "social affections" or concern for others as the true basis of economics. This economics takes its origin from the sarvodaya—welfare of all—vision, that is in the process of realization.

The critical function of realistic utopia is fulfilled not just by presenting a concrete picture of the ideal but also by exercising a "constant moral pressure on society to bring about a better world" (Chapter Two). A critical attitude to the status quo and exercise of constant moral pressure on society to move towards a better future make any utopia a dialectic, a process, a catalysing agent. Gandhi offered a valid critique of the economic system and suggested some alternatives in his *Hind Swaraj*. Some of the alternatives he suggested would entail constant moral pressure on society. His trusteeship, or responsible stewardship, for example, is an appeal to the good will of people who possess great wealth—often at the cost of the landless, the powerless and the voiceless— to be responsible stewards. Voluntary poverty and limiting wants are other examples of Gandhi's utopian economic ideal in the sense that they exert constant moral pressure on society and individuals so as to bring about changes. Sarvodaya economics becomes in some sense a dialectical process in Gandhi's hands: he "presents facts and possibility, the actual and ideal" by his (sometimes exaggerated) description of the evils of industrialization, by promoting small-scale industry and appropriate technology, by exploring the possibilities of self-sufficient village units where power and resources are decentralized, and by focusing on the ideal of economics with a human face—where trusteeship, swadeshi, appropriate technology, limitation of wants, meeting the basic needs of every person, and concern for others become the key issues to be dealt with.

The Gandhian economic ideals and principles we have discussed do not and cannot legitimate the status quo or conceal the existing economic situation or justify unjust socio-economic order; rather they situationally transcend the given and try to lead from the present to a realizable future. They seem to fit in well with the classification of utopia as opposed to ideology. If it can be agreed that utopias can never fully succeed since they show the "distance" between the current and the hoped for perfected future and that the decisive trait of utopia is not entire realizability but the preservation of opposition to the status quo (Chapter Two), then the whole sarvodaya vision of Gandhi, and sarvodaya economics in particular, is utopian. Gandhi's economics is "a constant ideal, that toward which we are directed, but which we never fully attain" (Paul Ricoeur, quoted in Chapter Two).

We concluded our brief description of "ideology-utopia" by saying that "a society without utopia would be dead, because it would no longer have any project, any prospective goals." The economic goals set by Gandhi for Indian society motivate a continuing human struggle to achieve them, which struggle in turn requires a confrontation with existing systems and structures. These ideals may appear to many as unrealistic and empty wishes or, in the words of Ernst Bloch, "abstract utopia" and "shear fantasies" (Chapter Two). But Gandhi was not day-dreaming or fantasizing in the abstract. He tried in his very own life to experiment with the economic goals he proposed, and to some extent showed that they are "really possible" and indicated concrete ways of reaching the goal. Again in the words of Ernst Bloch, they are "concrete utopias". Since the economic ideals and goals Gandhi envisioned demand a great deal of renunciation and sacrifices or, rather, they involve personal commitment and require a deep sense of "social affection", i.e., concern for others, the temptation for local, national or global economic planners and decision makers is to ignore and sidetrack such suggestions as Gandhi made then or Gandhians make now.

Gandhi, for example, conceived of trusteeship as a movement strong with moral imperative towards reforming and restructuring of economic systems. Though his appeal to the capitalists and the zamindars to become trustees and trusted friends to their tenants went unheeded, Gandhi still hoped for voluntary trusteeship and responsible stewardship. The reason is that Gandhi, like E. Bloch, thinks that the utopian function is the "principle of hope" for a human race which assumes responsibility for its own destiny" (Chapter Two). This is an eschatological hope, and for this reason Gandhi is a "Prisoner of Hope" (Judith Brown). And it is this hope that makes Gandhi's economic future horizon open, wider and flexible so that new economic experiments can be ventured upon. What makes Gandhi's economics utopian is thus also its hope-dimension, which takes future possible realization as the goal of ongoing economic dialectics.

As realistic imagination, utopia portrays the possible future, but it is more concerned with visualizing possibilities than with achieving them. It asks science or actual practice to test the feasibility of their realization. The end result of this utopian imagination is that it makes people sensitive to the breaking points of the present system and nourishes in them a longing for a new society and as such exercises a significant role in social change.

Gandhi's economic model nourishes in people a longing for a new society, where basic human needs—food and shelter—of every human being are met. The imagining of future of economic possibilities does not stop at merely meeting the basic needs of people, it hopes to change the traditional economic structures by presenting an ideal and challenging people to change in response to that ideal. The challenge is to place human persons and basic needs before everything else, to see economic equality, distribution of wealth and sharing of wealth as desirable, possible and even a moral responsibility, to work towards decentralization of power and resources, and to work for *Ramrajya* (the ideal polity, as we have discussed earlier).

Again, what makes Gandhi's people-oriented economics an utopian ideal is: economics as emerging from a life philosophy, i.e., an experiment with truth; never claiming any "finality" or "infallibility" about conclusions. Gandhi's economic experiments are "essentially creative and inherently constructive." It is utopian confrontation with the status quo that gives birth to new alternatives. Gandhi's individual dreams sometimes became India's dreams. Though the national economic agenda of the Congress Party and Nehru's regime did not pay much attention to the suggestions of Gandhi, Gandhi's economic dreams never lost their appeal. Gandhian economic ideals and projects may not work on a national or large centralized scale because his thrust and priority were toward village-India. The village emerges as the nucleus of social life in Gandhian scheme. Gandhi, therefore, promoted village and cottage industries, technology with a human face or a new technology that is relevant to rural India—demonstrating thereby a creative imagination, a constructive programme, a utopia that is realistic imagination.

There is also a very personal perspective in Gandhi's economic ideal that makes it unique and thus parts company with traditional economics. This personal element in Gandhi's people-oriented economy negates and transcends, in some sense shatters, the status quo and offers a different way of perceiving economy. Such personal perspective includes: individual metanoia or transformation leading to social transformation as when Gandhi pleaded for individual landlords and capitalists to be humanitarian, charitable, noble and patriotic; personal dedication or commitment to socio-economic changes; social affections, concern for others as the true basis of economics; non-possession and voluntary poverty for the service of others; and undying hope in the gradual reduction of wants both in personal and social life as a real possibility.

Looking forward to ideal living is an inborn propensity of human life. What Gandhi achieved in presenting a new vision of economics was to give expression to this human propensity. It was not humanly possible for Gandhi to present an ideal that is acceptable to all. There is no economic ideal (or model of economics) that is accepted by all. What is typical of Gandhi's utopia is its provisionality and this provisionality is reflected in his economics too. As long as we are not speaking of the ultimate ideal economics, not the perfect and finished product, and as long as we *are* speaking of an economics that is in a process of dialectics, we *are* speaking of Gandhian utopian economics. Scholarly research, publications and ongoing interest in academia for Gandhian economics and experiments being carried out in simple living and ashram life further confirm that it is valid to speak of a Gandhian utopian economy.

For many, Gandhi's economic alternatives, such as trusteeship, *swadeshi*, and khadi appear as fantasy. The reason is a prejudiced superficial study. As such trusteeship may be impractical but as an ideal of responsible stewardship, it may well be possible. We may never achieve hundred percent *swadeshi*, but some significant production and use of local products would instill and inspire self-respect and contribute to self-sufficiency; khadi may have failed to be commercially viable and not everyone will wear khadi, but Gandhi elevated "the spinning wheel as an economic necessity, a religious ritual, and a national symbol". As a symbol of self-reliance, self-suffering and simplicity, it will signify an economic priority and national symbol. Gandhi thought that the reintroduction of the spinning wheel in communities which had never made up for the loss of it, as either a tool or a symbol, might both answer a widespread economic need and serve as the symbol of a lost and regained identity. Later, when India was closer to political freedom and when Britain decided to support and invest in a new Indian industry, the wheel came instead to symbolize economic reaction. As Erikson comments, Gandhi "...could live in symbiosis with technology of his time and yet comprehend and exploit the fact that some such symbolic and pragmatic item as the spinning wheel could dramatically activate in hundreds of thousands of localities what was at the time not at all ready for industrialization" (Erikson 1970: 398).

Authentically human hope inspired Gandhi to transcend and transform the existing, often unjust, economics toward the horizon of an economics with human face which becomes concrete and real in genuine sharing. It is, in other words, economics of love waiting to be realized, and so it is utopian economics in that sense. Thus, what makes Gandhi's economic alternatives a realistic utopian ideal are: their focus on people as opposed to machine or material gain, their faith and hope in simplicity, i.e., simple lifestyle, self-reliance and self-sufficiency (at least in basic human needs), smallness—(see "Small is Beautiful", Schumacher, "Small is Possible", G. McRobie)—limiting the needs, and unfailing trust in the potential of human persons for *metanoia*, i.e., readiness for radical personal and social changes. Even so, such economic ideals are like Euclid's line—never fully actualized but having the potential to be actualized and the dynamism to lead society to new and fresh economic horizons. Such ideals are operative at the heart of any genuine hope for progress and, as innate human desire, inspire everyone for a better tomorrow.

References

1. E. F. Schumacher, *Small Is Beautiful: A Study of Economics as if People Mattered* (Great Britain: Blond and Briggs Ltd., 1973). The very title of the Book is indicative of the inspiration of Gandhi behind the theme discussed in the book.
2. Rajachandra was also known as Raychand. Gandhi records in his Autobiography: "In my moments of spiritual crisis...he was my refuge." M. K. Gandhi, *An Autobiography*, 75.
3. Gandhi wrote in his preface to the 1938 edition: "Let the reader bear in mind that it is a faithful record of conversations I had with workers, one of whom was an avowed anarchist." *CW*, 67, 169-70. This avowed anarchist, Gandhi later revealed, was no other than his life-long friend, Dr. Pranjivan Mehta. "I wrote the entire *Hind*

Swaraj for my dear friend Dr. Pranjivan Mehta. All the argument in the book is reproduced almost as it took place with him." *CW*, 71, 238.

4. "The Gandhian world-view (or philosophy of life) is, therefore, *radically spiritual* in the deepest sense of this phrase..." A. K. Saran, "Gandhi and the Concept of Politics...", 681.
5. Amartya Sen defined commitment in terms of "a person choosing an act that he believes will yield a lower level of personal welfare to him than the alternative that is also available to him." Amartya Sen, "Rational Fools: A Critique of the Behavioral Foundations of Economic Theory" in *Philosophy and Public Affairs* (Summer, 1977):317-344.
6. Devoted action detached of consequences was, of course, for Gandhi the essential message of the Gita.The ideal wholly committed man he found there described: "Although he is firm in his resolve, he is indifferent as regards success or failure of his action; that is to say, he is not anxious about its result". S. Narayan, ed., *Selected Works...*, vol. 4, 265.
7. "We must identify ourselves with the villagers who toil under the hot sun beating on their bent backs and see how they would drink water from the pool in which their cattle drink and roll. Then and not until then shall we truly represent the masses,and they will, as surely as I am writing this, respond to every call". Quoted by R. Iyer, *The Moral and Political Thought...*, 144.
8. For Gandhi Truth is the end whereas Ahimsa is the means. Even so for him, "realization of the goal is in exact proportion to that of the means". It follows that since, "means to be means must always be within our reach... Ahimsa is our supreme duty. If we take care of the means, we are bound to reach the end sooner or later". See Diwan and Lulz, Eds., 1985, 38.
9. For this presentation of the premises and principles of Gandhi's economics, I have heavily relied on Mark Lutz, "Human Nature in Gandhian Economics: The Case of Ahimsa or 'Social Affection'" in R. Diwan and M. Lutz, eds., *Essays in Gandhian Economics*, 28-53.
10. Gandhi may have been influenced in formulating the trusteeship doctrine by the life and example of Jamnalal Bajaj, whom he adopted as his fifth son. Coming from one of the richest families, Bajaj placed all his wealth and possessions at the disposal of Gandhi and his programme of fighting poverty and inequalities. see Malcolm S. Adiseshiah, "Gandhi and the Indian Economy Today", *Gandhi Marg* 13 (January-March 1992): 400.
11. "Politically it was a nonviolent civil disobedience or civil resistance

movement. Philosophically, it was a movement led by a force which is born out of an intense desire to follow the path of truth. Satyagrahi—a follower of truth—has to pursue the principle of non-hoarding or non-possession, the main thing to be borne in mind is, not to store up anything which we do not require. For agriculture, we may keep bullocks, if we use them, and the equipment required for them. Where there is a recurring famine, we shall no doubt store food grains. But we shall ask ourselves whether bullocks and food grains are, in fact, needed." Excerpt from a letter to Maganlal Gandhi, dated 15 March 1915, reproduced in S. Narayan, ed. *The Selected Works of Mahatma Gandhi*, vol. 5, 28.

12. "Gandhi has been misunderstood or misinterpreted by Marxists as a defender of private property and as being soft on capitalism. Clearly the concept of *aparigraha* is the strongest denunciation of capitalist forms". see Romesh Diwan and Sushila Gidwani, "Elements in Gandhian Economics", Notes, no.12, in R. Diwan and M. Lutz, eds., *Essays...*, 65.
13. Perhaps the most systematic presentation of the theory of trusteeship is the one by one of his closest associates, Shri Pyarelal, in a paper presented to the Seminar on Gandhian Outlook and Techniques, held in New Delhi in 1953. According to Pyarelal, Gandhi "summed up his trusteeship idea in the following formula: 1. Trusteeship provides a means of transforming the present capitalist order of society into an egalitarian one, it gives no quarter to capitalism but gives the present owning class a chance of reforming itself. It is based on the faith that human nature is never beyond redemption. 2. It does not recognize any right of private ownership of property except in as much as it may be permitted by society for its own welfare. 3. It does not exclude legislative regulation of ownership and use of wealth. 4. Thus under state-regulated trusteeship, individual will not be free to hold on disregard of the interest of society. 5. Just as it is proposed to fix a decent minimum living wage, even so a limit should be fixed for the maximum income that could be allowed to any person in society. The difference between such minimum and maximum incomes should be reasonable and equitable and variable from time to time, so much so that the tendency would be towards obliteration of the difference. 6. Under the Gandhian economic order the character of production will be determined by social necessity and not whim or greed."S. Naqvi,"Economic Thinking of Gandhi: The Concept of Trusteeship", in S.C. Biswas, ed., *Gandhi Theory and Practice...*, 219-20.
14. K. R. Rao,"The Moral Economy of Trusteeship", in J. D. Sethi, ed.,

Trusteeship..., 36. Extending this principle to the global level, Gandhi rejected the right of individuals, nations and all groups to monopolise resources to the detriment of the minimum needs of the majority. See *Young India*, 15 November 1928, 381.

15. One of them was worldly wise and the other three were otherwise. They had set out to make some money and were passing through a forest. In that forest they found a few scattered bones of a tiger. The first wise man whispered a mantra and arranged the bones into a skeleton. The second, with his mantric powers, put flesh and skin on the skeleton. The third uttered another mantra and infused vital breath into the body. The animal, as soon as it regained life, swallowed up the three wise men. The worldly wise man saved himself by climbing the top of a tree before the beginning of these "Experiments with Truth". Ganesh D. Gadre, "Trusteeship", in S.C. Biswas, ed., *Gandhi*, 123.
16. "Since 1974, the tax laws have been amended in the USA to encourage stockholders to introduce employees, consumers and others to become co-owners or take over their corporations. *Business Week* magazine reported in its 15 April 1985 edition, that as a result of these tax incentives, over seven million workers in over 3,000 corporations have now become co-owners". Shann Turnbull, "Trusteeship as Technique for Sustainable Industrialization", in J.D. Sethi, ed. *Trusteeship: The Gandhian Alternative*, 172.
17. "In Germany, co-determination has been explicitly accepted and put into operation, while in Japan it is almost a part of the economic culture. In Japan the word used is "consensus", which depends on the workers' complete loyalty to the firm; the workers' willingness to implement any agreement arrived at between labour and management; personal security of the workers; unrestricted mobility; guarantee of workers' training and up-gradation of skills, and democratic decision-making." J. D. Sethi, "Economic Task and Trusteeship" in J. D. Sethi, ed., *Trusteeship*, 165.
18. When he wrote *Hind Swaraj*, he was under the strong influence of Victorian socialists, who were at that time protesting against the evils of industrialization and the degrading conditions under which even women and children were forced to work for long hours under difficult conditions.
19. Vepa sums up Gandhi's attitude towards machinery saying that, "His opposition was not doctrinaire (except at the early stages when he wrote *Hind Swaraj*) but pragmatic: basically, his opposition was three-fold in nature: sociological, economic and political. Ram K. Vepa, *New Technology: A Gandhian Concept* (New Delhi: Gandhi Book House, 1975), 109.

20. Gandhi refers to the United States and says: "She has reached the acme of mass production, and yet she has not been able to abolish unemployment or want. There are still thousands, perhaps millions of people in America who live in misery, in spite of the phenomenal riches of the few..." *CW.*, 48, 165.
21. Romesh Diwan, "Total Revolution and Appropriate Technology", in R. Diwan and M. Lutz, eds., *Essays...*, 175-191; J.D. Sethi, "Technology, Society and Economy: A Gandhian Overview", in J.D. Sethi, *Gandhi Today*, 73-117.
22. "I have named it *intermediate technology* to signify that it is vastly superior to the primitive technology of bygone ages but at the same time much simpler, cheaper, and freer than the super-technology of the rich". E. F. Schumacher, *Small Is Beautiful*, 128.
23. Ram K. Vepa, *New Technology: A Gandhian Concept*, see specially Chapters: 3, 7, and 12.
24. P. L. Dhar, "Holistic Technology: A Conceptual Framework", *Gandhi Marg* 9 (March 1988): 755-763; and "The Gandhian Vision of Technology", *Gandhi Marg* 10 (January 1989): 648-655.
25. According to this model, there is a hierarchy of needs: 1. material needs—physical needs, safety, security etc.,; 2. social needs—self esteem, acceptance, affection etc.,; 3. moral needs—justice, service, love etc. P. L. Dhar, "Holistic Technology: A Conceptual Framework", 760.
26. *Speeches and Writings of Mahatma Gandhi*, iv Edn. (Madras: G. A. Nathan & Co., 1922), 336.
27. M.K. Gandhi, *From Yervada Mandir* (Ahmedabad: Navajivan Publishing House, 1957), 66.
28. "In your village, so long as you have got your village-barber, you are bound to support him to the exclusion of the finished barber who may come to you from Madras. If you find it necessary that your village-barber should reach the attainments of the barber from Madras, you may train him to that. Send him to Madras by all means, if you wish, in order that he may learn his calling. Until you do that you are not justified in going to another barber. That is Swadeshi..." *CW*, 13, 231.
29. "Most people are not interested in believing in any general normative economic model at all. And a few who do, take care not to allow their beliefs to interfere with their normal economic acquisitiveness. That is why in recent history no ideal model whatever, Communist, Cooperative or Gandhian, has materialized anywhere on a large scale". Raj Krishna, "Some Reflections on Gandhian Economics", in S.C. Biswas, ed., *Gandhi*, 233-47.

Four

Ashram to Village: An Experiment in Realization

The village occupied the centre of the social order envisaged by Gandhi. He approved the word "villagism" coined by J.C. Kumarappa to distinguish village-mindedness from city-mindedness. Gandhi felt very strongly that "if India is to attain freedom and through India the world also...the fact has to be recognised that the people have to live in the village, not in towns, in huts and not in palaces" (Pyarelal 1959: 4). Gandhi's village-mindedness and "ashramic" life were closely linked. Gandhi's "experiments with truth" start in the ashrams. Ashrams become the laboratories of experiments: truth, nonviolence, satyagraha, self-reliance, *brahmacharya*... Ashrams for him were the "nerve-centres" of his actions and involvement (socio-religious and political). The dynamics of Gandhian involvement and actions take their inspiration from ashramic philosophy. Ashram being the centre of action (experiment and service) for Gandhi, village work is just an extension of ashram life. This chapter, therefore, analyses Gandhian experiments with ashrams to see their significance for village reconstruction and reorganization: to see ashrams as mechanisms for applying to historical situations the utopian pressure for change.

Sources of Inspiration

Gandhi believed that ashramic life based on mutuality, simplicity and hard work would nurture attitudes and actions to reform society. Gandhi seems to have inherited a sense of community living from the tradition of the joint family that surrounded his early childhood. Basic human values of community living, such as tolerance, sharing and spirit of sacrifice for others, made a deep impact on Gandhi's life at an early age. His activities on behalf of the London Vegetarian Society brought him into contact with many men and women who advocated a return to the simple life. Though English society labelled them "eccentric",[1] for Gandhi they were a source of inspiration.

During his three years of student life in London, he came into contact with wide range of sources, learning, as Thomas Merton observes, to discover the wisdom of the East through the eyes of the West (Woodcock 1972: 22). He associated with socialists, anarchists, radical Christians and feminists. Gandhi has acknowledged his indebtedness to Henry Sumner Maine's work, *Village Communities of the East and West* in *Hind Swaraj* (CW 1: 178). Maine's work impressed upon Gandhi the idea that corporate ownership had been the norm rather than the exception in traditional Indian village communities. In a sense, Gandhi's initial theoretical knowledge of village community is what prevailed during the Victorian period, which depicted the village as a self-acting, egalitarian institution organized on the basis of collective ownership. The Western idealization of the village community failed to note the omnipresence of hierarchy and dominance in the village system. However, Gandhi in the light of his understanding of Maine's analysis, believed in the superiority of the ancient Indian civilisation over its modern form.

We have analyzed at some length the influence of Ruskin, Tolstoy and Thoreau on Gandhi in our first chapter. While in South Africa, Gandhi was certainly much impressed with the Tolstoyan idea of shaking free from the violence and coercion of the state and forming co-operative communities. The thrust of Tolstoy's writings was a plea for social renewal through service, renunciation and mutuality. Response to Tolstoy's teaching led to the establishment of small experimental communities in several parts of the world. Agricultural colonies run along his guidelines were initially restricted to Russia, but gradually the movement found support in North America, Britain, Palestine, the Netherlands and Bulgaria. Colonists tried to live by their own labour, to live in harmony with nature, and to devote themselves to serving their fellow humans. That Gandhi was impressed by such experiments is clear from the fact that in the trust deed of the Phoenix Settlement, which established the pattern of Gandhi's communal experiments. He acknowledged his indebtedness to Tolstoy by setting down the practice and propagation of Tolstoy's teachings as the main objective of the community.

No doubt, Ruskin's theme of self-renunciation for the common good impressed Gandhi; they both shared a fundamental concern for quality of life and dignity of labour and a distaste for the economics of material accumulation. The Gandhian concept of an ashram, moreover, is not far removed from Thoreau's idea of withdrawing to Walden Pond. As Mark Thomson concludes, "Neither Gandhi nor Thoreau — the latter at Walden Pond, the former through the communities or ashrams he established during his life—intended their respective withdrawals from mainstream society as quietist exercises in contemplative activity. For both it was an opportunity to rejuvenate the spirit and cleanse the soul through self-reliance, constructive work and simple life in harmony with nature" (Thomson 1993: 32).

The rationale or the philosophy of Gandhi's ashrams is withdrawal and renewal. Whether Gandhi was impressed by the ideal of *vanaprasthashrama* (i.e., retirement to the forest for contemplation after acquiring education and living a full life) is doubtful, because active involvement in the reconstruction of villages was one of the major concerns, if not the most important function, of the ashram. Gandhi drew inspiration from the ancient Indian traditions of *brahmacharya, vanaprastha* and *sannyasa*, as he did from the ideas of Ruskin, Tolstoy and Thoreau; but he always reinterpreted and adapted others' ideas from his own perspective so as to find concrete applications to changing situations. Thus Gandhi believed that the spirit of nonviolence and satyagraha could best be inculcated within the intimate communal environment of an ashram. The ashramic life, as envisaged by Gandhi, was by no means confined to an institutional structure. The lifestyle in the ashram was geared to help the individual to live in harmony with nature and humanity, based on self-reliance, creative activity and community service. To live such a life, Gandhi believed, was to conserve and rejuvenate the fundamental ties which have traditionally bound men and women together in organic communities. The constructive activities of individuals, whether collective or independent, were seen by him as a visible sign of their commitment to the community. Ashram for Gandhi was a laboratory for experimenting with his ideas, visions and ideals, a place to give effective expression to his views on society, politics, philosophy, morality and religion. We will now examine some of Gandhi's ashram experiments, first in South Africa and then in India.

Beginning of the Experiment

Gandhi's experiences of discrimination and oppression of non-whites in South Africa awakened in him the need to organize the non-whites to defend their rights. Twenty years in South Africa constituted a transforming experience for Gandhi: from a prosperous Anglophile lawyer to a nonviolent activist living a simple community life with his followers and prepared to sacrifice his life for the cause he believed in. It is in South Africa that he devised and gave concrete shape to his doctrine of satyagraha.[2]

More importantly, a desire to experiment with communal living began to grow in Gandhi soon after he reached South Africa. He began encouraging his associates to live in small communities. At one point he even invited his workers and companions to live communally with him in his large and furnished house in Natal. This initial experiment in communal living, however, was not encouraging. But his contact with a community of Trappist monks[3] provided him with a functioning example of micro-community. After a visit to the Trappist monastery Gandhi described the settlement as "a quiet little model village owned on the truest republican principles. The principle of liberty, equality and fraternity is carried out in its entirety. Every man is a brother, every woman is a sister" (CW 1: 182). The Trappist pattern represented for Gandhi a dynamic and creative fusion of ascetic ideals with the practical concerns of service to and management of the community. Though Gandhi was deeply inspired by Christian monasticism, his original contribution to ashramic life was one of "this worldly asceticism" by which he sought to awaken the masses to their social, cultural and economic traditions, "revalued in a dynamic way and purged of all inequities, as means to redress the oppressive social and economic conditions under which they laboured".

The Phoenix Settlement

Gandhi started his first community experimental centre at Phoenix near Durban, in 1904. He retained the name of Phoenix for the settlement, because, for him the name Phoenix symbolized the perennial character of the community experiment.[4] Though Gandhi was rarely there, he housed Kasturba, their sons and a nephew, Gokuldas, at Phoenix for long periods. Over the years the number of settlers swelled gradually. Gandhi looked upon Phoenix as "the common home" for all. "Phoenix thus developed into a little village, half a dozen families having come and settled and begun to increase there" (*Autobiography*, 259, 250-52). The household at Phoenix was managed on the principles of manual work, self-help and simple living.

Gandhi expected his family and others in the settlement to follow the asceticism and austerity he was convinced of. He tended to treat his family as a mere extension of his own austere nature. Gandhi's domination of the communities he established has come under strong criticism.[5] However, it is important to realise that a charismatic leader attains his authority and consolidates his "legitimacy" by constantly proving his personal strength in life. The initiators of utopian movements throughout history have invariably led their followers by virtue of their superior vision and personal example.

The common focus of all Gandhi's activities in South Africa, whether it be the operation of *Indian Opinion*, the Phoenix settlement and Tolstoy Farm, or the Satyagraha campaigns, was to refine a technique of action to alleviate the plight of the Indian community in South Africa. Speaking of his ultimate objective Gandhi, wrote in 1908:

> There is an obvious reason why the first duty of the Whites and the Indians living in Phoenix is to serve the Indian community. Indians must, of course, serve India...The Whites who have joined us were formerly engaged in their own avocations. There was no need for them to offer their services to the White community. Wishing to renounce their selfish pursuits and devote themselves to the service of others they decided to join the journal... (*Indian Opinion*, March 1908).

Service, not power, was Gandhi's ultimate goal in establishing centres such as Phoenix settlement. His asceticism and charismatic authority were "service-oriented", integral parts of his vision to improve the quality of his countrymen in South Africa. He sought to realise the Absolute through service and all other concerns, family or otherwise, were subordinated to that ultimate goal.

Gandhi's very presence was an inspiration at Phoenix. His love of simplicity, capacity of self-sacrifice and willingness to serve anyone in need of guidance or assistance, on many occasions inspired men, women and children of otherwise average ability and with no special talents to rise above their, "normal mental and moral stature to heights of great sacrifice and bravery" (West 1965). Not only did he promote the spirit of "universal service" in the settlement, but he was genuinely "ecumenical" in his religious outlook. Jews, Hindus, Muslims, Parses and Christians all participated in the "service", which was a blend of religious teachings and spiritual songs from the East and the West. One could very well learn the lessons of religious tolerance from the spirit prevalent in the settlement, for (Gandhi being a *Sanatana Hindu*) "no particular religion was given a superior position, the service each Sunday reaffirmed the universal bonds of love and truth upon which the community had been founded."[6]

Gandhi's departure from the Phoenix "came as a serious blow to the aspirations of those who remained at Phoenix". It appears that the Phoenix settlement could not contain Gandhi because he had a greater vision and mission to accomplish in India. Nonetheless, he remained an inspiration to Phoenix and similar experiments. Sushila Gandhi summed up the future and the real spirit of Phoenix in an interview: "The future is uncertain. Unless a miracle happens, I shall be the last Gandhi to work here at the Settlement...I must confess that I do not see eye to eye with all the teaching of the Mahatma. But I do believe in the spirit of all he did and said. And I have tried to live in this spirit...Who knows, like the mythical bird, this settlement may rise again to its former life and usefulness. The spirit is still there" (Goldie 1971: 19, 21).

Tolstoy Farm

Tolstoy farm was established as a corollary to the Phoenix settlement scheme. Kallenbach, Gandhi's associate, bought a farm of about eleven hundred acres, and offered it to Gandhi and the satyagrahis rent-free on 30 May 1910. The basic model for Tolstoy farm was Phoenix, a community where satyagrahis and their families would work to support themselves, and in the process learn to live a new and simple life in harmony with nature and one another. The driving force behind the experiment of Tolstoy Farm was the same as that of Phoenix; the emphasis was on communal living and co-operative cultivation. The watchwords of the Tolstoy Farm community were industry, economy and self-sufficiency. Gardening became obligatory for those not engaged in the kitchen. Without exception, everybody devoted some time to gardening.

Gandhi and Kallenbach were "role models" at Tolstoy farm by their example of renunciation and discipline and by their personal credibility and transparency. Gandhi's vicarious suffering—trying to expiate the wrong-doings of others by taking responsibility for their actions upon himself—seems to have bound the community and his disciples and supporters more closely to him. The lifestyle in Tolstoy farm was monastic to a great extent: "The time as well as the number of meals was fixed. There was to be one single kitchen, and all were to dine in a single row. Everyone was to see to the cleaning of his own dish and other things...Drink, smoking etc., were, of course, totally prohibited" (CW 29: 190). The settlers made their own furniture, clothes, and sandals. All wore trousers and shirts made out of coarse blue cloth and fashioned after a gaol uniform, which was suitable for labouring. The food served was vegetarian, prepared in Indian style and eaten with wooden spoons made at the settlement. In the context of austerity and simplicity, "the settlers learned to look upon one another as members of the same family..."

It is doubtful whether Gandhi wanted the continuity of the Tolstoy farm because there were no plans to continue the settlement after the end of the satyagraha struggle. He wrote to Maganlal Gandhi about his decision to remain at the farm: "My struggle will not be over when satyagraha struggle ends.

It is as it should be. That I shall have to stay on at Mr. Kallenbach's farm is something not expected..." (CW 29: 191). Gandhi was able to compromise the continuity with "provisionality". To be non-institutional is an essential aspect of being provisional. Tolstoy farm was an experiment with some specific goal. Gandhi believed that as a symbol of unity, sacrifice and strength the experiment of Tolstoy farm had proved invaluable. Gandhi stressed satyagraha as a means of returning to the natural condition of man; it was not merely a political technique of rebellion but an alternative medium of education and way of life. As a result, Tolstoy Farm was home for satyagrahis and it provided moral and economic support to active satyagrahis and was a training ground for potential satyagrahis.(In fact, on the basis of the spirit fostered at Phoenix and Tolstoy farm, he waged a series of non-violent campaigns against the South African Government with some success.)

The "Indian Experiment"

Experiences of frustration in achieving the goal of ashram experiments in South Africa in no measure dampened the spirit of Gandhi towards new and fresh experiments on Indian soil. He was however determined to continue the Phoenix experiment.

The ashram concept was deeply ingrained in Gandhi's total philosophy and vision. He saw ashram as a place to train young men and women to be ideal servants of the country. Self-realisation would be the ultimate goal, but this goal is achieved not through traditional quietist withdrawal from all social concerns, but through active social involvement and selfless service to the humanity. Deeply aware of the problems— poverty, ignorance, exploitation and oppression, illiteracy etc., — of the struggling masses in India's 700,000 villages, Gandhi sought to identify with them. Gandhi was convinced that sarvodaya can be realised only through caring for and serving the people at the bottom of the social ladder. Hence reconstruction of the villages, with the removal of poverty was the main challenge. His intention was to awaken the masses to his simple, non-violent technique of direct action and selfless service as a means of achieving the social and economic uplift of the poor.

In his search to find a suitable place for an ashram, Gandhi stayed at Santiniketan for some time.[7] But Gandhi soon realized that Santiniketan was not the right place for his experiments.

The Satyagraha Ashram was founded on 25 May 1915 at Ahmedabad, the former capital of Gujarat. Gandhi "had a predilection for Ahmedabad",[8] but it is ironical that funds for the ashram came from capitalists from Bombay and Ahmedabad. Gandhi regretted his inability to do without their support, and admitted that the monetary involvement of rich merchants and industrialists "greatly undermined the spirit of sacrifice upon which Sabarmati was theoretically based". Even so, he never discouraged benefactors.

The philosophy and the style of life of Satyagraha (Sabarmati) ashram were based on an unshakable faith in the principles of truth and non-violence. In order to pursue these ideals, Gandhi introduced a code of rules and observances in the ashram. These included a strict regimen of vegetarian food, manual labour, social service, celibacy, prayer and sleep. Ashramites took nine vows: truth-telling, non-violence, celibacy, control of the palate, non-stealing, non-possession, refusal to use foreign cloth, fearlessness and acceptance of untouchables. They do appear austere and the reactions to such an ashramic life "ranged from unreserved support to angry denunciation" (Thomson 1993: 100-101). These vows were intended "as practical aids to moral and spiritual growth." Gandhi intended Sabarmati (for that matter all other ashrams) to function as a catalyst of change in the society. He sought to break down caste ideology and remove the factors of alienation existing between the villager and the city-dweller, and between the manual labourer and intellectual worker. In his own words,

> I want to bring about an equalisation of status. The working classes have all these centuries been isolated and relegated to a lower status. They have been *shudras* and the word has been interpreted to mean an inferior status. I want to allow no differentiation between the son of a weaver, of an agriculturalist and of a school teacher (*Harijan* January 1938).

Gandhi's move to admit a Gujarati untouchable family into the ashram was a challenge to the traditional orthodox Hindu community and it created a lot of controversy in the ashram. The admission of the family also brought open rebellion from Kasturba and another woman. In response to Kasturba's complaints Gandhi told her to leave the ashram if she could not accept the situation and assured her they could part as friends. Gandhi persisted in his decision in spite of all objections from the family, friends and benefactors, because it was an important breakthrough in his programme "to undermine the dehumanizing ideology that human beings were impure by birth and that human function and aspiration could only be determined by caste" (Thomson 1993: 102).

Though Gandhi had declared the uplift of India's villages to be his main concern, his knowledge and experience of rural India were limited at this stage. What brought a revelation and real change in his "village-outlook" was the Champaran experience.[9] Gandhi realised the importance of education for village uplift and his concept of basic education began to take concrete shape in Champaran. The Champaran experiment crystallised many of his ideas concerning education and laid the foundation for further research.

The sarvodaya ideal of Gandhi acquired a coherence of thought and action in 1920, when he introduced a fourfold constructive programme through the ashram. By the end of 1929 he had established or reorganised twenty organisations to carry the message of non-violence to the cities and villages. It is to be noted, however, that though the ashram experimented with agriculture, Gandhi insisted on giving priority to the khadi programme.

A trend towards establishing ashrams after the pattern of Sabarmati started in the 1920s in order to facilitate the decentralization of the constructive work programme. The total number of the ashrams is not known. They are situated predominantly in rural areas. The ashrams and the services they rendered were considered as common property of the Indian people. Similarly, the ashramites were instructed to regard their time and energy as belonging to the nation. Speaking to a gathering of villagers in 1925, Gandhi summed up the rationale of the ashrams in simple terms, "The ashram is public property. You have a right to see it at any time you like. It is in your midst. And as long as you find that its activity is a helpful activity and serves your district, it is your bounden duty to help it in every way" (CW 26: 351).

The purpose of Sabarmati ashram was to function as a centre of service, experiment, action and change. But at times Gandhi himself felt frustrated about the progress made in the ashram experiment. "If I was to lay the foundation of the Satyagraha ashram today, I would organise it differently in the light of my experience to date", he said in 1925 (CW 28: 405-8). He was frequently absent from the ashram for long periods, attending to the many concerns of his political and non-political work. When ashramites complained about his absence, Gandhi had this to say: "It would be a sad state of affairs, indeed, if it were my physical presence alone which lent the ashram its life, for the mere body is bound to perish" (CW 14: 180). Gandhi's involvement in the political struggle may have had a disruptive influence upon the ashram and undermined the development of constructive work in general. But, as Gandhi himself admits, "...The external political activity is not my seeking. I, therefore, cannot give it up of my will..." (CW 25: 381). Nonetheless, it is to be remarked that, viewed from an over-all perspective of Gandhi's philosophy, political involvement is not an independent entity. Rather, it is an essential aspect of his sarvodaya. Sabarmati ashram was a centre of action. It organised the Dandi March — a twenty-four-day march of triumph for Gandhi's grass-root activism. Sabarmati played a leading role in the satyagraha campaigns at Bardoli in 1928, the Salt Satyagraha and subsequent civil disobedience campaigns. Even so, Gandhi wanted to devote more time and thought to village work and the uplift of India's disadvantaged communities. He wanted the ashramites to actively involve themselves in promoting khadi in villages and the ashram to remain in the forefront of khadi work, for he claimed that khadi offered an immediate, practicable and permanent solution to the prevailing unemployment and underemployment in rural India. Khadi for Gandhi was an effective economic symbol which eventually would lead to swaraj. His obsession for khadi bewildered the British and the educated urban Indian, but they had not witnessed the poverty and degradation of village people as he had. In fact, the total commitment to khadi work at Sabarmati hindered the development of other activities required for the reconstruction of the villages.

Several of the ashramites were employed in areas of work other than khadi, such as the cow-protection programme. Like khadi, it was begun for practical economic reasons. Gandhi's idea of cow protection included cattle breeding, improvement of the stock, humane treatment of bullocks, and establishment of efficient dairies and tanneries. The ashram programme, during the first decade, was confined to maintenance of large numbers of cattle, which were kept for ploughing, for manure and for milk. The main thrust of Gandhi's scheme was to communicate the results of these experiments to the villagers, and to assist in the establishment of dairies and tanneries on the ashram pattern to serve the rural population.

Though Gandhi was aware of the importance of agriculture to a dynamic economy, his experiment with agriculture was limited. He encouraged Maganlal Gandhi's farming programme at Sabarmati only to the extent that it enabled the ashram to be self-sufficient in fruit and vegetables. He was more concerned to promote the benefits of fruit orchards than develop new techniques of farming. The decision to cultivate cotton in the late 1920s expanded the involvement of the ashram in agriculture. Another area of agricultural experimentation at Sabarmati was closely linked to the sanitation programme. Gandhi had begun experiments in burying human excreta and converting it into manure at Phoenix. The work was continued at Sabarmati, and was later enhanced by a study of organic farming techniques made by an American disciple of Gandhi, Richard Gregg. Though a few experiments were tried, Gandhi became well aware of the fact that the ashram was unable to contribute anything substantial to the field of agricultural technology; for he wrote,

> Whilst it is wrong to think that I dislike all machinery as such, I do feel that we are not competent judges of the usefulness or otherwise of machinery however small it may be for the toiling millions...Let me tell you that in the ashram we have a variety of simple machinery in the way of ploughs, grass-cutting machines, grinding-mills, etc.

> But I am sorry to inform you that not much of our investment in this line had proved profitable or promising. This has happened because we are all amateur farmers. And this is judgment which I give you after an experience extending over a period of thirteen years.(CW 38: 7-8).

Gandhi was deeply convinced of the role of education in bringing about changes in the society and restructuring of rural India. Highly critical of the prevailing system,[10] Gandhi felt the urgent need of introducing a mass child and adult education programme which would impress upon people the dignity of manual work, the necessity of respect for the individual, and awaken in them the need of the disadvantaged classes. The new system of education envisioned by Gandhi was a process of self-realisation whereby every "pupil" comes to the awareness of the need for service to humanity, especially for the downtrodden.

Gandhi's plan was to establish a national school where boys and girls would be trained to serve their country. Surrounded by an atmosphere of simplicity, manual work and service, their training as potential satyagrahis would thus be inextricably bound up with ashram life. In 1920 Gandhi launched a major educational experiment by founding the *Gujarat Vidyapith*. As an outgrowth of the ashram, the Vidyapith was established to serve a complementary function.[11]

Did Sabarmati achieve the ideal of Gandhi's educational system? His approach to education was denigrated as "anachronistic" or "retrograde" by members of the educated classes. As Judith Brown observes, "In attacking Western education and castigating lawyers and doctors, Gandhi was challenging the vested interests of his educated contemporaries, the very people who were the heart of the new politics, and controlled the Congress. It was hardly likely that they would find such an opponent congenial company" (Brown 1972: 45). The pedagogic principles of Gandhi, derived basically from the ancient ashramic system, may be impractical for formal and professional education. Gandhi had a dislike for highly disciplined formal education and therefore the methodology employed by him was non-intellectual and non-professional. Nonetheless, Gandhi's criticisms of the prevailing education system — i.e., not enough people were receiving education, there were great imbalances of social and geographical nature, much of the education was irrelevant to India's needs, too many people were being educated to an unnecessarily high level at great cost of the country, and education was failing to produce attitudes conducive to the all-round development of the nation—seem valid even today. It is interesting to note that Tagore, a contemporary well-known educationist, shared with Gandhi a dislike of highly disciplined formal education. Though both Gandhi and Tagore employed non-intellectual and non-professional methodology, Tagore more avidly pursued cultural learning, while Gandhi trained youth to be efficient instruments of public service rather than cultured aesthetes.

Sabarmati provided a supportive community to develop and consolidate constructive activities; and also to serve as a training ground for satyagrahis. To get the support and co-operation of the orthodox Hindus in India, Gandhi introduced a rigid system and code of conduct in Sabarmati. Over-emphasis on rules and regulations of the ashram seem to have stifled individual initiative and creativity. As Mark Thomson opines, "Gandhi's myopic attitude to marriage and sexual relations undermined the stability of the ashram and the constructive work programme in general".[12] Nevertheless Sabarmati remained the centre of satyagraha campaigns and other constructive programmes; it provided Gandhi with a "workshop in which he laid the ground-work for the social organisation and economics of his envisaged village community".

Village Worker

The constructive programme was part of the Congress Party policy, but Gandhi soon realized that the success of the constructive programme could not depend on the guidance and finance of central or regional organisations. Congress men gave lipservice to the constructive programme mainly to take advantage of Gandhi's political acumen. Disenchanted with Congress activities, and disappointed with its performances, Gandhi stepped up his vociferous campaign to focus attention on the plight of the poorest and weakest people in the villages. He began to depend more on colleagues capable of organising mass action without the need for political machinery. Though in the over-all sarvodaya vision of

Gandhi, politics, religion and other developmental actions were closely linked, the village was his priority, and reconstruction of villages through constructive programme was his major concern. This is clear from what he said in his letter to Jamnalal's friends after his death in 1942: "Neither he nor I had any attraction for what is called politics...My real politics was constructive work..." (Parvate 1962: 160), and from what he told a social service organisation in a speech in 1931,

> Till today we worked in a wrong way — we did all our work in cities and formulated all schemes keeping cities in view. We stayed away from village folk, hence they have so far regarded their privations as the result of divine wrath and could think of no other causes. Institutions of public service should be located among the people, be partners of their joys and sorrows and render service by spreading knowledge among them (CW 45: 391).

In an effort to get more in touch with rural India, Gandhi took an extensive tour of India at the end of 1933. This tour helped him to broaden the perspective of village work. It became apparent that both Harijan and caste-Hindu would be better served if the village work programme had as its main object village reorganisation and reconstruction, rather than concentrating all resources on Harijan uplift. Gandhi's decision to dissociate himself from the Congress in 1934 was a logical consequence of his commitment to the constructive programme and of his dissatisfaction with the Congress version of constructive programme. (Nehru was disappointed with Gandhi's decision, but Gandhi argued that politicisation without reconstruction would not lead to the non-violent society of a self-reliant Indian Commonwealth.) For Gandhi the constructive work programme became the acid test for anyone claiming to be a fighter for freedom. He argued that the cause of freedom would be lost unless young people turned from the frivolous pleasures of youth in favour of the simple, hard-working conditions of village life.

In outlining the requirements for village workers, Gandhi emphasized the workers' personal identification with the villagers and the realities of village life. This identification calls for a total "being" and a genuine "giving". Total "being" is living for the villagers and adopting the same standard of living of the villagers; genuine "giving" is an active expression of love through personal service.

Many village workers and the general public began to see Gandhi as the embodiment of the constructive work programme. To this he reacted by saying that "what gives us hope and courage...is undying faith in a cause or principle irrespective of persons from whom it is derived" (*Harijan* March 1933). He did recognise the tendency of "hero-worship" and "making of mahatma or saint" as a threat to the success of the work programme. Even so, a large proportion of village workers depended upon him for their inner strength.

It can be assumed without doubt that the village and its uplift had the topmost priority in Gandhi's sarvodaya vision. But it was not within the scope of his agenda to outline the details of the future action programme for the generations to come. Gandhi's sarvodaya mission being an going process, his ideals work as inspiration to any village worker, though he was himself unable to dedicate his time and energy totally for the uplift of any one village. Figuratively speaking, Gandhi's charisma took him to every village in India to such an extent that wherever village is mentioned, there Gandhi is referred to as well.

Sevagram: The Village of Service

It was not Gandhi's intention to set up a separate institution at Segaon (later named as Sevagram) on the line of his previous ashrams. He explained that he wished the entire village and its surroundings to become his ashram. He planned to build nothing but a home for his co-workers, and he intended that this should serve as a model for what its surroundings might become. If Sevagram became an ideal centre of rural life, Gandhi hoped, the success of village programme need no longer rely entirely on his personal faith. Perhaps all India would consider the concept of sarvodaya a practical ideal if he could arouse the social awareness of the villagers. Beside transforming the "uncompromising village into a model one" and setting an example to fellow *gram sevaks*, he also hoped to detect flaws in his approach to village work.

But the Segaon experiment brought home ever more clearly to Gandhi the extent to which he had become "the victim of his own charisma". Another ashram was being formed around Gandhi. He wanted to work quietly secluded from the national politics and the excessive attention of his devotees. People from all walks of life came to see him. Not only did Gandhi discourage contact with the outside world during the experiment, but many people who sought to join the ashram or to meet him personally were warned of the harsh realities of village life. Still Gandhi was not able to achieve his objective of living alone in the village; instead his cottage became overcrowded. The many administrative concerns of the constructive work programme and the changing political situation continued to demand his attention, and therefore he was unable to perform much physical work in Sevagram and surrounding villages. Eventually Gandhi was forced to abandon work in the village completely in 1940s due to the pressure of national politics and freedom movement. A possible and feasible alternative was to delegate capable leaders to carry out the ashram mission Gandhi had envisioned. It appears that such delegation of capable leaders was not prominent in Gandhi's style of action.

Though Gandhi's intention was not to establish another ashram at Sevagram, the population of Sevagram swelled over the years and this called for more institutionalisation and regimentation. As the administration became more difficult, rules regulating every aspect of ashram life were laid down. Gandhi seemed to place a disproportionate emphasis on the issue of sexual continence and *brahmacharya,* which not only created confusion and conflict among his co-workers, but diverted attention unnecessarily from the main question of village uplift. Undue importance given to community living, observances of rules and regulations of ashram life and indiscreet selection of followers to live in the ashram, deeply affected the quality of village work. Munnalal Gandhi complained that Sevagram had become a *dharmasala* (resting place) for the weak-minded, and Gandhi himself remarked that the ashram "was some kind of *shambhoomela,* consisting of all types of curious and abnormal persons who would ordinarily be regarded as 'cranks' in society" (CW 65: 213). The greatest obstacle to Gandhi's work in Sevagram, according to

Mahadev Desai, was this unusual crowd of people who gathered about him, "each good in his own way but not fit to bear or even to share the burdens he has taken upon himself".

What kept Gandhi going was his commitment to the sarvodaya ideal; a vision, he thought, was being realised through the uplift of the millions living in the villages of India. Ashram community, therefore, stood for Gandhi as a "prototype" of village community and thus a model village: a village which lacked nothing in the way of hygienic comforts, proper food, proper sanitation, and proper medical care etc. In his own words,

> ... Sevagram is to me a laboratory for *ahimsa*. If my experiments here were successful and I could find a solution for the little problems that confront me here, I am sure the formula would provide me a solution for the bigger issues that today face us in the country. That is why I am so reluctant to leave Sevagram. It is my laboratory for *satyagraha*. It is there that I expect to discover the key to India's independence, not in Simla or New Delhi (CW 72: 211).

Self-Help Experiments

Self-sufficiency in food and improvement of diet, were integral part of village reconstruction. Gandhi took keen interest in the efficient cultivation of the whole village land. In order to provide the people of Sevagram with a practical demonstration in various improved agricultural techniques, a section of the ashram land was brought under cultivation. Crops such as sugarcane and papayas, which ordinarily were not extensively cultivated in the district, were introduced at Sevagram. At Gandhi's insistence, bee-keeping was introduced at Sevagram, which not only established a honey industry but also greatly enhanced the production of fruit and vegetables. Gandhi hoped the villagers would follow the agricultural practices introduced in the ashram. But it was the villagers' inability to do so that highlighted perhaps the greatest failings of the Sevagram experiment. In spite of the ideal of simplicity and various austerity measures introduced in the lifestyle of the ashramites, Sevagram never achieved self-sufficiency, instead it relied on outside support for its survival.

Animal husbandry was another agricultural experiment at Sevagram. *Goseva* (cow-service) became part of this experiment. The programme of cow protection, which includes experiments in the proper use of hide and carcass, cattle-breeding to increase milk yield etc., in Gandhi's view, was "a symbol of sound rural economics". The ultimate aim of Gandhi was to develop a co-operative dairy in the village; but with all the caste factions prevalent in the village, it was nearly impossible to instill any spirit of co-operation in the village. *Goseva* programme at Sevagram was often linked to the removal of untouchability.[13] But the reactionary opposition of orthodox Hindus remained the greatest obstacle to the *goseva* programme.

Gandhi never lost faith in khadi as the only industry "with the economic potential to serve as a permanent remedy and safeguard against unemployment and under-employment". Though the potential of khadi was never fully realised at Sevagram, Gandhi did not give up hope that the village would eventually become a model for khadi production and village economics. During Gandhi's years at Sevagram the khadi programme in the village met with a degree of success, though he was not content with the results. In association with AIVIA (All India Village Industries Association), Gandhi introduced number of industries to promote local products. They were: village earthen pots instead of factory-made china, reed pen instead of steel pen, handmade paper instead of ordinary paper, *babul* or *neem* twigs instead of the tooth-brush, leather goods made in villages out of village-flayed cattle instead of factory-tanned hide, ordinary village *jaggery* (or *gur*) instead of factory sugar, and hand-pounded whole rice instead of mill-polished rice.

Sevagram as a Laboratory

Gandhi initiated a movement with the intention of developing Sevagram into a model village, but it was left to his colleagues to nurture its growth. Many ashram activities did bear fruit, but Sevagram did not develop into a model village. Sevagram was a laboratory, like all Gandhi's communities, in which he experimented with ways and means to combat the poverty and oppression that pervaded village India.

Sevagram may be taken as an expression of Gandhi's love for villages and his enthusiasm for constructive work. Whether Sevagram was an experimental village or a "symbolic village" — i.e., to popularise the ideal of village work without actually doing it in concrete terms—or whether Sevagram remained a model for constructive work or a rural nerve centre for directing the nationalist campaign, is not easy to answer. There is a distinction between a successful experimental institution (like an agricultural university or an experimental village) and a successful "model" village. Sevagram was, if anything the former; and should not be expected to be the latter as well. "Model" village is the necessary "by-product" of such experimental institutions. Gandhi faced the career-long dilemma: to direct a national movement or to experiment with rural life. Both needed his attention, not to do either optimally meant restricting the effectiveness of the other. He may have made the best of the dilemma. Ideally, he needed someone of great ability to handle the constructive side full-time — to which he could contribute from time to time—while he gave primary attention to the national public role. But such a leader of the constructive programme would not have shared all of Gandhi's values.

Gandhi's attempt to elevate politics and community work to a spiritual plane was not understood by the majority of his followers. Gandhi's involvement in politics and that of his so called followers are somehow two different things. From the beginning, Gandhi's emphasis was on swaraj and village reconstruction. While Nehru and Congress were preoccupied with power, Gandhi devoted energies to the realisation of the non-violent society. "About political matters, I merely offer advice and then forget about it", he told the Gandhi Seva Sangh in 1937. "I do my writing for the constructive programme and for it I work" (CW 65: 133). He was not interested in "power politics" but in politics as constructive work. But to his displeasure, a significant proportion of his co-workers did in some way become involved in politics. He was adamant that the members of the Gandhi Seva Sangh should not be associated with factional politics, nonetheless many members of the Sangh took up membership as a means to enhance their political careers. One reason why the constructive programme could not achieve the success initially intended was the lack of community workers who were self-motivated, determined and willing to serve the poor without hope of gain. Gandhi himself recognised that many people at Sevagram and elsewhere, involved in the constructive work organisations, were inspired more by a desire to achieve some renown for themselves by association with him than by a wish to serve the really poor in the villages.

Sevagram, nonetheless, remained a centre of satyagraha action. For example, it was in the forefront of the "Quit India" satyagraha in 1942. The political awakening that occurred among the villages surrounding Sevagram during the Quit India movement was a logical consequence of Gandhi's presence and action at Sevagram. Such awareness made the villagers conscious of their role in attaining freedom for the country and consequently their participation in total sarvodaya. In this sense, ashrams in general and Sevagram in particular were nurseries of sarvodaya ideal and action programme. Nehru saw the ashram concept merely as a potential for arousing political consciousness among the villagers. But Gandhi's vision went way beyond politics into the genuine liberation of each human being. Through the ashram concept, he envisaged a liberating process carried out by constructive work. Political involvement for Gandhi was an immediate need, whereas constructive programme is to be an on-going process. In the over-all sarvodaya perspective of Gandhi, politics, religion and other developmental works were closely linked. But village was his priority and reconstruction of villages through constructive programme his main concern. This becomes clear from what he said: "My real politics was constructive work...", and "...I would stop all writing and simply bury myself in village and there work away for all I am worth, and that I should love to do in perfect silence" (*Harijan* September 1935).

Gandhi was certainly aware of the symbolic importance of his decision to settle in Sevagram, which would focus the public gaze on village work rather than his press image. For him the true symbols of the village experiment would be the work done and the social awareness required to appreciate its value. But in many respects the Sevagram experiment revealed the extent to which he had become the victim of his own charisma—his charisma could not be limited to one village or ashram. He lamented not being able to perform more physical work in Sevagram and surrounding villages. It appears that he was struggling with the idea of giving/ showing an example of ideal village life by living in a village. However, the duration of Gandhi's sojourns at Sevagram became shorter, until the pressures of politics during the 1940s forced him to abandon work in the village completely. Even so, he advised the ashramites to "share their sorrows, understand their difficulties and anticipate their wants" (*Young India* September 1924), and to serve the villagers in a spirit of love. He also advised the sincere workers among them to leave Sevagram and settle down in the villages of their choice. The ideal of putting a *gram sevak* in each village remained Gandhi's ultimate objective.

Gandhi admitted the flaws in his approach to politics and constructive work in his speech on 25 August 1946 on the eve of his final departure from Sevagram. His words, as Mark Thomson comments, "...highlighted the inherent ambivalence towards politics that had undermined Gandhi's constructive work activities throughout his long career" (Thomson 1993: 234). Gandhi expresses the sublimity of the idea set before the people and also the prophetic and utopian nature of such ideals, i.e., that they may never be realised in their entirety, though there is an ongoing struggle towards their realisation:

> When the Ashram was first started in Kochrab we set before us certain ideals. Some ideals are before us today. What is our duty in terms of these ideals in the face of the conflagration that is raging in the country today? Let us be humble and confess that we have not got the strength today to meet all the expectations that the people entertain of us. But we are sincerely striving for it. If we had fully realised the principles for which we stand, we should have rushed into the blaze and offered the purest sacrifices which might have conceivably quenched the flames... The acme of *satyagraha* for us would be to lay down our lives for the defence of India's just cause. Let us then pray to God to give us the requisite purity and fearlessness in the true sense of the term, to make our sacrifice worthy of the

altar. Then alone shall we be worthy of the name of the Ashram (*Harijan* September 1946).

Village and Basic Education

Education, understood as "creating awareness", was essential to the sarvodaya ideal and action programme of Gandhi. Therefore, he developed a methodology that is described by Gandhi as "Basic Education" or *Nai Talim* (New Way). Gandhi envisaged under this programme a complete restructuring of the Indian educational pattern. *Nai Talim* was closely linked with the constructive programme. As Saiyidain puts it, "Educational reform...is also social reform and reconstruction in the widest sense of the work" (Saiyidain 1950: 16).

In his critique of the existing system of education, Gandhi says that it is defective, that it "is based upon foreign culture to the almost entire exclusion of indigenous culture, it ignores the culture of the heart and the hand, confines itself simply to the head, (and) real education is impossible through a foreign medium" (Ramana Murti 1970: 337). Speaking of the use of textbooks he observes that it is not through the textbooks that the lad learns what is right and wrong in the home life. He even went to the extent of saying that, "If I had my way, I would certainly destroy the majority of the present text-books and cause to be written text-books which have a bearing on and correspondence with home life, so that a boy as he learns may react upon his immediate surroundings" (Ramana Murti 1970: 337). About the primary education, he has this to say, "... the present system of primary education is not only wasteful but positively harmful. Most of the boys are lost to their parents and to the occupation to which they are born. They pick up evil habits, affect urban ways and get a smattering of something which may be anything but education" (Ramana Murti 1970: 363).

In order to remedy the situation, Gandhi suggested education by means of vocational or manual training. Education should be self-supporting, and be vitally related to India's rural heritage. He wanted "the whole process of education to be imparted through some handicraft or industry." The introduction of manual training will serve a double purpose in a poor country like India. Firstly, that education should enable the recipient to be self-supporting in later life, and, secondly, that education should in itself be self-supporting. As Gandhi says, "I am very keen on finding the expenses of a teacher through the product of the manual work of his pupils, because I am convinced that there is no other way to carry education to crores of our children".

The whole plan of basic education "springs out of nonviolence." "If we want to eliminate communal strife and international strife," Gandhi observed, "...If India has resolved to eschew violence, this system of education becomes an integral part of the discipline she has to go through...We cannot, will not, think in terms of exploitation, and we have no alternative but this plan of education, which is based on nonviolence" (Ramana Murti 1970: 366). Another purpose of this Basic Education is to help reduce the exploitation of villages by the cities and to promote a healthy and moral relationship between the city and village. In Gandhi's own words, "...Whilst the child will be encouraged to spin and help his parents with agricultural jobs, he will also be made to feel that he belongs not only to his parents but also to the village and to the country..."

It is to be noted at this point that Gandhi did not promote manual work merely for the joy of creation or pursuit of knowledge, but for the overall development of the individual. The Sevagram education plan was proposed as a means of sustaining the ideals of social service and citizenship through the activities of children from the earliest formative years.

The self-supporting aspect of Basic Education generated great controversy among educationists and the public in general. Some went even to the extent of saying that it is a legalised child labour,[14] and some others criticised the scheme for transforming the child into a wage-making machine. Despite such criticisms, the Wardha Scheme or "Basic National Education" received national attention.[15] For example, in a comprehensive resolution, the Indian National Congress endorsed the Scheme and initiated the formation of the Hindustani Talimi Sangh (All-India Board of Education). In 1939 the Bihar Government started thirty new basic schools in the district of Champaran, the Bombay Government introduced Basic Education in fifty-eight district board schools and twenty eight other schools, in Gujarat, Maharashtra and Karnataka. In view of extending the scope of Basic Education to "everybody at every stage of life", the third All India Basic Education Conference, held at Sevagram, made plans for the future of Basic Education.

But somehow, as Mark Thomson observes, "opposition to the Wardha Scheme in Government and Congress circles appeared to harden after independence". The Government's stress on formal academic education, urbanisation and industrialisation pushed aside craft instruction merely as a subsidiary in its overall programme. *Nai Talim* was village-oriented to provide the majority of Indians with the basic education necessary to make them self-reliant within the existing system. This ideal was never fully realised due to poor teachers, inadequate textbooks, the reluctance of middle-class parents to send their children to schools which prescribed manual work, or a combination of all these factors. As Ram K. Vepa puts it, "Perhaps, the implementation of the scheme was largely by people who were not in tune with its ideals: whatever the reason, the 'Basic Scheme of Education' of Gandhiji has for all practical purposes remained a dead letter even after independence" (Vepa 1975: 253).

Fragments of a Vision

Our rather comprehensive analysis of Gandhi's experiments with ashrams— The Phoenix Settlement, Tolstoy Farm, Sabarmati and Sevagram—as means of entering into the inner fabric of villages, shows how genuinely village-minded Gandhi was. He certainly had a vision about the future of village-India; he initiated a process of village reconstruction, rural uplift, a sarvodaya. Gandhi abhorred dogmatism for the same reason that he discouraged monuments to himself: his philosophy of provisionality and dynamism calls for changes in outlooks, attitudes and action programmes. There is no such thing as authentic "Gandhism". Original Gandhian ashrams could have continued as nerve centres of sarvodaya action, but the Sabamarti and Sevagram ashrams have been transformed into museums and national shrines. On the twenty-eighth anniversary of Gandhi's death, his grandson, Arun Gandhi, wrote: "The Ashrams where Bapu lived, worked and from where he gave inspiration to 400 million people have been turned into showpieces; there is nothing Gandhian about them".[16] Despite the failures of Gandhi's followers to further develop his ashrams as vehicles of community activism, other Gandhian ashrams, which have been founded by men and women dedicated not only to Gandhi but to the ideals he stood for, have continued to serve people in various ways.

The network of ashrams that developed was perhaps the major outcome of the ashram experiment. Most of these ashrams function as centres of service to the villages. Gandhi himself shifted the emphasis from the role of the ashram as an institution to that of the village worker, who orders his life around the ashramic ideal. Ashrams were needed as supportive communities for the village worker. They were necessary to provide basic social services, to train villagers to be community workers and teachers among their own people, and to educate adults and children to be clean, healthy, independent minded citizens, self-reliant and proud of their cultural and religious heritage. Gandhi's vision is alive and active in Gandhi ashrams spread far and wide in India. The vision is ever dynamic because, "it has grown much since Gandhi's time, with new faces, new issues, new ideas, new techniques, new failures, and new successes. Though in some ways it may have fallen back from the standard Gandhi set, in other ways it has gone beyond him" (Shepard 1987: 10).

Writing about sarvodaya and organizations, B. P. Pandey gives a list of fifty-two ashrams as centres where sarvodaya ideals are their objectives (Pandey 1988: 150-52). The list is not exhaustive. As part of my research I made a random selection of a few ashrams in three states of India: Bihar, Tamil Nadu, and Kerala (my home State). Following is the summary report of my field visits and assessment.

Samanvay Ashram in Bodhgaya extends its outreach programme through 150 centres in 83 villages with 4,000 children, according to the News Bulletin privately circulated from the ashram (Sundrani 1990: 44). The ashram was founded by Acharya Vinoba Bhave in 1954 to promote harmony among people of different castes, creeds and statuses. But the dedication and hard work of Dwarako Sundrani for the last 38 years, to reach to the weakest section in Indian society (the Musahar and the Bhoktas) have made headway in Bihar State. Non-formal education, agricultural programmes and housing projects introduced and implemented by the ashram have generated hope, dignity and pride among the people with whom the ashramites work. Through the programme of education in the line of *nai talim*, Samanvay Ashram has made significant achievement in this area. As a result, the Government of Bihar has decided to designate a compact area in which to demonstrate non-formal education. The Government has also declared the ashram the training centre for all teachers in the district. The ashram has succeeded in bringing the message of liberation to the lowest in the society by productive education and self-help programmes. Nonetheless, the ashram and its activities entirely depend on donations from people in India and abroad. The ashram has a long way to go towards achieving self-sufficiency. Dwarako Sundrani and Baikuntha Pandey (coordinator of developmental works in the ashram) are very hopeful and confident that programmes initiated by Samanvay Ashram will eventually lead to sarvodaya.[17]

At Khadigram, Jamui in Bihar, Acharya Ramamurti has concentrated all his energies on outreach to villages and deliberately dismantled the traditional ashram activities. The activities of the ashram range from education of children, agriculture and self-help programme for women, to promotion of local arts, dramatics and music. At Khadigram simplicity was more marked; one was left with a sense of almost puritanical devotion and unobtrusive kindness. Ramamurti's vision is to make Khadigram the centre for experimenting in agriculture and agro-industries, and for studying the problems connected with *gramdan* extension work[18].

Gandhigram, which is "the Sevagram of the South",[19] combines two streams, namely, Gandhigram constructive programme and academic studies. The founders of Gandhigram University, who were experienced in village developmental work under the guidance of Gandhi himself, managed to involve the academic community in this movement. The Rural Institute, deemed a university, is the result of their effort. By comparison and contrast with other Gandhian projects, Gandhigram may appear a "Mega project" in Gandhian terms. The developmental activities cover a large spectrum of projects and programmes, such as social welfare, education, Kasturba hospital, socio-economic programme, teda projects, carpet projects and intensive extension work. Gandhigram, in its long journey in search of a way to alleviate poverty, has finally settled down to the spinning wheel as a sustainable solution. The houses of over 1,500 spinners and nearly 500 weavers give a powerful witness to Gandhi's dream of self-reliance through khadi. Other enterprises, such as processing of cereals and pulses, the extraction of oil, both edible and inedible, the preparation of soap, the manufacture of steel furniture, the concoction of different herbs with a range of other natural ingredients to meet the *ayurvedic* system, seem to flourish at Gandhigram and have given hope to the more than 3,000 families who engage themselves in such industrial pursuits. The Lakshmi College of Education is built on the principles of basic education, which is not only craft-centred but environment-based. The development activities in Gandhigram, in addition to stressing the need to nurture the eco-system, have also started to work out a strategy for limiting the population. Apart from adopting the usual sterilisation techniques, a new thrust is being given to implement an integrated programme of health and sanitation. The thrust of Gandhigram is to fight against unemployment, underemployment, alarming increase in population and to keep an ecological balance. Gandhigram stands as a living and dynamic witness to the sarvodaya vision and constructive programme initiated by Gandhi. Such a living and dynamic witness has brought new hope and life to nearly 246 villages spread over 16 blocks in Tamil Nadu. In order to save Gandhigram from growing into a mega-project, there is need to decentralise its activities to different centres and villages.

Gansoville (Gandhian Society Villages Association) is a humble attempt in Amaravathi Pudur, Tamil Nadu by some Jesuits to evolve and demonstrate a working model of rural reconstruction on a Gandhian social pattern that could help the socially and economically weak to become self-reliant and socially integrated. Though in its infancy (begun in 1977), Gansoville has a small livestock programme of goat-rearing in 21 villages, an environment programme of afforestation in nearly 100 hectares and a training programme for rural employable and income-generating skills, such as: agriculture, poultry, tailoring, gem-cutting, masonry and carpentry. Gansoville has not yet made any significant contribution towards self-reliance in its 19 years existence, in spite of the undying hope and dedication of Ignatius Jesudasan and his team.[20]

Navodaya Danagram at Puthukode, not far from Kozhikode, in Kerala, is the brainchild of Radhakrishna Menon, its founder, mentor, and guide. Started in 1958-59, it was built on the cornerstones of basic education, social change and economic development. It still has to go a long way towards self-sufficiency because it depends on foreign charities and other outside help, though Radhakrishna is hopeful that, "within a few years, the coconut on our common land will mature. The annual crop will earn enough to fund all Danagram's development needs. Then we won't depend on outside funds" (Shepard 1987: 97). The village has fifty families (a total of 350 people). Living and working as a community, Dhanagram demonstrates the value of communal harmony and the fruit of cooperative enterprise. Through *Sevamandir* ("Temple of Service"), basic education primarily took the form of agriculture. Another aspect of basic education is that students help run the school. The students at Sevamandir have their own government, with executive, legislative and judiciary. At Danagram, new values are growing out of old traditions, material gains are bringing incentive for further development, education is stimulating minds in living a full and creative life. As Mark Shepard concludes, "... Danagram was basically a form of social education, a way of teaching people to live and work in harmony..." (Shepard 1987: 102). One leaves Danagram with a deep sense of appreciation for the achievements brought about by Radhakrishna's restless energy and commitment to Gandhi's sarvodaya.

Centre of Science for Villages (CSV) was started in Wardha, in 1976 by Devendra Kumar, an associate of J. C. Kumarappa (who was Gandhi's right hand in his village industries movement and principal spokesman of his economic philosophy). The Centre seeks to continue the work Gandhi and Kumarappa, started in the thirties, of utilizing science for improving the rural economy. With the help of technologists and grass-root workers, researches are undertaken to find ecologically sound and socially just solutions to rural economy. Once a new technique appropriate for the area is evolved, it is tried out in the villages through an extension programme to see how it can be accepted by the people and assimilated by the rural economy. CSV has evolved more than fourteen such technologies which are novel in character and have wide applicability.[21] Based on the philosophy of "appropriate technology", CSV has started functioning from where Gandhi had started his rural technology campaign. CSV has established a healthy link between science and technology and mud huts. It basically is a technology transfer agency. What is happening today is that in India as a whole most techniques and technological innovations for productivity and production processes are being geared to the urban economy. By contrast, CSV attempts "to bring about technologies which can utilise resources presently available in the villages and yet make it possible to increase the productivity at that point and then gradually change the prevailing culture of poverty" (Kumar 1983: 16). CSV's success in introducing appropriate technology in village India is a revolutionary move to make Gandhi's dream of Indian villages come true. There is urgent need for nurturing and multiplying such Technology Transfer Centres the country over, if we want to fulfil India's role of finding alternatives to the present system.[22] It is now commonly felt that agriculture by itself is not in a position to employ the increasing population and fulfilling the optimum needs of the village. CSV therefore bases its philosophy of action on a Gandhian principle that the industrialisation (understood as Appropriate Technology, one that is environmentally sound and leads to social justice) of the villages is a must for removing rural poverty. Efforts of rural technology and industry will eventually lead towards the fulfilment of the Gandhian dream, where everyone happily lives a life of sharing with nature and fellow being in such a way that develops the individual, the community and natural environment to their full.

Glimpses of Hope

Gandhi's ashram experiments were intended to spread the gospel of village-mindedness and village-reconstruction to the people of India. Despite apparent failures with the experiments,

Gandhi continued to spread the message of village-mindedness through his writings and active involvement in constructive programme. Hundreds of ashrams, i.e., experimental centres, established in various parts of India witness to the ongoing process of the realisation of sarvodaya. Though South Africa witnessed the genesis of Gandhi's satyagraha and ashram concepts, he declared that his main objective was the uplift of India's downtrodden (*antyodaya* leading to sarvodaya).

The ashram concept was not new to India's Hindu masses, but Gandhi's cross-cultural synthesis of ascetic and communal traditions of the Christian and humanistic West, challenged the religious orthodoxy of many in India. Quite a few of Gandhi's ideas, such as the removal of untouchability, sanitation reform, uplift of women and co-education, and men and women living together in his ashrams, were unacceptable to many Indians. Opposition did not deter him from pursuing his vision. Support and patronage he received from prominent businessmen and intellectuals such as Gokhale and Tagore reassured him in his endeavour. Gandhi's idea was that ashram life would foster an active asceticism; while self-realisation remained the ultimate goal of the ashramite, active service to society was the means to that end. In his view, the ashramite who ordered one's life around a refined asceticism, and yet remained active in society and politics, was an irrepressible agent of social change.

Ashram was a centre of action, of service to the needy. Removal of ignorance and illiteracy by means of education — so as to arouse the masses out of their fatalism and inertia to awareness of their individual and national duties, rights, and dignity — was of topmost priority in Gandhi's action programme. But the demands of the political struggle severely handicapped Gandhi's non-political work,[23] and increasing institutionalisation of the ashram and constructive work organisations led to the routinisation of Gandhi's ideas. This stifled individual initiative and creativity by promoting a rigid orthodoxy and code of conduct that dogmatised and rigidified the dynamism and evolutionary nature of Gandhi's vision. But ashrams were needed as supportive communities for the village worker. They were necessary to provide basic social services, to train villagers to be community workers and teachers among their own people, and to educate adults and children to be clean, healthy, independent-minded citizens, self-reliant and proud of their cultural and religious heritage. The Gandhian ashrams also played a supportive role in the satyagraha campaigns.

The work done by the Gandhian ashrams is scattered and insufficient in terms of bringing about a total liberation (sarvodaya) in India, especially in village India. But in some areas at least the ashrams remain "the only source of succour and hope to the poverty-stricken people they serve" (Thomson 1993: 272). Most of these ashrams are not self-supporting and do not attract the young and the elite intellectuals; the work done by some ashrams is merely "relief" rather than uplifting, liberating and constructive. Nonetheless, there is a growing awareness and interest in India and the world over for grass root action for "people-oriented development", "people's participation in decision making and democracy", ecology and environment, simple living, nature-oriented living, "appropriate technology"(science for village), small (village) industries as opposed to industrialisation etc. The network of ashrams (some of them quiet but effective) that developed in post- independent India seem to proclaim the vision and message of sarvodaya society: non-violent, village-minded, self-reliant, liberated and liberating.

Ashram to Village: Realizing the Experiment

Ashram was not an end in itself for Gandhi. He wanted the ashramites to go and settle in villages and work as instruments of change. It was Gandhi's mission to rebuild the Indian society based on the village system. He wrote in 1936: "I would say that if the village perishes, India will perish too. It will be no more India. Her own mission in the world will get lost" (*Harijan* August 1936). He was not only aware of the obnoxious realities of Indian villages, but he acknowledged the same in his vivid descriptions of them.[24] But he was confident that the prevalent situation could be transformed by villagers themselves, provided proper help and guidance were extended to them.

He enunciated the basic principles of village swaraj, such as trusteeship, *swadeshi*, bread labour, self-sufficiency, decentralisation, co-operation, equality, *nai talim* etc. His conception of an ideal village, thus, was comprehensive, encompassing the economic, political, social, and educational dimensions. Gandhi's conception of village uplift would not have been congenial to the modern (urban-industrial) notion of "development" but would be to the post-modern perspective of "quality of life". By advocating village reconstruction, ideal village and self-sufficient village, Gandhi was not attempting to give a once and for all solution to the plight of the poor or to the problems of growing urbanization in India. He was only suggesting alternatives to remedy the existing contrast between rural and urban, rich and poor in India. Gandhi would see constructive "development" not in terms of urbanization, but in terms of helping the poorest of the poor, in terms of *antyodaya* and sarvodaya — total liberation of the human being[25].

Gandhi never lost sight of his vision that *Ramrajya*, a non-violent social order, "...can be built on self-contained villages...," because, "...Rural economy, as I have conceived it, eschews exploitation altogether and exploitation is the essence of violence". Gandhi was of the opinion that the nearest approach to civilization based on non-violence was the erstwhile village republic. He, therefore, believed that the main task before an independent Indian government would be the humanisation of village society:

> Man is not born to live in isolation but is essentially a social animal independent and interdependent. No one can or should ride on another's back. If we try to work out necessary conditions for such a life, we are forced to the conclusion that the unit of society should be a village or call it a manageable small group of people, who would in the ideal be self-sufficient (in the matter of their vital requirements) as a unit and bound together in bonds of mutual co-operation and interdependence (Pyarelal 1959: 8).

The present *panchayati raj* in India was originally based on the Gandhian programme, though, as Indira Rothermund observes, "... the people lost sight of the core of the principle and the principle itself remained elusive" (Lal ed. 1981: 12). By *panchayati raj*, Gandhi meant a harmonious, non-violent society and state where power, both political and economic, is distributed and decentralised, where self-sufficiency in basic needs is fundamental, where each individual is respected and recognised for one's human dignity and equality. This was the sarvodaya society Gandhi envisioned, the village swaraj he dreamt for. This obviously is a vision that is being realised. In his view, sarvodaya ultimately depended upon individual effort and self-reliance.

Gandhi wanted to project his sarvodaya ideal through ashrams to village India for communities founded on voluntary association and sustained by spontaneous organic growth were a prominent feature of his ideal society. The educative function of the ashrams carried out through *nai talim*, was to create social awareness of the rights and responsibilities of citizenship, and to awaken the people to their innate power to change the social and physical environment. Gandhi's ashram concept may have been based on the principle of withdrawal and renewal common to Hindu and Christian ascetic traditions, but self-realisation through active service to society was the ultimate ideal of every ashram.

Gandhi was well aware of the evolutionary nature and the provisionality of his ideals, but the increasing institutionalisation of ashrams by his followers dogmatized his ideal. In this process a provisional utopian ideal may have become a rigid ideology. The provisionality comes from its thrust for villages for the needs of the villages change and so too the constructive action programmes for the villages. Ashrams can outlive their usefulness — Sabarmati was disbanded in 1933 — and venture into new action programmes for creating sarvodaya society.

Gandhi's view was that sarvodaya could only be realized if planning came from the grassroots level because it was here that relevant programmes could be developed in terms of the day to day needs of the people. His ashramic ideal was to promote village life based on service, self-reliance and creative activity. His ashrams were living laboratories wherein he and his colleagues experimented with ways and means of enabling India's villagers to live in dignity and freedom. The Gandhian experiments continue to inspire people, especially those who are engaged in a struggle for liberation in the India of today, to conduct their own experiments.[26]

The ashram-village experiments Gandhi initiated and those that continue in some form as Gandhian experiments give concrete expression to Gandhi's utopian ideal of sarvodaya. Ashram-village experiments are to be seen as a liberative and liberating praxis. Such experiments are logical and ontological because an ideal merely in the abstract is no ideal in the full sense. The dialectic between ideal and actual is an ontological reality of potentiality and actuality that is at the basis of any change. As a result, positing any ideal logically presupposes (intends) actuality in some degree. The sarvodaya ideal of Gandhi, for that matter any of the ideals of Gandhi, must not be seen in the abstract. The sarvodaya ideal as concretized in ashram-village experiments shows that its realizability to some extent is a possibility. As an experimentalist, Gandhi never worried about the success of his experiments. The reason is that he was aware that an ideal by its very nature transcends the actual and that full realization of any ideal would make it stop being an ideal; if an ideal is fully and totally realized, then there is no more possibility of its realization, no more "becoming", no more pressure for change. For Gandhi, experiments are like Euclid's line (cited in Chapter Two)—"no one has so far been able to draw it and never will. All the same, it is only by keeping the ideal line in mind that we have made progress in geometry". What is important is to keep the ideal in mind. This is true of every ideal. In Gandhi's sarvodaya worldview, ashram experiments and ideal village experiments were ideals like Euclid's line.

We said above (Chapter Two) that sarvodaya, understood as a "realistic utopia", is a process of realization that explores areas of new possibilities for the well- being and harmony of humanity. What Gandhi does is to explain the ashramic ideal as a process of such realization: for him, ashram is the centre of action and village is an extension of ashram life. Life in the ashram is based on simplicity of living, hard work and concern for others. There is collective ownership or responsible stewardship in the ashram. There is fundamental concern for the quality of life and dignity of labour and a distaste for the economics of material accumulation. For Gandhi, ashrams were laboratories for experimenting with his ideas, ideals and visions. Those experiments become concrete, visible and testable in ashrams.

Though Gandhi was influenced to some extent by Christian

monasticism as well as by traditional Indian asceticism (Hindu, Jaina and Buddhist) in his ashram idea, his original contribution to ashramic life was "this worldly asceticism". By introducing this worldly asceticism, Gandhi intended to awaken the people to their social, cultural and economic traditions. This new conception of asceticism is innovative in two ways, namely, as a breakaway from traditional asceticism and thus as a negation of an existing system (not necessarily oppressive) and as a transformation in some measure of the existing system of ascetic lifestyle. Self-realization would still be the ultimate goal, but this goal is achieved not through traditional quietist withdrawal from all social concerns, but through active social involvement and selfless service to humanity. The ideal of this worldly asceticism thus gains the characteristics of concrete utopia. The new vision presented by Gandhi through the ashram ideal may seem less than "shattering"; yet it surely is not conservative, but new and revolutionary. It is progressive and offers possibilities and ventures for better being and better living for humanity. Ashram for Gandhi was never exclusive; the ashrams and the services they rendered were considered as common property of the Indian people. Speaking to villagers, Gandhi said, "the ashram is public property. You have a right to see it at any time you like. It is in your midst. And as long as you find that its activity is helpful and serves your district, it is your bounden duty to help it in every way" (CW 26: 351). Gandhi not only promoted the spirit of "universal service" in the ashrams but encouraged an "ecumenical" community. Jews, Hindus, Muslims, Parsees and Christians all participated in the "service", which was a blend of religious teachings and spiritual songs from the East and the West. The educative function of the ashrams, carried out through *nai talim*, for instance, was a definitive break from traditional understanding of education and was revolutionary in this sense, that it was intended to create social awareness of the rights and responsibilities of citizenship, and to awaken the people to their innate power to change their social and physical environment.

The essence of the realistic utopian phenomenon being "the critical intention to break through the existing conditions and achieve a better future", (Chapter Two) Gandhi's ashram ideal is a realistic utopia because the ashram concept, though not new to India's Hindu culture, in Gandhi's version of it challenged the religious orthodoxy of many in India. Ideals held high in the ashrams, such as the removal of untouchability, sanitation reform, uplift of women, co-education, and men and women living together in his ashrams, were novel and unacceptable to many Indians. Gandhi's strong conviction was that the ashramites who ordered their lives around this worldly asceticism, and yet remained active in society and politics, were irrepressible agents of social change. Thus the ideal of ashram fulfils in some sense a critical function by presenting a concrete ideal and, by the example of the ashram residents, exercising some degree of moral pressure on its environing society to change its practices so as to bring about a better world.

Gandhi was convinced that India's heart beats in its villages and that ashrams are nerve centres of sarvodaya praxis. Such theoretical/symbolic convictions and consequent experiments with ashrams and village ideals fundamentally challenged the status quo. Though Gandhi may not appear overly critical of the status quo, his actions were, nonetheless, critical of the system: e.g., his satyagrahas and other nonviolent actions against oppressive colonization. Even those more overtly political action programmes were centred around ashrams. Gandhi becomes more critical of the present by projecting a constructive image of the future and presenting it as a model, an ideal and an alternative. He was aware of the dialectics at work in ashram lifestyle and model villages. His ideals did at times turn into ideologies and thus stopped being utopian. At times, regimentation, extreme austerity and institutionalization may have destroyed the provisionality, creativity and future-orientedness that made ashram and village ideals an utopian vision. Gandhi anticipated this danger and realized that his role as a charismatic leader was to initiate and inspire others. "Phoenix settlement could not contain him", for example. Just as an utopian vision operates in a dialectic, an utopian visionary functions in a dialectic: he/she has to outgrow the present and there has to be a constant outgrowing or transcending. It is the dynamic of utopia that it can never fully succeed since it shows the distance between the current and the hoped for future. Therefore the decisive trait of utopia is not full realizability but rather the preservation of genuine opposition. The ideal ashram remains a future possibility and the model village exists in potency. Society cannot effectively function well without such ideals or utopias because they are at the root of change in the society.

With Ernst Bloch, we would say that "the material world is essentially unfinished, the future is undetermined and therefore that the future constitutes a realm of possibility" (Levitas 1990: 87). Such possibilities are not mere formal possibilities but real possibilities for Bloch. Being an anticipation of the future, utopia works as a catalyst of the future. There is, of course a danger of such anticipation becoming escapist fantasy or mere wishful thinking. What is at issue is hope understood "essentially as a directing act of a cognitive kind". Gandhi's utopian sarvodaya ideal, with its inbuilt village reconstruction programmes and ashramic experiments, is an anticipation of the future, for, as "prisoner of hope" (Judith Brown) and as prophetic visionary, he had the insights to set realizable goals and to indicate concrete ways of reaching them. These goals are concrete utopias in so far as they "actually influence people's thoughts and actions". It was this hope in the better future that moved Gandhi towards new and fresh experiments in Indian soil even after experiences of frustration in achieving the goal of ashram experiments in South Africa. It is again the very same hope that keeps ashram experiments going in India and maintains village reconstruction as a priority. Such "authentically human hope" (Bloch 1986: 82-84; Baum 1975: 171, 282). is the driving force for creative vision and effective change in society; and this hope is existentially and theologically viable because, in the words of Gregory Baum, "in hope alone do people authentically relate their yearning to the future. Only if the day-dream is accompanied by hope does it release the potentialities of matter, direct action and enable people to create the new" (Baum 1975: 282).

In our discussion of utopia as vision, we said that utopia has both positive and negative characteristics: it contains truth, so far as it contains *telos*, the goal and purpose of existence; but it also contains untruth, in that it forgets that estrangement is a condition of human existence. Though utopia opens up new possibilities which would have been lost without utopian anticipation, utopia sometimes tends to describe impossibilities as real possibilities. There would seem to be a substantial element of untruth and impossibility in picturing the whole of India as a cluster of self-sufficient, autonomous but interdependent villages, or seeing ashram life as a prerequisite for village workers or for village reconstruction, or expecting to establish perfect equality, liberty and fraternity in the ashrams. The truth is that we need ideals and models and that village reconstruction in Gandhian style is possible on a small scale and that ashram experiments continue to promote grassroots village development, self sufficiency, village industry and village-mindedness. What is important is to maintain a healthy tension between the negative content (which inevitably leads to failure and disillusion) and the positive power (the power of transformation: "the root of its power is the essential ontological discontent of man in every direction of his being"). Utopia attains its quality of transcendence as a result of this inbuilt tension. With Paul Tillich we would say that "utopia is always and necessarily suspended between possibility and impossibility". True, Gandhi's ashram experiments and his followers' further ashramic experiments met with failures in achieving their set goals and there probably is no resoundingly successful model village to be pinpointed, but even failed or faltering experiments do not mark an end of utopian ideals or prove the impossibility of their realization. Instead, those experiments open up new possibilities and create new hope; because failures may occur, not because the goal is wrong or impossible but because the means may have been wrong. The brief study of ashrams in this Chapter shows that Gandhian ashram-village experiments achieve partial, relative, limited and temporary success, some very significant and others rather insignificant. Such achievements in Gandhian terms are utopian signs of hope for tomorrow.

The exploratory, inventive and normative nature of utopia reveals the power of the human mind to picture the possible, to transcend the actual and the ability to cross the borders of the unknown. The importance of these utopian functions is that the thrust for progress and development in the society as a whole is based on these functions. They critique and evaluate the present in the light of a new future that works as ideal or norm. Therefore, such norms and ideals lie at the root of any progress in society. Gandhi's "ashram-village" functions as normative and ideal for village reconstruction in India. By proposing normative or ideal ashram-villages that are utopian in the sense that they reveal new and potential possibilities for future realization, Gandhi invests great hope in village-India. But Gandhi's individual dreams failed to become India's dreams. Despite the failures of Gandhi's followers to further develop ashrams as vehicles of community activism, the network of ashrams that developed was perhaps the major outcome of the ashram experiment. As centres of service, ashrams are needed as supportive communities for the village workers. The work done by the Gandhian ashrams may be insufficient in terms of actual and total liberation—sarvodaya—in village India, because the work done by some ashrams is merely "relief" rather than developmental and constructive. Some of the ashrams may like to maintain or conserve traditions, like home-spinning, other ashrams are "essentially creative and inherently constructive" (Bondurant 1965: 192) in their outlook and action programme. What is at work here is the utopian dialectic of conservation-revolution. Emergence of new alternatives is the end result of such healthy confrontation, constantly challenging the society to venture upon new goals and ideals.

Personal *metanoia* leading to social change, which is typical of Gandhian utopia, seems to be the key to the realizability or even to the possibility of utopia. Gandhi's ideals of ashram and village cannot and do not work as a piecemeal solution to India's socio-economic and religio-cultural problems. The down-to-earth personal agenda—commitment and dedication to the ideals and a firm hope in their realizability in some form and one's constant nonviolent satyagraha to its realizability in personal and social milieux—makes those ideals difficult, challenging, at times brands them as mere fantasy or wishful thinking. Because of the strong personal elements—personal commitment and sacrifice for sarvodaya—in Gandhi's utopian ideals, their effectiveness and realizability have less appeal to the public. There is a symbolic "dying" to one's selfish motives, interests and needs (limiting of needs) and a symbolic "rising" to the awareness of social reality of equality, liberty and fraternity and their practical realization. This process of "dying" and "rising" is at the centre of Gandhian utopian dialectics of progress and change. Gandhian utopia conceives that "change must ultimately stem from the heart" (Lal 1990: 239). This change from the heart, in other words, is self-realization—God realization too—which inspires a person to commit to the sarvodaya praxis, dedicate oneself to the welfare of *Daridranaryana* (God as the poor). The purpose of ashram experiments is also to bring people to this self-realization and the consequent personal dedication to sarvodaya and village reconstruction. In Gandhi's case, ashram experiments came as expressions of his self-realization and ashrams served as centres of this self-realization.

The reason why national policy-makers and planners in India fail often to give priority to village reconstruction and grassroots developmental projects may be the lack of public appeal mentioned above. Gusfield has an answer to this dilemma when he speaks about the transforming capacity of utopias. He says, "as Gandhi believed, it was necessary to have men who sought to change others by the force of their vision and the exemplary life with which they brought that vision into existence on a *small scale* (italics is mine). Such men do not seek to change laws, or create new institutions, but transform society by transforming attitudes and feelings in an essentially apolitical fashion: by an *utopian appeal*" (Plath 1971: 85) (italics mine). Gandhi's ideal ashrams and model villages constitute such an utopian appeal. Response to this appeal is "personal", "small", "hopeful" and "simple". It is easy to loose sight of the personal-simple-small-hope aspect of the Gandhian utopian ideal, especially when minds—personal, national and global—are set on "bigness", "speed", "anonymity" and "unhealthy competition".

We concluded above from our brief sketch of the history of utopia that "utopia has always existed and utopia will continue to exist as a vision to guide humankind to a better future". Model villages and ideal ashrams of Gandhi are the confirmation of the existence and continuity of utopia. As any society needs utopia to keep the momentum of progress in focus, Indian society needs model villages and ideal ashrams as utopian ideals in her particular journey towards sarvodaya.

Ideals and models are logico-ontological presuppositions of empirical realities. And in the dialectic of change—actual-potential, potential-actual—these models and ideals get realized and actualized in the present and in history. The existence of ashrams and villages is self-evident, especially in India. By proposing ideal ashrams and model villages, Gandhi reaffirmed the truth that an utopian ideal, i.e., hoping for a better future, is an inborn "human propensity". Gandhi's conception of the ideal village was comprehensive, encompassing economic, political, social and educational dimensions. His firm hope for *Ramrajya*, i.e., building a harmonious, humanely prosperous nonviolent social order on self-contained villages ("village republics") makes Gandhi an utopian visionary. The *panchayati raj* and village swaraj that Gandhi envisioned may never be realized in their entirety, but they are needed as utopian ideals and models for ashramic experimentation and for radical village reconstruction. Gandhi's own limited experiments with ashrams, the continuing ashram experiments by dedicated followers of Gandhi and the village reconstruction efforts by other Gandhians keep alive and operative the hope of realizing the Gandhian realistic utopia.

References

1. A number of them lived on the basis of self-help: building their own cottages, designing and making their own clothes, footwear, furniture, and above all else, growing their own food. Mark Thomson, *Gandhi and His Ashrams* (Bombay: Popular Prakashan, 1993), 12.
2. Between 1907 and 1914, Gandhi initiated a number of civil resistance movements which revealed the effectiveness of organised nonviolent resistance against a more powerful opponent.
3. These Trappist monks lived at Mariam Hill near Pinetown, sixteen miles from Durban. The monks lived in communities on the basis of voluntary poverty, self-renunciation and constructive work. *CW*, 1, 180-6.
4. Speaking of the significance of the name Phoenix, Gandhi says,"Its significance, as the legend goes, is that the bird Phoenix comes back to life again and again from its own ashes, i.e., it never dies. The name Phoenix...serves the purpose quite well for we believe that the aims of Phoenix will not vanish even when we are turned

to dust...At present our whole structure and behaviour are those of the bird Phoenix". *CW*, 10, 69.

5. Robert Payne, *The life and Death of Mahatma Gandhi* (London: The Bodley Head, 1969), 188-9 & 239-53. Some writers accuse him of being domineering and insensitive to the needs of his family and of obstinately refusing to heed the advice of his friends. See for example, Ashe Geoffrey, *Gandhi: A Study in Revolution* (London: Heineman, 1968), 88-9.
6. Passages from the *Bhagavad Gita* and the New Testament were read, English hymns were sung, and Gujarati *bhajans* (sacred songs) would be chanted by those who knew the language. A small hymn-book, printed and bound at the Phoenix Press, and containing eighteen hymns from many sources, had been specially arranged for the "universal service". Mark Thomson, *Gandhi and His Ashrams*, 63.
7. Santiniketan in Bengal was an experimental school founded on ashramic principles by Rabindranath Tagore at the turn of the century. Before the establishment of the Satyagraha Ashram in Ahmedabad, the group of relatives and co-workers from Phoenix who had departed from South Africa ahead of Gandhi in 1914 had been living in Santiniketan. Tagore welcomed Gandhi and invited him to take over supervision of the ashram school programme. Gandhi introduced a self-help programme at Santiniketan, but the new system clearly hampered the method of teaching followed at Santiniketan. The austerities introduced by Gandhi reduced the time and energy available for teachers and pupils to pursue literary interests and such activities as art, music and dancing, all of which were specially emphasised by Tagore. See Sasadhar Sinha, *Social Thinking of Rabindranath Tagore*, (Bombay: Asia Publishing House, 1962), 74-85; Kathleen M. O'Conneell, "Tagore as Educator: Setting, Strategy and Method"(Ph.D. thesis, University of Toronto, 1995), 143-47 and 283; see also M. Thomson, *Gandhi and His Ashrams*, 93-94.
8. "I had a predilection for Ahmedabad. Being a Gujarati I thought I should be able to render greatest service to the country through the Gujarati language. And then, as Ahmedabad was an ancient city of hand-loom weaving, it was likely to be the most favourable field for the revival of the cottage industry of hand-spinning. There was also the hope that, the city being the capital of Gujarat, monetary help from its wealthy citizens would be more available here than elsewhere." M. K. Gandhi, *Autobiography*, 329.
9. In response to a request by Rajkumar Shukla, a peasant from Champaran in Bihar, Gandhi visited the north Indian district to investigate the grievances of the villagers in the face of exploitation by British indigo planters. There he came in touch with the suffering

of people: dietary deficiencies, insufficient clean drinking water, illiteracy, poor sanitation, lack of medical care etc.

10. In Gandhi's view, the so-called "liberal" pattern of education introduced by the British reinforced divisions and compounded inequalities which plagued Indian society. "It has sapped the energy of the nation, it has shortened the lives of the pupils. It has estranged them from the masses, it has made education unnecessarily expensive. If this process is still persisted in, it bids fair to rob the nation of its soul." *Young India*, 5 July 1928.
11. Gandhi persuaded Kalelkar and J.B. Kripalani to take charge of the project, and under their guidance it became a working proposition. Kalelkar introduced spinning, weaving and other manual crafts into the curriculum in order to make the students more village-minded. A Mahavidyalaya was established as a constituent college of the Vidyapith. Under the charter of this institution of higher learning a new academic degree was created equivalent to a "Bachelor of Rural Science". Mark Thomson, *Gandhi and His Ashrams*, 162-63.
12. Gandhi expected young men and women to sublimate their sexual urges merely by taking a vow, the practice of which was confined usually in the Hindu tradition to male ascetics able to live as hermits away from the company of women. Evidently many potentially dedicated community workers were confused and disillusioned by Gandhi's precept that human being could choose sex or service, but not both. Mark Thomson, *Gandhi and His Ashrams*, 125.
13. When Gandhi learnt that Harijans who skinned carcasses were not paid, but ate the carrion as their reward, he determined that the job be put on a cash basis. He arranged training classes for tannery, shoe-making and other leather manufacture. Thus the Harijans at Sevagram learnt to make much more money from the industry.
14. Dinkar Desai, of the Servants of India wrote that "the basic craft is given such predominant place in the Wardha Scheme that it loses its real educational value. The predominance is so pronounced that craft teaching is sure to degenerate into the worst form of child labour." Dinkar Desai, *Primary Education in India* (Bombay: Servants of India Society, 1938), 78-81; also cited in Mark Thomson, *Gandhi and His Ashrams*, 239.
15. In October 1937, a small conference of educationists met at Wardha to discuss the plan of education Gandhi had been propounding in the columns of *Harijan*. The conference appointed a committee of educationists with Dr. Zakir Husain as its chairman, to prepare a detailed syllabus. Their report, which embodies what is known as the Wardha Scheme, or "Basic National Education", was submitted

to Gandhi on 2 December 1937. *Harijan*, 30 October & 11 December 1937.

16. Arun Gandhi, "Gandhi Ashrams: No Gandhian Spirit", *The Illustrated Weekly of India*, 97 (1 February 1976): 17. It is a view shared by others. Evelyn Wood, writing on the failure of "neo-Gandhians" to communicate Gandhi's ideals to the people, wrote of his own attitude to Sabarmati and Sevagaram: "To be frank, he (the author) must admit that the lunatic fringes of the Sabarmati and Sevagram Ashrams repelled him so intensely that, much as he loved, admired and enjoyed working with Gandhi, he avoided the ashrams as far as it was possible to do so", *Gandhi Marg* 4 (April 1960): 122.
17. "... we have taken a basic approach to sarvodaya..." Dwarako Sundrani in his letter to me dated 19-8-1991. Dr. Baikuntha Pandey, during the personal interview with him said that the non-formal education programme sponsored by the ashram has brought new life and new hope into the lives of thousands of villagers in and around Bodhgaya.
18. See the "Annual Report" (*Varshik Prativedan*) 1988-89 and 1990-91, published from Khadigram, Munger, Bihar, in Hindi. See also Erica Linton, *Fragments of a Vision: A Journey through India's Gramdan Villages* (Varanasi: Sarva Seva Sangh Prakshan, 1971), 32-41.
19. Gandhigram, in Dindigul District, in the state of Tamil Nadu, India, was founded by late Dr.(Mrs.) T.S. Soundram. Shri Devandra Kumar considers Gandhigram the Sevagram of the South. Devendra Kumar, *Four Phases of Human Progress* (Gandhigram: Gandhigram Press, 1985), 1.
20. In my interview with Rev. Jesudasan, S.J., he came through as a convinced Gandhian. Besides his active involvement in rural reconstruction, he also tries to give shape to "A Gandhian Theology of Liberation." See I. Jesudasan, S.J., *A Gandhian Theology of Liberation* (New York: Orbis Books, 1984).
21. Some of the techniques evolved by CSV are: scientific handling of the rock bee; utilization of the trunk of banana plant for making into pulp, paper boards and other pulp products; steam cooker using only one handful of charcoal for cooking a full meal for one family; parabolic solar reflector; production system of the blue green alga-spirulina (which is highly nutritious human food to fight malnutrition among children and the weak); a hand-flush, manure-giving rural toilet... See, *Science for Villages*, Nos.145-148 (July, August, September, October, 1991): 21.
22. India's uniqueness lies in the fact that though it is a country of villages (78% to 80% live in its villages) it has a well-developed city

civilization with its urban complexes of industry and commerce, science and technology etc., and where the rural-urban economies could be made complementary. A solution to the exploitative and unjust system seems to lie in an economy of ecological balances, conservation of non-renewable mineral sources, more and more self-expression and psychological satisfaction in all human endeavours, economic equality and social justice and closer human contact with each other and the living nature surrounding us.

23. "His ability to exploit hitherto untapped political resources propelled him to the leadership of the freedom struggle...Gandhi's plea that true freedom would not come from political independence alone but from sustained and constructive social change, fell on deaf ears..." Mark Thomson, *Gandhi and His Ashrams,* 266.
24. "Instead of having graceful hamlets dotting the land, we have dung-heaps. The approach to many villages is not a refreshing experience. Often one would like to shut one's eyes and stuff one's nose; such is the surrounding dirt and offending smell". M. K. Gandhi, *Constructive Programme: Its Meaning and Place* (Ahmedabad: Navajivan Publishing House, 1948), 15.
25. Gandhi never visualized an ideal village in the city because for him village occupied the cnetre of the social order he envisaged, and also because for him the heart of India beats in India's villages. Even so, two (realistic utopian) possibilities emerge for the rural-urban Indian scenario. One is that the present slum set-up ("bustees") in the cities may be treated as villages in a modified sense and "urban village" reconstruction programmes may be introduced, as is done in rural villages. Secondly, helping the city poor to improve their standard of living through meeting their "basic needs" is basic sarvodaya praxis of total liberation.
26. "The life of Mahatma Gandhi provides a concrete model of a hermeneutic circle, in which the interiority and liberation mutually encounter in an open ended process of experiments. His involvement with the Freedom Movement and his commitment to *satyagraha* throw new light into the experiences of the *Upanishadic* seers...The Gandhian experiments inspire us to conduct our own experiments in our struggle for liberation in the India of today. It is in this context that the action groups and the ashramites who are searching for alternatives are called to collaborate and create the path of liberation with interiority." Xavier Irudayaraj, "Interiority and Liberation", in Felix Wilfred, ed., *Leave the Temple: Indian Paths to Human Liberation* (Maryknoll, New York: Orbis Books, 1992), 124.

Five

Continuation of Legacy

Gandhi abhorred dogmatism because it takes away the provisionality and evolutionary nature of his ideal. Hence he was also against any sect or cult built in his name. He wrote: "there is no such thing as "Gandhism", and I do not want to leave any sect after me. I have tried in my own way to apply the eternal truth to our daily life and problems" (Gandhi 1961: 3-4). But Gandhi lives today through his philosophy and teaching. Sarvodaya ideal being one such vision that is in a process of realization, this chapter concentrates on the "face-lift" sarvodaya has undergone through the leadership of Vinoba Bhave and Jayaprakash Narayan during the years after Gandhi's death. Vinoba and Jayaprakash, more than most others, have put sarvodaya on the map.

The *bhoodan-gramdan* (land-gift, village-gift) movement brought a new dimension to the earlier Gandhian constructive programme and brought the concept of sarvodaya into focus. Though Vinoba advocated the politics of *loka-shakti*, no one looks upon him as a politician but as a "spiritual revolutionary." Jayaprakash Narayan, J.P. as he was often called, on the contrary, is the intellectual exponent of the politics of sarvodaya. While Vinoba stood for "mild experiment" (Fox 1989: 168). J.P. believed in *sampurna kranti*, i.e., "total revolution". The focus of our discussion of Vinoba and J.P. is sarvodaya as an utopian ideal in process of (practical) realization. Therefore, it is important to keep in mind, at this stage, the strength and weakness of sarvodaya, namely, the experimental nature, infinite possibility of interpretation and application, and its dynamic scope for ongoing development.

New Face of Sarvodaya

The vehicle for the development of the theory and practice of India's nonviolent revolution[1] has been the sarvodaya movement, which is the direct descendent of Gandhi's constructive programme and of the institutions and persons involved in it. After Gandhi's death, a first conference of constructive workers was held in March 1948. It was decided to form a rather loosely structured fellowship of *lok sevaks* (servants of the people), called "Sarvodaya Samaj", i.e., Society for the Welfare of All. The purpose of this Samaj was also to unite the various organizations of constructive Gandhian work formed either during his life time or immediately after his death. As a result, four organizations with specific target groups and field work joined hands in the Akhil Bharat Sarva Seva Sangh (All India Association for the Welfare of All), established in 1949. There were others, like the Harijan Sevak Sangh, Kasturba Memorial Trust, Gandhi Smarak Nidhi, Gandhi Peace Foundation etc., among which there were a variety of informal connections, though a unified approach was still missing.

Liberation from foreign domination was not the sole aim of Gandhi's "Independence Movement", as is clear from his sarvodaya vision, which is total liberation or welfare of every human being in all aspects. Independence obviously gave more freedom to Indians; at the same time, it placed on them the responsibility of building a new nation. In the post-independent disillusion of India—over massacre of Hindus and Muslims, rehabilitation of a flood of half-starved refugees, poverty of the masses, the land hunger of the landless...—need was strongly felt for pursuing Gandhi's vision and for charismatic leadership. Under such circumstances, Vinoba Bhave opened up a new vision to the whole country.

Mild Experiment

Born into a Brahmin family in Maharashtra in 1895, Vinoba, encouraged by his mother, a devout Hindu, had shown early signs of an impulse towards self-realization (or God-realization) through the traditional path followed by sannyasis in India—one sign being his taking the *brahmacharya* (celibacy) vow at the age of ten. He was deflected from pursuing the well-worn path of the sannyasi in 1916, when — with his nationalist sympathies aroused by Gandhi—he joined the Gandhi Ashram at Sabarmati, at the age of twenty-one. For the next forty years, Vinoba devoted himself to spiritual studies and to various kinds of constructive work. Gandhi noted that Vinoba had never been in the limelight on the political platform. With many co-workers he believed that silent constructive work was far more effective than the already overcrowded political platform. Gandhi considered Vinoba as his spiritual heir, insofar as Gandhian Philosophy allowed for such a position at all. Gandhi had a very high opinion of Vinoba. He told C. F. Andrews in 1917, "He (Vinoba) is one of the few pearls in the Ashram. They do not come like others to be blessed by the Ashram, but to bless it, not to receive but to give" (*Gandhi Marg* January 1958: 64). Due to his discipleship and close association with Gandhi, Vinoba in his life and work has been inevitably linked with Gandhian thought. He never failed to pay tribute to Gandhi and admitted the influence Gandhi had on his life. Speaking of his relationship with Gandhi, Vinoba wrote:

> I rarely mention Bapu's name. Since others do it so frequently, it is but proper for me to desist from it. But my soul is witness to the fact that I am a child of his. I was a mere boy when I approached him in 1916. Since then I have lived under his sole sway and none other's. I have laboured a great deal to assimilate the ideas he has given us, the wealth of thought he has bequeathed to us from the beginning to the end. I can claim to have practised thoroughly the ideas he placed before us (Tandon 1981: 4).

However, a closer look at his thought reveals that he was an independent thinker in his own right. As Ishwar Harris puts it, "A Gandhian in his vision, yes indeed, but it was with a 'Bhaveian' twist that he implemented his ideas" (Diwakar and Agarwal eds. 1984: 1). His independence is very obvious in the *bhoodan-gramdan* movement.

The Bhoodan-Gramdan Movement

It was in the village of Poochampalli in Telengana District on 18 April 1951 that the idea of *bhoodan* (land-gift) was born: the landless untouchables had approached Vinoba and asked for his help so that they might be given some eighty acres of cultivable land, which they needed for their bare subsistence. Vinoba then thought "that perhaps a few men may obtain land that way, but it would not solve the problem. So I suddenly turned to the people of the village and asked whether there was somebody among them willing to give land to his brethren so that they may not die of starvation; and a man came forward and offered a hundred acres of land" (Koestler 1966: 301). Vinoba generalized this unique example and translated it into a national scheme of *bhoodan*, or land gift, whereby he hoped to solve the subsistence problems of the landless in India.

The Telengana incident, neither planned nor imagined, was a pleasant surprise to Vinoba and made him think that therein lay the potentiality of solving the land problem of India. This movement, which later developed into the *gramdan* (village-gift) movement, as Vinoba repeatedly said, was not a mere movement for equitable distribution of land. It was a further step towards establishing a sarvodaya society. Thus it became part of a comprehensive movement, sarvodaya. It took some time for Vinoba to sort out the place of *bhoodan* in the broader picture of sarvodaya activities. Once he determined that it was land-gift activity around which all sarvodaya activities could be woven and given the form of movement for the reconstruction of man and society, he never deflected from tackling the basic problem of land, which affected the life of some thirty percent of the population in the countryside constituting the agricultural landless labour class. He trekked the length and breadth of the country for land-gift for some 4,500 days, covering some 7,500 kilometres.

For Vinoba, the *bhoodan* movement was based on the fundamental presupposition that land belongs to God and that man is its steward. As a result, Vinoba criticized private ownership and believed in collective sharing of natural resources. He went as far as to say that those who claim the right to property are enemies of God. For Vinoba, the basis of the sarvodaya philosophy, of which *bhoodan* is one aspect (albeit Vinoba's own contribution), is belief in God as an absolute power and the conviction that the Absolute abides in each individual. There is no doubt that Vinoba saw the gift of land as a sign from God, indicating the way in which nonviolent social change could and should be pursued. Vinoba recounted on a number of occasions in later years what went through his mind after he received the first gift of land:

> That night when I went to bed I could not sleep. I was thinking over the event. What has happened to me today? A man came forward and donated a hundred acres of his land without any compulsion. Is there a sign from God in this?...I could not believe that people would offer that amount of land...But a voice from within myself told me that, if I doubt, if I do not put my faith in the power of love and God, then I must abandon my belief in nonviolence and follow the violent way...so, if you go begging in the name of God, you will get a response (Koestler 1960: 30).

The initial enthusiasm and goodwill of Vinoba, his fellow-workers and donors of land brought great success to the movement. During the first years, the initial target figures were far exceeded so that it was considered possible to gather all the fifty million acres Vinoba needed by 1957. The scale of expectation propelled the movement into an even more ambitious scheme. The achievement of the movement made JP remark that, "In India it is one of the biggest things that has happened since independence—*the* biggest thing, I should call it" (Narayan 1960: 32). Though the movement began as an individual activity of Vinoba, its success first in Telengana, where he secured 12,000 acres of land in fifty days, and then in the regions that lay between Wardha and Delhi, when the gift averaged about 300 acres per day, infused a sense of confidence in Vinoba as well as in the Gandhian workers associated with it, and also in those who were watching its progress. As Vishwanath Tandon observes, "Thus a personal activity assumed the form of a movement, reminding the people of the political movement of Gandhi. This was rather a very remarkable achievement for a constructive work movement".

The beginning of the *bhoodan* movement may look accidental, but, in an effort to underline the real meaning of *bhoodan* as a step towards a new caring and sharing society, Vinoba devised other *dan* (gift) programmes which include the following aspects:

> *shramadan* (gift of labour), i.e., the contribution of part of one's labour to certain sarvodaya project.

sadhandan (gift of things), i.e., subsidiary means of production, such as bullocks, to enable *bhoodan* donees to till their new land.

sampattidan (wealth-gift), i.e., the dedication of part of one's property or income to the Movement.

buddhidan (intellect-gift), i.e., the dedication of one's mental abilities and knowledge to the realization of sarvodaya ideals.

jeevandan (life-gift), i.e., giving of one's whole life and energy to the cause of the Movement (Ostergaard 1985: 16; Kantowsky 1980: 20).

Taken together, these *dans* signified that everybody had something to share with others; some might have more than others, but there were to be no "have nots". Of these *dans*, *sampattidan* was potentially the most significant because behind it lay Gandhi's theory of trusteeship, interpreted in a socialist way. In the words of a resolution of the Sarva Seva Sangh: "The basic principle behind *sampattidan yajna* is that such means of production as are not directly in the hand of the producers should vest in the society of village community...The one-sixth share now claimed leads to the recognition of the principle that any individual possessing property and wealth is not its owner but only a trustee holding them for the whole community" (Ram 1954: 492-93).

Vinoba takes the idea of *bhoodan* far beyond the narrow confines of gift of land and the distribution of land, to the realm of total gift of the human being to the welfare of the society. He therefore calls it *yajna* (religious sacrifice). In explaining the aims of *bhoodan*, he says: "This problem is not such that only the big landowners can take part in it. This is a *yajna*. In a *yajna* everyone should give. Therefore, all those who have land should give. Small owners, like Sudama, should give a little. But all should give" (Diwakar and Agarwal 1984: 50). Vinoba was able to comprehend the whole of humanity within his vision of *bhoodan* and the participation of every human being: "Nowadays everybody is giving land, and you should also give your share. If you have land, you should give some land. If you have wealth, you should give wealth. Wealth is not only money. Those who have books should give books; those who have time should give *samay-dan*;

those who have strength should give *shram-dan*;...But it should be the case that everyone has given" (Diwakar and Agarwal 1984: 51).

What was implicit in the idea of *bhoodan* was the more radical idea of *Gramdan*, gift of village. *Gramdan* grew naturally out of *bhoodan* as the case in which the whole or a major part of a village was to be donated by not less than seventy percent of the villagers, who were to relinquish their right of ownership of their lands in favour of the village. The village would be vested with a power to equitably distribute the total land among its families with a provision for revision after some intervals. *Gramdan* thus tried to accomplish a social revolution through communal decision, whereby individual ownership of land should be abolished altogether; the land is "villagized". The objective here was to make the village one family, in control of its own independent economy and polity. Once the landowners had made a gift of their private property to a village corporation, it would be managed to ensure the welfare of all. What happens in *Bhoodan* is that individual land donations are accumulated and then redistributed to the landless, but the concept of private ownership is maintained for both the givers and the receivers. But in *gramdan*, all the village land is to be pooled and vested in the community. In the words of Ostergaard, "the movement from *bhoodan* to *gramdan* represented a move from a basically individualist programme (and one which could be criticized for increasing the fragmentation of land holdings) to a basically socialist programme" (Ostergaard 1985: 18). Speaking of *gramdan* villages, Kantowsky observes that, "In such a village the landless labourer ceased to be a recipient of acts of charity and was elevated to the status of an equal among all the other members of the *gramdan* community. If that scheme had succeeded on a grand scale, then India would have made a great stride towards the Gandhian goal of village autonomy and village government. Such were the hopes of the mid-fifties" (Kantowsky 1980: 19).

Gramdan was introduced as the basis for establishing *gramswarajya* (village autonomy). Because of its more radical character, *gramdan* proved harder to promote than *bhoodan*. Nonetheless, by the early 1960s some 6,000 of India's 550,000 villages had accepted this concept, but most of these villages were small, very poor and confined to low-caste and tribal areas. But, by 1971, more than 168,000, or very roughly 30 percent, of India's villages had been pledged to *gramdan*.[2] *Sulabh* (easy) *gramdan* was introduced at this stage, as a modified or simplified *gramdan*. From then on, a distinction was made between ownership and possession. The new concept was much less radical than the original and gave significant concessions to the principle of private property. Though all land donated to the village was to be vested in the village community, up to nineteen to twenty percent of it could remain in the possession of the donors, who could pass it on to their heirs. The advantage was that *sulabh gramdan* prevented village land from passing out of the control of the community; the means of production were controlled by the villagers themselves and could not be taken over by outside capital. A village may be declared *gramdan* if 75 percent of the adults consent and if 75 percent of the landowners, owning at least 51 percent of the land, agree to make over their titles to the village assembly, consisting of all adults in the village.

This modified idea of *sulabhdan* proved successful; *gramdans* were no longer confined to marginal villages, and large areas of the country became involved in the movement. *Gramdan* grew into *blockdan*, to *Districtdan* and even to *Statedan*.[3] *Sulabhdan gramdan* movement was specially conducted in Bihar state under the personal guidance of Vinoba from 1965 to 1969. Of the 140,000 villages the Movement claimed to have reached in 1969, 60,000 were in the northern state of Bihar, where the movement had pooled a great deal of its efforts and resources. With nearly ninety percent of its villages covered, Bihar was proclaimed the first *Statedan* in India. In terms of statistics, much was achieved in regard to the *gramdan* idea, but it was largely on paper only. But before we come to an assessment of the movement, a few more observations are in order.

As a process of development, the movement has three distinct stages for the development of a village: 1. *prapti*, where land is acquired in favour of *gramdan* and the ownership of the donated land is transferred to the village assembly; 2. *pushti*, where village assembly is set up, land titles are legally transferred to the village assembly and the distribution of one twentieth of the land among the landless is carried out; 3. *nirman*, where development and social reconstruction of the village proceeds under the aegis of *Gram Sabha* (village assembly). But the process seems to have stalled on its way due to lack of leadership and shift of emphasis in the very programme. Vinoba retired to his Paunar Ashram, leaving a band of a few trusted workers to complete the process of *gramdan* in selected areas. The sarvodaya workers were more or less on their own and could not draw on the saintly image of their leader. Moreover, for him, rural reconstruction was secondary, whereas what mattered was the change of attitude, which would by itself lead to socio-economic results. For he wrote, "Let it be understood clearly that increasing agricultural production is certainly not the aim and object of *bhoodan* and *gramdan*. That would be only incidental. Its main object is to widen man's loyalty to the entire society" (Bhave 1957: 18).

Allied Activities

Though *bhoodan-gramdan* has been a unique and major innovative contribution of Vinoba to Gandhian sarvodaya, there are other allied activities in which Vinoba was interested. References have already been made to *dans*, such as *sampattidan*, *shramadan*, and *jeevandan*. Such activities made the *dan* programme total and comprehensive. The establishment of a *Shanti Sena* or Peace Force—an idea originally mooted by Gandhi—came to the realization through Vinoba. The *Shanti Sena* was set up to act as a nonviolent police force (particularly in the context of communal conflicts), though the response was not very encouraging. The movement continued to emphasize production of khadi as a village industry. Some other prominent programmes are *acharyakul* (association or family of teachers), *stri shakti* (women's-power), science for villages, nature cure, *kushta seva* (service of lepers), and cow protection. But none of these programmes, despite their ingenuity, captured the imagination of the public or excited as much interest as *bhoodan* did.

Reluctant Leader and Mild Experiment

In spite of his saintly character and worldwide reputation, Vinoba is not spared criticism. One major criticism that has surfaced from within the sarvodaya movement is that Vinoba lacked the dynamism of Gandhi. What they say is that Vinoba was primarily an ascetic, and not a social activist. Consequently, he could not provide a dynamic leadership to the Gandhian movement with which he was associated. This criticism may be a reaction by those who preferred the activism of JP over Vinoba. But one would agree with Indira Rothermund, that Vinoba was forced to function as a leader after the death of Gandhi. As he himself said: "Circumstances compelled me to come out and be audacious enough to be an initiator" (Diwakar and Agarwal 1984: 113). He was not willing to play the specialized role which calls for effective skills of a leader of an organization. He described *bhoodan* and *gramdan* as "people's own movement" and he withdrew from any further involvement and reverted to his original role of *rishi* (sage) of the old Indian tradition who withdraws to a forest at a ripe old age.[4] But this act of renunciation left unfinished and incompleted his work of building the *bhoodan* and *gramdan* movement into model villages of mutual co-operation and independency. Vinoba had hoped to bring about a rural communitarian society, characterised by harmonious relations between the individual and the group and participatory democracy. But he was not able to accomplish much in this regard, nor did he succeed in institutionalising the concept of trusteeship or communalization of land.

The basic outlook of Vinoba on politics, organization, leadership, satyagraha etc., seems to have affected the momentum of *bhoodan-gramdan* radically. In the *bhoodan* movement, Vinoba refused to create a party, but did welcome the support of the parties as were already in existence. Vinoba believed that the *bhoodan* programme, as a precursor of a far reaching comprehensive social change, would receive ready support, as it was already on the agenda of the political parties, and that all the parties would readily join it. Detached from power and party politics, Vinoba wanted to develop a new consensual "politics of the people." This new politics is one of truth and love and the hallmark of this new politics is consensus. In developing the new politics, i.e., *lokniti* (politics of the people) as distinct from *rajniti* (politics of the state), Vinoba's position was in line with the advice given by Gandhi to constructive workers in 1947: "We should keep ourselves aloof from the old kind."[5]

As *lokniti* suggests, Vinoba's view is basically anarchistic. Echoing the sarvodaya-swaraj concept Vinoba asks:

> If I am under some other person's command, where is my self-government? Self-government means ruling your own self. It is one mark of swaraj not to allow any outside power in the world to exercise control over oneself. And the second mark of swaraj is not to exercise power over any other. These two things together make swaraj—no submission and no exploitation (Bhave 1962: 13-14).

In his gradualist anarchism, Vinoba visualizes three distinct stages: first, a free (i.e., independent) central government; second, the decentralized self-governing state; and third, pure anarchy or freedom from all government. With political independence, India entered the first stage; and with the introduction of *Panchayati Raj* institutions, it is proceeding into the second stage. The third stage, the stateless society, will develop to the extent that the people become more self-reliant and create new self-governing institutions. Two questions remain to be answered at this stage: 1. Why did Vinoba advise that the movement be officially halted in 1974? 2. How does one interpret Vinoba's highly ambiguous stance during the Emergency?

Vinoba seems to have been more interested in the number of pledges than in the programme's actual performance. He emphasised the act of changing minds alone, but he failed to distinguish between lip-service and true change of heart. Satisfaction with pledges gave way to a sense of failure. Faced with the "politicalization of the movement"[6] (Vinoba discouraged any such move; instead, he stood for "the spiritualization of politics"), Vinoba seemed to shift his emphasis to the propagation of *devanagari* as the script for all of India's different languages, cow protection, the *acharyakul* (organization of teachers) etc. He appeared to place the *devanagari* programme above that of *gramdan*: "We have done a lot through *bhoodan* and *gramdan*, but as the population increases and the land gets further fragmented, the people fifty years hence will forget all about our work through *bhoodan*. But if the *nagari* script is adopted and gains currency in

India through our efforts, that will be a permanent monument to our work. I find this (work) more revolutionary." Vinoba's shift of emphasis from *bhoodan* to *devanagari* may be seen as his acceptance of defeat, i.e., "failed experiment", or as his failure or unwillingness to pursue the real cause. Because there is no great deal of revolution in promoting *devanagari* script; and also it is hard to find any link between *bhoodan* and *devanagari*. At this stage two case studies deserve our attention, namely those of P. Mukherji[7] and of T. K. Oommen.[8] Mukherji concludes the analysis of one single village in these words, "a parasitism of the rich adherents to the *bhoodan* ideals became evident, village hospitality was exploited by outsiders and visitors, the Sarvodaya leadership became apathetic and idea of *gramdan* lost its emotional appeal for most of the villagers". Oommen made a careful study of four successful *gramdan* villages in Rajasthan. Summarizing his findings in the economic sector, Oommen concludes that, "there exists hardly any difference in the pattern of land-holding between the experimental *gramdan* and control villages. A substantial portion of land in *gramdan* villages is concentrated in the hands of the upper class who are usually the upper castes too, in the case of caste-Hindu village" (Oommen 1972: 98). The village democracy that Vinoba hoped to establish, in *gramdan* villages, "is a far cry in *gramdan* villages". Vinoba himself retired to his ashram and by 1972 reconciled himself to the fact "nothing spectacular could be expected from *gramdan* in the foreseeable future" (Kantowsky 1980: 86). Finally, in 1974, Vinoba recognized the de facto situation of the previous five years and advised that the movement be officially halted.

The original concept of *bhoodan*, which developed into *gramdan*, was revolutionary in its nature because it involved the radical, essentially socialist idea of the "villagization" of land. And *gramdan* had been the basis of the concept of *gramswarajya*—a new polity, economy and society. But the movement's involvement in the Government's programmes, such as "20- point programme", where the distinction between *bhoodan* land and other land available for distribution, such as Government surplus land, mostly resulting from ceiling legislation, was effectively obliterated, considerably reduced the revolutionary nature of the movement because *bhoodan* was supposed to be an act of love, signifying a change of heart on the part of the donor; it could in no way be equated with land compulsorily acquired by the Government.

Vinoba avoided altogether the "confrontation tactics" of Gandhi's experiment; as a result "he allowed himself, without protest, to be used by politicians (especially Mrs. Indira Gandhi)". Vinoba's highly ambiguous stance during the Emergency and his tacit support of the same may be attributed to his predilection for the Nehru family,[9] Vinoba's disagreement with JP and Vinoba's inability to judge the craftiness and vested interests of politicians. He did confess his ignorance of politics when he wrote that,

> "...Baba [i.e., Vinoba himself] doesn't know anything about politics. Gandhi knew that Baba was ignorant of politics, but still had faith in him. Gandhi himself had possessed faculties for both politics and spirituality. He publicly declared that Nehru was his political heir. The position of spiritual heir he reserved for Vinoba. For the last 25 years I have tried to act according to the duty placed on me. I don't claim total success. Only God knows how successful I have been, but Baba has tried his best to promote spirituality. So Baba will not give his opinion about political matters" (Ostergaard 1985: 147).

We said at the beginning of this section that Vinoba's problematic understanding of politics, organization, leadership and satyagraha did not help the growth of the *bhoodan-gramdan* movement. Vinoba was of the view that satyagraha should be interpreted positively to mean nonviolent assistance in right thinking rather than negatively as nonviolent resistance to evil. His approach was not one of confrontation but "gentle, gentler, gentlest". Vinoba did not accept Gandhi's satyagraha as an appropriate mode of action today. He even went to the extent of saying that, "Satyagraha as practised by Gandhi has therefore become quite irrelevant in India". Thus Vinoba's view on satyagraha made *Bhoodan-gramdan* experiment a very 'mild experiment'.

Vinoba was against setting up an all-India organization. However, he was not altogether against setting up some organisation; what he opposed was centralised organizations, those organizations which issued orders and handled centralized funds. Organizations could function at the local level, that is, on a decentralised basis, giving opportunity to local workers to meet, discuss, exchange ideas and plan action. Vinoba has been criticized for his lack of emphasis on organization. It is a fact that he underplayed the importance of organization, with the result that his movement remained limited in appeal to individual land-owners. Though thousands of landless people listened to and were convinced of Vinoba's pronouncement that land, like water, light and air, is created by God and therefore should be available to everyone, the movement failed to give an organized expression to it. As one of the critics pointed out,"the deprived and the landless had no realization of their own strength through the movement". Instead of creating organizations of the landless with a view to branching off into the more militant aspects of nonviolence, Vinoba preferred gentler mode of nonviolence and finally retired from action altogether.

Whether Vinoba visualised the institutional permanence of the *bhoodan-gramdan* movement is debatable. As a "reluctant leader", he failed to produce institutional permanence, though, as a spiritual revolutionary and "spiritual heir" to Gandhi, his thrust was the change of attitude, which would by itself, he hoped, lead to socio-economic results. JP's observation appears quite valid:

> "Vinobaji did something miraculous for some years. It appeared as though a new Gandhian process of social change and reconstruction had emerged. But after his stormy *Bhoodan* experiment not even a mild breeze blew, not to speak of mighty 'storm' of *Gramdan*, *Gram-Swarajya* or any other constructive experiment. Later he withdrew into his inner self, and started the experiment of 'action' in the form of 'inaction'" (Narayan 1977: 83).

Vinoba and Sarvodaya

Bhoodan (and other *dan* movements) stem from the ideal of sarvodaya and they are concrete manifestations of sarvodaya. *Bhoodan-gramdan* movement brought a new dimension to the earlier constructive programme, and brought the concept of sarvodaya into focus. Vinoba continued what Gandhi started, building a nonviolent social order, and his *bhoodan* movement was undertaken in the same spirit in which Gandhi promoted his various campaigns. Basically his innovations were of a spiritual nature because, as a "spiritual revolutionary", Vinoba represents "the priestly wings of sarvodaya",[10] and consequently he tried to spiritualize politics, economics, science, religion, etc. He also wanted to revitalise the Gandhian idea that all land belongs to God (Gopal), that is, the concept of a communitarian society built upon a nonviolent order. And the *bhoodan* movement revealed that he could, at least initially, establish a rapport quickly and effectively, with what is often described as a "revolution through love".

Vinoba was not merely a follower of Gandhi. He subjected Gandhi to a slow process of "refinement", which has been viewed by some as the unfolding of the "essential Gandhi". The spiritual metamorphosis of the social, political, economic, and the overall character of the essential Gandhi at the hands of Vinoba, as Devadutt puts it, "is too subtle and too sophisticated, too imperceptible to be easily identified and hence precisely and concretely articulated"(Diwakar and Agarwal 1984:176).

Ostergaard is of the view that Vinoba represents "revolutionary Gandhism"[11] because "*Bhoodan* was, and *Gramdan* now is, only part of the immediate programme of a movement which aims at a 'total revolution', a complete revaluation of values, leading to the establishment of the Sarvodaya society not only in India but also, ultimately, throughout the world" (Ostergaard 1971: 148). But the situation now is different. There are some Gandhian organizations which undertake *gramdan* work. But this is only project work. It is not a movement. *Bhoodan* has either got institutionalized in the form of voluntary agencies sustained by foreign aid or has been handed over to state administration.

Vinoba, as a reluctant leader, failed to accept the confrontational element inherent in the Gandhian vision. This enabled the Congress to own Vinoba; as a result he came to be known as the "*sarkari*" or "government" Saint. Vinoba's refusal to admit confrontation made the voluntary land reform movement impractical because it depended on well-meaning or bad-faith resolution, and it had no means by which to transform this consciousness into revolutionary social practice. In sum, through *bhoodan-gramdan*, Vinoba took Gandhi's sarvodaya vision in a mild reformist direction. This takes us to look at sarvodaya from a different perspective: total revolution.

From Socialism to Sarvodaya

Born in 1902, Jayaprakash Narayan (JP) was, as he later put it in his *Prison Diary*, "bitten by the bug of revolution" during his high school days. His ideological progression is remarkable. As a student he changed over from science to sociology, as a political worker he started with Marxism and arrived via socialism at a sarvodaya interpretation of reality. Since the very beginning of his career as a politician, JP faced the problem of rapid social change. For him massive and rapid social change and revolution were synonymous. "In fact, it is the search after revolution that took him first to Marxism, then democratic socialism, later Sarvodaya and finally to total revolution" (Prasad 1992: xiv).

JP's political life began in 1921, when he walked out of Patna College to follow Gandhi's call for non-cooperation with all institutions aided by the British Government. He went to the United States in 1922 to continue his studies. In the United States, JP came in close contact with Marxist circles. He returned to India in 1929 as a convinced Marxist with his master's degree in Sociology from the University of Ohio. The first step on his return to India was to contact Gandhi. Though initially he disagreed with Gandhi's philosophy of nonviolence, he joined the Congress and in 1934 the Congress Socialist Party was founded as an integral part of Congress, with JP as its General Secretary. JP's disillusionment with the communists began when he found out that the Indian communists, under the instruction from Moscow, decided to oppose the national liberation movement led by Gandhi. At this stage JP did not give up Marxism, but tried to rationalise his thinking within the framework of Marxism.[12] But eventually he moved away from Marxism toward a Gandhian position.

It was in the "Quit India" movement of 1942 that JP first clearly emerged as a national leader. His militancy, the spectacular escape from jail, and his organization of underground resistance, helped to make him a national hero. JP's concept of free India goes way beyond the mere "transfer of power" from an alien to a native ruling class, to the building up of a "*gram raj*, a self-governing village, a village republic". Such villages should be "centres of struggle and resistance during a revolution and would constitute the bricks with which the structure of the free Indian republic could be built" (Narayan vol.1 1978: 86). His move towards Gandhian position appears ever more pronounced when he wrote in "Means and End" that "the greatest thing he (Gandhi) taught us was that means are ends, that evil means can never lead to good ends and that fair ends require fair means" And elsewhere JP says, "We have all been deeply influenced by Gandhiji. I do not mind saying that I have been rediscovering him lately and understanding him. I believe he was one of the most vital thinkers of the modern age. I am sure there is a great deal to learn from him today and also tomorrow. I am sure, had he lived, he would have evolved further, as he ceaselessly did, and we would have today a clearer picture of the method he would have followed to achieve the goals that we jointly share..."(Narayan 1964: 80). Then in "Socialism and Sarvodaya" JP commented that the Sarvodaya plan[13] "is a concrete programme of basic social revolution...it is the first attempt to picture concretely a new social order..."

In an article published in 1953, JP develops his suggestions and maintains that the Gandhism alone can offer a genuine solution to India's problems since, "both socialism and communism are faced with failures. Communism, where it is victorious, has ended up in state capitalism and dictatorship, the very antithesis of communism. Socialism, in western Europe at any rate, has lost its pristine idealism and become only a parliamentary or legalistic creed. Thus, both the method of violence and parliamentary action have failed. Gandhism offers the third alternative of revolution by nonviolent mass action" (Narayan vol.1 1978: 160).

Vinoba's initial success in obtaining *bhoodan* hastened JP's conversion to sarvodaya. At the annual sarvodaya conference held in Bodhgaya in 1954, he announced that he would devote all his further time and attention to the movement and its philosophy. He became the movement's first "*jeevandani*", the first to dedicate his whole life to this single cause. He felt that there was no work of greater importance than *bhoodan*. As a result, in 1952 JP announced his decision to renounce power politics. JP's sojourn for twenty years in the *bhoodan* movement may appear to some people as typical of "a man in the wilderness." But he was in fact searching for an answer to his questions. JP hoped that the *bhoodan* movement might, with the collaboration of Government agencies, resuscitate the village and its economy because he felt that the village rather than the city should become the centre of the national effort. This, however, proved to be wishful thinking on his part. Neither the Government nor the *bhoodan* movement, with its method of persuasion and conversion, was able to create a situation suitable for development.

Total Revolution

Since Vinoba had retired to his ashram by 1969 and was no longer actively involved in the day-to-day direction of the sarvodaya movement, JP became its unofficial leader and spokesman.[14] JP's leadership was of different nature. Though the *bhoodan* movement got some initial success through the charisma of Vinoba and later JP, the movement could not survive as an ongoing revolutionary process. There obviously was difference of emphasis between Vinoba and JP right from the beginning, which eventually led to differences over strategy and tactics and a rift in the sarvodaya movement.

It is to be noted that the concept of total revolution is not something novel. Karl Marx had used this term more than a century and a quarter before JP popularized it.[15] The idea of total revolution was implicit in many of Gandhi's writing and speeches (Ganguli 1973: 145-261). "Gandhi was indeed", as G. Ostergaard observes, "in modern parlance, an advocate of total revolution" and "a social as well as political revolutionary; he did seek radical changes in the structure of society, polity and economy and also in the modes of thinking and individual behaviour" (Ostergaard 1985: xv1-xvii). Vinoba expanded the idea further. He declared in 1951: "My aim is to bring about a threefold revolution. First, I want a change in people's hearts, secondly, I want to create a change in their lives; and thirdly, I want to change the social structure" (Tandon ed. 1981: 91).

It has been aptly observed by G. Ostergaard that JP's movement for total revolution was "a continuation of the preceding movement for non-violent revolution through *bhoodan* and *gramdan*." JP was indeed fully justified in remarking on one occasion: "There is hardly any difference between sarvodaya and Total Revolution. If there is any, then sarvodaya is the goal and Total Revolution the means. Total Revolution is basic change in all aspects of life. There cannot be sarvodaya without this" Ostergaard 1985: 404). Without using the term "total revolution", JP himself had been emphasizing since the mid-forties the need for a social revolution which would not merely bring about a change in the structure of society, but also an improvement in the character of the individuals comprising it. After he joined the *bhoodan* movement, he laid particular stress on it. In an article published in 1969 he also used the term "total revolution" to describe the objective of the sarvodaya movement in India. Referring to the *bhoodan* and *gramdan* programmes, he wrote: "Gandhi's nonviolence was not just a plea for law and order, or a cover for the status quo, but a revolutionary philosophy. It is indeed a philosophy of a total revolution, because it embraces personal and social ethics and values of life as much as economic, political and social institutions and processes" (Prasad 1972: 2). Thus, total revolution is a further extension of Gandhi's thought on socio-economic problems and technique of change in the context of the modern social reality. JP's contribution is, as Nageswar Prasad says, "that he discovered something quite unconventional in Gandhi. This unconventionality was most pronounced in Gandhi's thinking on the social and economic arrangement of the society, as also in the whole technique which he developed to attain his ultimate goal. It is this unconventionality of Gandhi which gives him a distinctive revolutionary character. The author of the total revolution only tried to build upon it with a great emphasis on specific components of the whole concept" (Prasad 1992: 141).

Sampurna Kranti: An Utopian Vision

We have stated above that total revolution (*sampurna kranti*) is a further extension of the Gandhian approach to social change and that social change in the Gandhian scheme is a very comprehensive and inclusive term. Gandhi meant not only a change in the social framework but a qualitative change in the behavioral-attitudinal and psychic texture of the individual also. JP developed Gandhi's "unconventional wisdom and technique" into a total revolution. "Total revolution" as a concept was put forward by JP in the wake of the Bihar movement (1974). And as the movement acquired greater intensity and coverage, the concept assumed greater content and form.

Like Gandhi, JP recognised the necessity of change in the individual, the individual who takes upon himself the task of changing society. "One of the unstated implications of satyagraha would be self-change, that is to say, those wanting a change must also change themselves before launching any kind of action," JP says in his *Prison Diary 1975* (Narayan 1975: 34). In this lies the key to JP's total revolution. JP's faith in the change of the individual as the precondition for change in the society was a Gandhian approach. But JP believed that the transformed individual and the social framework are to interact so as to lead to an all-round change. A process of simultaneous change, therefore, is the *sine qua non* of a society expecting a revolution.

Speaking further on the components of total revolution, which is to be brought about by peaceful means, JP says that it "will embrace all aspects of individual and social life". According to JP, such a revolution will be "a combination of seven revolutions: social, economic, political, cultural, ideological or intellectual, educational and spiritual. Though it was impossible for JP to go into the details of such a revolution, he offered a vision for the future, a new agenda for social reconstruction and the birth of a new humanity. But JP's picture of the new social order remained broadly the same as he depicted in *A Plea for Reconstruction of Indian Polity* (1959) and *Swaraj for the People* (1961). What he pleads for in *A Plea for Reconstruction of Indian Polity* is a model for democracy, based on an integrated concept of society and providing the fullest possible scope to the individual to participate in the management of his affairs, without the intermediation of political parties. In JP's ideal society, parliamentary democracy will be replaced by a new kind of polity which he describes as communitarian or partyless democracy. This new polity, however, is part of the larger project of social construction, which in fact is the re-creation of human community, where people live together in meaningful relationship of sharing, participation and fellowship. The new socio-political system must be so devised as to provide a congenial environment for fostering these qualities.

JP followed the same line of Gandhi's thinking in his approach to the constitution of power from the base. What led him to support the *panchayati raj* experiment was the approach to decentralisation of power. He strongly felt that the political structure of the community must correspond to its social structure. The base of the new social organization will be the local or primary communities—"self-governing, self-sufficient, agro-oriented, urbo-rural local communities". He thus advocated the creation of formal structures at the village, block and district levels. Most of the power, in his scheme, rests with these structures. These structures are governments at their respective levels in the sense that they are independent in the sphere of operation and yet interdependent in relation to other tiers. In such a polity, participation of the largest number in the decision-making process is guaranteed. He also made recommendation with a view to reforming the present system of election: election should be so conducted that political parties do not play any role in them up to the district level; even at the state and national levels, the candidates must be selected by the people themselves and not by parties; he raised the issue of the corrupting role of money in the entire election process; the constituents must be vested with the power to recall a legislator if he or she does not behave.

The political structure sketched above will require for its base a new kind of economic structure. JP was of the view that social revolution basically included economic revolution[16]—and, in a sense, "social equality meant economic equality and equality of status". Though JP recognized the social reality underlying the caste configuration in Indian society, total revolution, he believed, should break the caste barriers. It must evolve new norms and practices, replacing those based on caste. For example, inter-caste dining, abolition of dowry system, archaic marriage rules and regulations, all must enter the area of total revolution.

In his new conception of economy, he pleaded for

decentralised economy and the need for limiting of wants. Otherwise, "the need for more and yet more will lead to mutual conflict, coercion, spoliation, war and also a system of production that will be so complex as to bind democracy hand and foot and deliver it to a bureaucratic oligarchy." Speaking on the economic relationship, JP recorded in his *Prison Diary 1975*, that, "(it) includes technological, industrial, and agricultural revolutions, accompanied by a radical change in the present pattern of ownership and management" (Narayan 1975: 95-96). The new economy JP envisions is to develop an agro-industrial community based on an organic blending of agriculture and industry.

When JP constantly used the term "total revolution" during 1974-79, he made a few additions to the above picture. He stressed the need for change in the political and economic system and pleaded for the abolition of the caste system and the abolition of dowry. One another important emphasis was on the need for a radical transformation of the educational system. Because, in his vision of cultural revolution, a new ideological and thus an intellectual revolution was inevitable. Any change in the belief system or value system of society begins with an intellectual revolution. By far, the most important variable in the cultural change is education. Revolution in education was one of the most salient demands of the agenda of the Bihar movement. In his critique of the existing system of education, he thinks that the system is extremely elitist in character leading only to a meaningless proliferation of institutions. According to JP, education must be a powerful element of social change and it should be closely linked to national development. It should be biased in favour of the masses rather than in favour of the upper classes. It must create a new kind of awareness among the submerged and weaker sections of our society, so that they feel fully integrated with the society. He, therefore, suggested more active participation of educational institutions in social service and national development programmes; and introducing more adult education and non-formal education and universalization of elementary education for all children.

Praxis of Revolution

What mode of action did JP propose to usher in a total revolution? In JP's scheme, the usual constitutional devices are not adequate to bring about radical changes in the society. From 1973-74 onwards, JP began to advocate openly a basic change in the whole system so as to overcome the malaise into which the country had drifted during two decades of Congress rule. JP's dream was to go beyond the passive revolution accomplished by independence from Britain and make it an active revolution, a fundamental reorganization of Indian society, along what he understood as Gandhian lines. For JP, this revolution was well within the scope of sarvodaya vision, for he says,

> Those who think that sarvodaya is made up of goody-goody people, who no doubt talk about nonviolent revolution but do not mean it seriously, are in for a surprise. I cannot remain a silent spectator of misgovernment, corruption and the rest, whether in Patna, Delhi or elsewhere. I have decided to fight corruption...to fight for a real people's democracy (Ostergaard 1985: 76).

This revolution could not come about simply through democratic elections, legislation, and government administration. It would require "people's direct action," in the form of peaceful disobedience and non-cooperation—"satyagraha in its widest sense."

It was educated young people in particular whom he asked to play an active part in the struggle to come.[17] Encouraged by students' agitation in Gujarat,[18] he expressed the view that the country was fast heading for a new revolution: "There is another 1942 movement in sight to change the course of history." JP accepted the leadership of the Bihar students' movement from which a struggle against the State government soon emerged. He turned the Bihar movement into an experiment of total revolution. The agitation in Gujarat was non-partisan, whereas Bihar student politics had long been closely associated with party, faction and caste politics of the State. But JP's condition for accepting the invitation to guide and direct the student movement was that it should be non-partisan. The pledge for the movement's activists, expressed a belief in "a non-political people's movement", and

JP's programme for building up the Jan Sangharsh Samitis (Peoples Struggle Committees) stipulated that care should be taken to see that all office-holders were non-political.

The student movement was not to be confined to the students but to be grown as an all-India movement. JP had deep belief in the endless strength of the people;[19] he therefore suggested the formation of people's committees at the grass roots. These people's committees were conceived of as organs of people's power. They had a two-fold function: they were supposed to mobilize the energies of the people in constructive channels. It is in this constructive role that JP visualized a healthy interaction between the power of the people and the State. *jan shakti* (people's power) and *rajya shakti* (state power) are supposed to supplement each other. Yet another function for the people's committees is to resist the injustices and tyrannies of the State, individual, or a group of individuals. Non-violence, as an extra-constitutional weapon, therefore, was to be invoked. In JP's agenda, a system of people's administration was to be instituted at the village, *panchayat* and block levels.

Establishment of *Janata Sarkar* (People's Government) from the village upwards to at least the district level was in the scheme of JP as part of empowering the people. Dissatisfied with the present system of administration JP said:

> We have to snatch the initiative from the hand of the politicians, from the parliament and the legislatures and give it back to the people...Salvation will not come from the legislators. Salvation will not come even from the military or others. It will come from the people, if they follow Gandhi...The people should not think in terms of *Sarkar* as an organization separate from them. That the people are the government, they must realise this. People in villages and cities should manage their affairs... (Prasad 1992: 75).

Considered conceptually, *janata sarkar* assumes that in the ultimate analysis sovereignty vests in society. The elected representatives are trustees, because in the context of democracy the exercise of the right to vote means that the society decides to lend, not give, power to an elected representative for a specified period of time to implement a mandate. The *janata sarkar* cannot function if people do not have sufficient self-awareness and self-confidence. Therefore, *janata sarkar* should mean a movement to generate self-respect and self-confidence among the people.

Through the struggle committees and *janata sarkar*, the Bihar movement was trying to make people conscious of their rights and organize them to fight for their rights. But the formation of *janata sarkar* at the village, *panchayat*, and block levels, and a people's assembly at the State level could be interpreted as providing for "parallel government".[20] JP's attempt to consolidate the Bihar movement and to spread it to the rest of the country resulted in the imposition of the Emergency (1975-1977; JP was arrested on 26 June 1975): the total revolution had been, to all appearances, successfully repressed. (Declaration of national emergency was an extreme political weapon used by Mrs. Indira Gandhi, the then Prime Minister of India, to terminate the experiment with total revolution.)

Journey Unfinished

JP's total revolution is a grand vision of society. It is based upon Gandhi's basic ideas and it envisages unconventional methods of changing society with altogether unconventional techniques. A close study of JP's philosophical journey reveals that he was concerned with comprehensive social change which he, eventually described as "total revolution". Total revolution, therefore, is an all-enveloping process of change in the individual as well as in the society. JP's "ideas were an interesting blend of realism and utopianism" (Ostergaard 1985: 123). The realism was expressed in the acceptance of certain hard facts, such as the existence of political parties and their vested interests, in the relegation of partyless democracy to a distant future, and in the expectation that miracles would not happen. There was a clear determination to move from "where we are at" and there was the desire to consider carefully "the next step".[21] The utopianism was expressed, in the vision of a radical, participatory democracy, partyless democracy and in the idea of "people's power".

As there is no "finished product" in the dynamics of change, the goal of total revolution is distant and extends into the future of realizability. Total revolution is an ongoing process; "As with partyless democracy so with several other goals of Total Revolution like the abolition of the caste system or the end of all exploitation of the weaker sections by the stronger sections of society, the struggle for Total Revolution is bound to be a very long one. The final end may never be achieved. Indeed, there is nothing like a final end. For Total Revolution of JP's conception is a permanent revolution and is expected to move on towards higher and higher goals" (Prasad 1992: 17). If partyless democracy seems utopian, can anything different be said about the stateless society which was the ideal of both Marx and Gandhi? As Gandhi once said, there is no harm, but every good in an ideal being idealistic. For, in trying to reach that ideal, humanity is likely to come nearer and nearer to it without ever completing the journey. Though his revolutionary experiment with Gandhian utopia precipitated division and rift in the sarvodaya fold, JP was convinced that total revolution was within the frame of sarvodaya vision.

Changing Sarvodaya

Sarvodaya ideals and the thrust of the movement have gone through remarkable changes under the leadership of Vinoba Bhave and Jayapraksh Narayan. Such changes have led sarvodaya through the mild experiment of *bhoodan*, introduced by Vinoba, to total revolution, initiated by JP. The history of the sarvodaya movement after Gandhi's death indicates that the movement was clearly manipulated by political parties. Vinoba, from the beginning, claimed to be against any move to "politicalise the movement" and discouraged any such move. Yet Vinoba's tacit support of Indira Gandhi and her Emergency seems to contradict "the spiritualisation of politics" he advocated. (One of Mrs. Gandhi's tactics was to re-authorize Vinoba as the spiritual head of the Gandhian sarvodaya movement and to get him to speak out in favour of the Emergency.) When JP and his movement of total revolution became a threat to the apparently autocratic regime of Indira Gandhi, she began to question publicly and attack the personal integrity of JP and accused him of creating a rift in the sarvodaya movement. But, for JP's part, he never wanted to create a division in sarvodaya. For, JP explains, "...There is complete understanding between me and Vinobaji and each of us knows the limits of our agreement and disagreement. While there is a vast area of agreement between us, there is a tiny area not so much of disagreement as of differences of approach to certain problems. There is absolutely no difference in matters of principles...(Ostergaard 1985: 77). But the two leaders operated on different wave-lengths; the styles of action were markedly different. The pre-mature withdrawal of Vinoba from active involvement into *maun* (silence), change of priorities in favour of propagation of the *devanagari* script and, later, cow protection and his tacit support of the Emergency (when his vow of silence ended in December 1975, Vinoba labelled the ongoing Emergency an "era of discipline" *anushasan parva*), contrasted sharply with the revolutionary nature of JP's movement, with its political involvement in opposition to the ruling Congress party. This division of priorities precipitated the formation of a "JP wing" and a "Bhave wing" in the sarvodaya movement. This was inevitable in the context of Indian political consciousness.

The sarvodaya movement had been known for its quality of uniting people and keeping equidistant from all political parties. But the Bihar agitation placed sarvodaya in opposition to the Congress party and the CPI (Communist Party of India), and identified it with the Jana Sangh, the RSS (Rashtriya Swaymsevak Sangh),[22] the SP (Socialist Party), the CPM (Communist Party-Marxist), etc. According to the CPI, the real forces behind the movement were the RSS, the Jana Sangh, and the Ananda Margis—all indiscriminately labelled "fascist": the rest, including JP's sarvodaya group, were mere facade. Mrs. Gandhi herself reflected the CPI line. The nature of the relationship between the movement and the main opposition parties in Bihar is a highly disputed subject.[23] JP's association with Jana Sangh was an open issue and he did pay tribute to the Jana Sangh as the best organized party in India.[24] JP wanted the movement to be partyless, although he was aware that it was difficult "to mix the two that are unmixable", that is, to have a partyless agitation with political parties participating in it. His ideal was that the opposition parties had to merge their identities in the movement, although ultimately they would find reward in it. But mention is to be made that, "...he (JP) has repeatedly shunned power and preferred to devote all his time to the Sarvodaya movement". The vast support given by the people of Bihar to JP, it was felt, was precisely because of JP's non-party character, because he was identified as a "*lok nayak*" (leader of the people), rather than as an ordinary politician, and "the success of the Bihar movement and the support it received throughout the country had been based on JP's reputation for integrity, distaste for power politics, and, above all, his insistence that the movement was a revolution in the sense of challenging the *status quo*, for changing social values, not another form of party politics" (Ostergaard 1985: 200).

Nonetheless, both Jana Sangh and the Akhil Bharatiya Vidyarthi Parishad (All India Students Association), which had RSS connections, were to become compelling forces in JP's experiment with total revolution. JP's dilemma[25] was that he needed the support of the opposition parties to advance with the movement of the total revolution, although in principle he did not approve of power politics, sectarian thinking and militant religiosity. But he did acknowledge and even defended the participation of the Jana Sangh and the RSS in his movement for total revolution.[26] On the other side, Hindu nationalist associations publicly endorsed JP's movement. For instance, Balasaheb Deoras, the supreme guide of the RSS, likened JP to both Gandhi and the recently deceased RSS chief Golwalker. Nana Deshmukh, former RSS pracharak and a power in the Jana Sangh at the time, was all with JP through the mass protest.

Moreover, JP was instrumental in the formation of the Janata Party, though he may have believed that there was protection against rampant Hindu nationalism in the four-party coalition. On the day that Morarji Desai was sworn in as Prime Minister of India, all the Janata MPs assembled at Gandhi's *Samadhi* at Rajghat and solemnly swore "to complete the work initiated by the *Mahatma*" (Ostergaard 1985: 284).

In the midst of this process the utopian ideal of total revolution was appropriated and utilized in the interests of the party politics and sectarian appeals. JP no longer directed the movement; instead the parties and associations that constituted the movement directed JP. Even Gandhian thinking became transformed into Hindu nationalism by 1980. Indeed, G. Ostergaard suspects that the policy of the Congress government (under Indira Gandhi and afterwards her son Rajiv) aimed to split the Gandhian voluntary movement. Thus, in effect, there became a Congress-oriented Gandhian movement (Vinoba's and his successors') and an opposition-oriented Gandhian movement (JP's and his successors'). The political leanings of the leaders of the Gandhian movements and the political manipulation of a supposedly apolitical movement by politicians left many Sarvodayaites disappointed and confused. The movement lost much of its appeal as a liberative movement of the oppressed, of the least and the last; in other words, a great deal of its *antyodaya* and *sarvodaya* nature was lost. On the contrary, the movement became subordinated to Hindu nationalist ideology.

A strong Hindu vision and a nationalism that conceives of India as a Hindu nation seem to be growing in India since the early 1980s. Hindu nationalists maintain that "Hinduism is in danger" and that India is endangered, too. They feel that their nation grows weaker under Muslim, Sikh, Untouchable, and Christian demands. As a result, new associations embracing Hindu nationalism have sprung up and existing ones have grown more militant. Communal violence and confrontation have become commonplace now. Mushrooming of communal organizations (Hindu, Muslim and Sikh) appears to be a common phenomenon today[27]. *Hindutva-vada* (Hinduness doctrine) of militant Hindus advocates a Hindu India ("*Hindia* for the *Hindians*", in the words of R. Fox), in which all Indians are, or should be, Hindus in essence. In the words of Kuldip Nayar, "The Rashtriya Swayamsevak Sangh, which controls the Bharatiya Janata Party and the Viswa Hindu Parishad, has never believed in secular principles. It has always stood for the Hindu rashtra, to the exclusion of Muslims" (Nayar 1992: 2). Elsewhere Nayar says, "The Hindus, who constitute 82 percent of the population, could have had a Hindu rashtra when India won freedom. But they preferred secularism because that was the ethos of the national movement led by Mahatma Gandhi" (Nayar 1993: 2).

With its extreme militant and fundamentalist outlook, such Hindu nationalism does violence to Gandhi and Gandhian thinking, it may be argued. As R. Fox explains, "Hindu nationalism embeds Gandhian thinking by intertwining certain strands of it and discarding others. The resulting Gandhism is a new but insubstantial growth, weaker and smaller than the original, in which utopia is not sustained. No longer is there a comprehensive view of Truth and God and revolutionary experiment that supports a set of particulars for India: personal discipline, decentralization, village development, indigenous and primary education, and other aspects of what once was Gandhian utopia..." (Fox 1989: 248-49). But then the question arises, is there any hope for a new Gandhian utopia?

The experiments of Vinoba and JP are indications of infinite possibilities to which sarvodaya as an utopia is open to. The individual *metanoia*, which is the key to any meaningful social change in Gandhi's vision of change, was very strong in the original *bhoodan* movement, but Vinoba did not seem to insist on this individual aspect of *bhoodan*. Again Vinoba avoided altogether the "confrontation tactics" of Gandhi's experiment and was contented with "mild experiment", which in some way ended in failed experiment and ideology. Even so, the utopian ideal of equal access to natural resources—"land, like water, light and air is created by god and therefore should be available to everyone"—remains valid. In spite of Vinoba's so-called revolutionary agenda—"My aim is to bring about a threefold revolution, first, I want a change in people's hearts, secondly, I want to create a change in their lives; and thirdly, I want to change the social structure" (Tandon 1981: 91), — *bhoodan* could not survive as an ongoing revolutionary process. Vinoba retires from action and started the experiment of 'action' in the form of 'inaction'.

JP was of the view that Gandhism offers the third alternative of revolution by nonviolent mass action and he maintained that the Gandhism alone can offer a genuine solution to India's problems. As a vision of the future, JP's total revolution is comprehensive and opens itself into a wide spectrum of new possibilities—a combination of seven revolutions: social, economic, political, cultural, ideological or intellectual, educational and spiritual. JP offers hope and vision for the future, a new agenda for social reconstruction and the birth of a new humanity. JP's ideal society may never be fully actualized, but by proposing partyless democracy and a re-creation of human community where people live together in meaningful relationship of sharing, participation and fellowship, he not only critiques the past and present but transcends the present into a hope-filled future. Decentralization of power and right distribution of power are radical ways of recognizing "people's power" (*jan shakti*).

The birth of a new humanity with inter-caste dining and abolition of the dowry system, archaic marriage rules and regulations, is an ongoing vision or utopia in the socio-religious fabric of India. So too the decentralized economy, need for limiting wants and development of an agro-industrial community based on an organic blending of agriculture and industry may not become active and effective too soon. But JP was well aware of the importance of intellectual revolution as the fundamental requirement of any change and hence he promoted education that is biased in favour of the masses rather than in favour of the upper classes.

In his praxis of revolution, JP kept in focus the utopian dialectic of healthy tension and change. In his words, "I have decided to fight corruption...to fight for a real people's democracy" (Narayan vol.4 1978: 115-17). *Janata Sarkar* and *Jan Sangharsh Samitis* are realistic expressions of JP's belief in endless strength of the people and the need to empowering people for total revolution and sarvodaya.

The political leaning of the leaders of the Gandhian movement, the political manipulation of the sarvodaya movement by politicians, the strong Hindu vision and nationalism that conceives India as Hindu nation and the engulfing nature of Hinduism in general appropriated the sarvodaya movement to the Hindu nationalist ideology. There is need to free sarvodaya from such narrow ideology and sectarian thinking and to reorient it to a global scenario. There is need to develop the concept of *lok sevak* (=someone who identifies himself or herself with the oppressed and is willing to help them in the nonviolent struggle for liberation), *gramswaraj* and *lokswaraj*, non-party alternative (basic to sarvodaya revolution of finding an alternative for the existing system), people's party, people's power and people's candidates etc. The possibilities, that Gandhian utopia offers do not merely call for a regeneration of Gandhian utopia, instead, offer a challenge to those who have placed their faith in the status quo and to those who stand for radical changes to the status quo. The unfinished journey of Gandhi, Vinoba, JP and other followers of the Gandhian ideal of sarvodaya social order is an ongoing journey to a realistic utopia of sarvodaya society. The "open endedness" of Gandhian utopia thus leads us to new realms of infinite possibilities. Among these are theological implications of sarvodaya and its ecological impact, which we shall discuss in our concluding chapter bringing sarvodaya to its global relevance.

References

1. The term "nonviolent revolution" was in fact coined by Gandhi, although he did not use it often. Two of his references to it may be noted. In one, he declared: "Some have called me the greatest revolutionary of my time. It may be false, but I believe myself to be revolutionary- a nonviolent revolutionary." (The quotation was used as the epigraph to an article by JP in *The Times* (London), 13 October 1969. In the article, JP argues that Gandhi's nonviolence "is indeed a philosophy of total revolution, because it embraces personal and social ethics and values of life as much as economic, political and social institutions and processes." In the other, Gandhi wrote: "A nonviolent revolution is not a programme of 'seizure of power'. It is a programme of transformation of relationships ending in a peaceful transfer of power." *Harijan*, 17 February 1946.
2. R. N. Mishra, *Bhoodan Movement in India* (New Delhi: S. Chand, 1972), 108.
3. A "block" is a group of about 100 villages in the government's Community Development Programme. *Blockdan* is defined as a block in which 85 per cent of the revenue villages or 75 per cent of the population (excluding that of the towns) have declared for *Gramdan*. A "district" is one of the 300 or so main administrative units of the country. (There are nearly 500 districts in India according to the statistics of 1990). See *Manorama Year Book, 1990* (Kottayam, Kerala: The Malayala Manorama Company Ltd., 1990). *Districtdan* is achieved when all blocks in a district have met the condition of *Blockdan*. *Statedan* refers to a state in the Indian Union in which all districts have met the condition of *Districtdan*.
4. Nehru once said, "I regard Vinoba as a great *Rishi* in line with Indian tradition. We may not realize this today, but history will reckon him as an eminent *Rishi*, equal to any of the *Rishis* who

sanctified this land in the past." Shriman Narayan, *Vinoba: His Life and Work* (Bombay: Popular Prakashan, 1970), 330-41.

5. This does not imply that nonviolent revolutionaries should not seek the cooperation of political parties and of the state in promoting the programmes of the movement, even though, when the new society was fully developed, there would be no role for parties and no place for the state. It also did not imply that nonviolent revolutionaries should not intervene in elections. Their intervention, however, was to be strictly non-partisan and educational, helping to inform voters of their rights and duties and beyond that, trying to persuade them to practice the new politics, for example, by getting *gram sabhas* in a constituency to put up a single agreed candidate who would thus be returned unopposed. See G. Ostergaard, *Nonviolent Revolution*, 16.
6. To some sarvodaya workers, the close involvement with the Government of a movement which was committed to voluntary action and which was seeking to achieve a stateless society appeared to be a radical contradiction. But JP on joining sarvodaya had carefully explained that renunciation of "power and party politics" did not mean renunciation of politics as such. In line with Gandhi's advice that constructive workers should seek to guide political power and mould the politics of the country without taking power them selves, JP therefore continued to take a keen interest in political affairs. Certain sarvodaya workers had apparently gotten tired of wandering in the political wilderness of Grand Alliance, which had been so decisively beaten in the recent election. Other sarvodaya workers, however, feared that identification of sarvodaya with such politics would besmirch the fair name of Gandhism. See G. Ostergaard, *Nonviolent Revolution*, 42-50.
7. Partha Mukherji, "*Gramdan* in Village Berain: Sociological Analysis," *Human Organization*, 25 (Spring 1966): 33-41; See also D. Kantowsky, *Sarvodaya*, 82.
8. T. K. Oommen, *Charisma, Stability and Change: An Analysis of Bhoodan-Gramdan Movement in India* (New Delhi: Thomson Press, 1972).
9. He regarded Nehru as his 'brother', trusted him, believed (contrary to much evidence) that Nehru was earnestly trying to carry on Gandhi's work, and, though critical of many aspects of his policy, always expressed particular criticisms in studiously moderate terms. This general attitude towards Nehru he transferred to Mrs. Gandhi, who made use of the relationship to her own political advantage. Vinoba, it was reported, was left with the impression that the Prime Minister's (Mrs.Indira Gandhi's) views were those of a

member of Sarva Seva Sangh. "Baba thinks that, although she is a party politician, the mental attitude and values of Indira Gandhi as a person are near to his own." Devendra Kumar Gupta, on the "Indira-Vinoba Dialogue," *People's Action*, February 1974.

10. Iswar Harris, in explaining the spiritual dimension of Vinoba's thought, says that, "Jayaprakash Narayan and Vinoba Bhave represent the prophetic and the priestly wings of *sarvodaya*. Both received their inspiration from Gandhi...In Vinoba, the priestly nature dominated the prophetic. Priests have pastoral concerns, love of humanity, and sacrificial spirit. Prophets are reformers, decisive in action, and bold in decision-making. As a *sannyasin*, Vinoba had developed what I have termed a 'priestly nature.'... Vinoba gave a total freedom to the prophetic element in *sarvodaya* to thrive and make its impact. He did not hinder its growth, nor did he speak against its prophet." Iswar Harris, "The Spiritual Dimension of Vinoba Bhave's Thought", 17.
11. G. Ostergaard differentiates three types of Gandhism: 1. **Political Gandhism**: represented by the khadi and Village Industries Commission and the official programmes of Community Development and Panchayati Raj. 2. **Institutional Gandhism**: finds expression in a number of independent and voluntary organizations, such as Kasturba Memorial Trust and the Harijan Sevak Sangh which are concerned to promote particular aspects of the Constructive programme... 3. **Revolutionary Gandhism**: expressed mainly through the Sarva Seva Sangh. In their general approach to the problems of social reconstruction, those workers associated with the Sangh have come closest of all to carrying on Gandhi's work along the lines he suggested in the last years of his life. See G. Ostergaard, "Indian Anarchism: The Sarvodaya Movement", in *Anarchism Today*, 147-48; see also *Nonviolent Revolution*, 4-5; and Buddhadeva Bhattacharya, "Vinoba Bhave—An Ideologue of Sarvodaya: A Marxist Appraisal", in *Vinoba*, 133.
12. JP wrote, "the socialist movement in India must evolve its own picture of socialism in the light of Marxist thought, of world history since Marx's death and of conditions in this and our historical background. Marxism is a science of society and a scientific method of social change that includes social revolution. As such there can be no room for dogmatism or fundamentalism in Marxist thought.... If Marxism is a science, Marx could not have propounded ultimate truths, but only made approximations to them." Bimal Prasad, ed., *A Revolutionary Quest: Selected Writings of Jayapraksh Narayan* (Delhi: Oxford University Press, 1980), 119-20.

13. In December 1949, two hundred constructive workers met in Wardha and endorsed the programme which was published on 30 January, 1950, as "the Sarvodaya Plan".
14. Vinoba's announcement to return to his ashram in Paunar, near Wardha suggested that he was relinquishing his close direction and guidance of the movement, but it left unclear who, if anybody, was to lead the movement. As Ostergaard opines, "If there was to be one successor to Vinoba, JP was the obvious candidate." Ostergaard, *Nonviolent Revolution*, 29. But Vinoba did not designate JP as his successor. Vinoba foresaw some form of "collective leadership". A survey of sarvodaya activists made in 1965 showed clearly that most of them regarded JP as the best person to provide leadership and guidance to the movement in the event of Vinoba's death. See G. Ostergaard and M. Currel, *The Gentle Anarchist* (Oxford: Clarendon Press, 1971), 216-20.
15. K. Marx, F. Lenin and V. Lenin, *On Historical Materialism* (Moscow, 1972), 83. Writing in the *Poverty of Philosophy* (1847), Marx remarks: "Meanwhile the antagonism between the proletariat and the bourgeoisie is a struggle of class against class, a struggle which carried to its highest expression is a total revolution."
16. "Social" in the Marxian sense also includes "economic". Social revolution, therefore, is basically an economic revolution in the Marxian formulation. Nageswar Prasad, "Total Revolution and Social Change," 150.
17. In an appeal to Youth Power, in December 1973, JP asked persuasively: "Will our youth continue to look on idly at this strangulation of the democratic process at its very birth? Surely there cannot be a more important issue which could move the youth power in India to the national arena and play a decisive role in establishing the primacy of the people and securing their victory over power of money, falsehood and brute force." Quoted from G. Shah, "Revolution, Reform or Protest? A Study of the Bihar Movement", *Economic and Political Weekly*, XII (1977) Nos.15, 16 and 17.
18. Students' agitation at Ahmedabad in December 1973 against the decision to raise cafeteria charges by 41 per cent soon acquired a wider dimension. A month later, students all over Gujarat came out against the inept, inefficient, and corrupt government. By the middle of March, the Gujarat government gave in to the pressure from the students, and it dissolved the state assembly. It is not certain exactly what influence JP had on the students in Gujarat. JP's biographers Bhattacharjea and Vasant Nargolker, see no link

between JP's appeal and the student's struggle in Gujarat. See Vasant Nargolkar, *JP's Crusade for Revolution*, 82-83. According to Brahmanand, it was only after JP's appeal- "Youth for Democracy"- to the students in 1973 that they started a movement against food shortages, rising prices, and official corruption. See Brahmanand's "Search for an Ideology", in JP's *Towards Total Revolution*, Vol. 1, cxxvi.

19. "...The people is like Hanuman. There is endless strength in the people. It is a question of expressing this strength; of organising it; of giving this strength a voice; of giving it limbs...the people appear to be absolutely unconscious; dead! and the same people the very next moment perform unimaginable feats—thrones topple, systems perish, governments change, society gets transformed. The people do all that." Quoted in G. Ostergaard, *Nonviolent Revolution*, 276-77.
20. Even such an enthusiastic supporter of JP as Nargolkar doubted whether it would be possible to set up a system of parallel government without resorting to violence and without organizing armed revolutionary guerrilla bands. "A nonviolent attempt to set up a parallel government is in theory not impossible" he suggested, but, " in practice...it would presuppose a tremendous amount of constructive work among the masses, a well developed sense of unity, solidarity, discipline and cooperation amongst the rebelling people, wise leadership at the lowest level...the programme of the establishment of a nonviolent parallel government is bound to remain only embryonic or even conceptual". Vasant Nargolkar, *JP's Crusade for Revolution* (New Delhi: S.Chand, 1975), 141.
21. "All utopianism is related to reality; no utopianism is unrelated to reality. Utopianism derives its model from reality itself, not by an indiscriminate imitation of reality". Amlan Datta, "JP and Social Change", in N. Prasad, ed., *JP and Social Change*, 234. See also G. Ostergaard, *Nonviolent Revolution*, 123.
22. The *Rashtriya Swayamsevak Sangh* (RSS), a Hindu nationalist association began in 1925 as a cultural association working for Hindu revitalization. As a cultural association it avoided political engagements but worked hard to develop grass-root cadres of committed and disciplined Hindu nationalists. Highly militant in its philosophy of action, it claims to be an organized force in India like the Army...(The Jana Sangh party, from its inception in 1951, was closely associated with the RSS). R. Fox, *Gandhian Utopia*, 218-220.
23. The opposition parties rallied quickly in support of the movement's political demands and, at an early stage, formed a coordinating

committee to express this support. Some observers maintain that the Jana Sangh was the main political force within the movement from the very beginning and that it increased its grip as the months went by. Narayan Desai, the Shanti Sena leader who acted as one of JP's principal lieutenants, maintains that the role of the political parties was never strong and that it became increasingly less important as the movement developed. JP stated that it was not possible to keep political parties from coming into an open mass movement, but that he kept the party influences low and gave the movement a non-party character. See JP, *Prison Diary 1975*, 56-57; see also G. Ostergaard, *Nonviolent Revolution*, 114.

24. Addressing a large contingent of the party's members in Delhi, JP declared that the party was neither fascist nor reactionary, adding, in words later to be used against him, "but if it is to be wrongly branded as such, I am also a fascist or reactionary". G. Ostergaard, *Nonviolent Revolution*, 163.
25. Some commentators see JP as a puppet of the Jana Sangh and RSS, and others see him as taking over an ongoing social movement and harnessing it to the so-called fascist right. The fact of the matter is, as R. Fox opines, "clearly, J.P. out of necessity initially accepted the support that existed 'on the spot' in Bihar. As the movement went on, he found he could not revolutionize the students away from their previous affiliation, and instead, just to keep the movement going, he would have to come closer to affiliating with these organizations himself". R. Fox, *Gandhian Utopia*, 223.
26. To put it in JP's own words, "To my knowledge, there is no Anand Margi in any of the Sangharsha Samities... As for RSS, it too is not formally part of the movement, though I daresay there are many members participating. The Bharatiya Jana Sangh is certainly a constituent... the Vidyarthi Parishad, too...If all these add up to the RSS being a part of the movement, I have no quarrel with it". *Ibid.*, 223.
27. Government estimates in 1987 placed the number of communal organizations (including Hindu, Sikh, and Muslim associations) at more than five hundred, whereas in 1951 they numbered less than a dozen. They had estimated membership in 1987 of several million. In 1961 only 61 Indian districts (out of 350) experienced communal violence, but by 1979 there were 216 districts affected by it, and the estimate for 1987 was 250 districts. See R. Fox, *Gandhian Utopia*, 237.

Six

Recapitulation and Promise: Sarvodaya as an Ideal for Liberation Theology and Ecology

A. Recapitulation

Gandhi visualized a society which he called by various names, like *Ramrajya, swarajya* or sarvodaya. The ideal society which he wanted to establish was totally egalitarian and based on fundamental concepts of truth and non-violence. What we have discussed in the preceding chapters of this book clearly points to the fact that Gandhi's vision of the future transcends the immediate future, conventional socio-economic and political structures, traditional developmental models and mere national independence. The realistic alternatives Gandhi offered as sarvodaya lifestyle, we call realistic utopias. This vision is holistic through-and-through in its completeness and integral in its unification. Gandhian utopia — vision of life — is essentially futuristic, a hope for the future. This utopia, i.e., vision for the future, is embedded in his autobiography, his philosophy of life, *The Story of My Experiments with Truth,* which is radically future-oriented. Gandhi's experiments with truth challenge the "Absoluteness" of B(b)eing and Reality in general and of cultural traditions and systems of thought in particular. Gandhi thus introduced the notion of "already and not yet" into his utopia, an ideal that is in the process of being realized. It may be difficult to explain the nature of the final product or to work out all the details of this process, but the process has begun and it is ongoing and never ending. All concerns of Gandhi and all preoccupations finally aim at sarvodaya: the welfare of all.

Sarvodaya is both an ideal — vision — and a praxis — action

programme for the welfare of all. These two functions of sarvodaya are complementary: as an ideal it sets sublime goals and inspires people to engage in an action programme to achieve the goals. Those goals are being realized, i.e., realistic utopias. We have employed the category utopia to understand and explain the effectiveness of sarvodaya as a dynamic entity-cum-process because it helps us to make fair and reasonable assessments of the effectiveness of sarvodaya (and of Gandhi's work overall) in the past and, even more importantly, of how it enables us to identify the continuing potential of Gandhian sarvodaya as an utopian ideal within India (for social, economic and political reform and liberation theology) as well as on a global scale pertaining to sustainable development and ecological lifestyle.

What makes sarvodaya of Gandhi realistic utopia is the presence of provisionality, open-endedness, untiring hope in the future, creativity, explorative and experimental nature that make any ideal a realistic utopia. It is again the dialectic of known and unknown, possible and impossible, actual and potential at work in sarvodaya ideal, which make it an ongoing programme of progress and change. We have picked a few actual and possible sarvodaya realizations, namely in the area of economics and ashram-village experiments to show that, while people-centred economy is an ideal Gandhi thought suitable to India, Gandhi's village-oriented communal living experiments were based on sarvodaya vision, which believes in a praxis that starts at the grass-root level and grows into total development of human beings. It is beyond any dispute that Gandhi visualized and worked for self-sufficient villages, economics with a human face, priority for the human person as opposed to mere material progress. Gandhi advocated a holistic economics which rejects the principles of self-interest and avarice as the foundation of economic activities and relations and replaces them by "social affection" or concern for others as the true basis of economics. It was authentically human hope that inspired Gandhi to transcend and transform the existing, often unjust, economics into the horizon of an economics with a human face which becomes concrete and real in genuine sharing. It is, in other words, economics of love waiting to be realized, and so it is utopian economics in that sense.

The ashram-village experiments Gandhi initiated and those that continue in some form as Gandhian experiments give concrete expression to Gandhi's ideal and praxis of sarvodaya. For Gandhi such ashram experiments and ideal village experiments were ideals like Euclid's line. Model villages and ideal ashrams of Gandhi are the confirmation of the existence and continuity of utopia. As any society needs utopia to keep the momentum of progress in focus, Indian society needs model villages and ideal ashrams as utopian ideals in her particular journey towards sarvodaya. The *panchayati raj* and village swaraj that Gandhi envisioned may never be realized in their entirety, but they are needed as utopian ideals and models for ashramic experimentation and for radical village reconstruction. The continuing ashram experiments by dedicated followers of Gandhi and the village reconstruction efforts by other Gandhians keep alive and operative the hope of realizing the Gandhian realistic utopia.

The ways Vinoba and JP tried to experiment with sarvodaya may have had their drawbacks. Even so, such experiments as *bhoodan* and total revolution stand as examples of new possibilities of sarvodaya experimentation and practical realization. Though the "mild experiment" of Vinoba in some way ended in failed experiment or failed ideology, the utopian ideal of equal access to natural resources—"land, like water, light and air is created by God and therefore should be available to everyone"—remains valid. So too, people's democracy, *janata sarkar* and *Jan Sangharsh Samitis* are realistic expressions of JP's belief in the endless strength of the people and the need to empower people for total revolution and sarvodaya. The unfinished journey of Gandhi, Vinoba, JP and other followers of Gandhian ideal of sarvodaya social order is an ongoing journey to a realistic utopia of sarvodaya society.

B. Promise

What brings sarvodaya to its global relevance is its theological implications and its ecological impact. In his sarvodaya vision, Gandhi projected a model for the India of tomorrow. Thinking, planning and acting in the context of a colonized India, Gandhi was immediately concerned with the independence of India from foreign domination; but his far reaching vision penetrated into the very soul of India. Sarvodaya, therefore, is a rising of every human being, welfare of all, freedom from all that makes any human being less of a human being. In other words, it is a total liberation. Gandhi gives a theology as well as methodology of liberation, which is universal in its scope and meaning and can be applied to the theory and practice of the liberation theology movement. Though the integral liberation which Gandhi envisaged for India is not fully realized, the method he evolved remains a potent and comprehensive, but under-exploited resource. Gandhi's commitments to liberataive praxis and identification with the exploited stem from his basic theology: Truth-realization or God-realization. Gandhi did not propound a theory of environmental protection or ethics, but Gandhi's sarvodaya-utopian mode of holistic discourse is appropriate for holistic-integrative approach to ecological issues. Gandhi visualized eco-villages, ecological living, i.e., life attuned to nature and an environmentally friendly technology. Through voluntary simplicity, small self-sufficient communities, people-centred development etc., Gandhi "initiated an invisible tide, a surge of new ideas and actions that might herald a truly Gandhian revolution in the world of today" (Ananthu 1991: 482).

Sarvodaya: A Model of Indian Liberation Theology

Quest for liberation is as old as human civilization itself. History holds in high esteem some of those who committed their lives to the liberation of the oppressed. Ideals of Moses, Buddha, Jesus, Mohammed, Marx, Gandhi and Martin Luther King inspire millions the world over to initiate, participate in and continue the process of liberation. The need for liberation is ever more urgent because of the oppressive tendencies of socio-economic, political and religious structures and systems. Victims of these oppressive structures cry for liberation. Societies or people in general, seem ordinarily to tolerate and live with such oppressive structures. But charismatic leaders and visionaries may become turning points in this respect. And, as liberator of the oppressed, Gandhi even declared that in the liberation of the oppressed lies the liberation of the oppressors as well.[1] Liberation is a pressing challenge in India today. It is a matter of delivering the lives of the masses of men, women and children from death, destruction and inhumanity. It is a question of survival for the least, the oppressed, the voiceless.

What direction should India follow in order to achieve the total liberation of humanity and of every human being is a complex question. There is no magic answer to this question, but one can suggest possible projects toward a solution. Throughout the history of India, various forces and movements of liberation have emerged. Buddhism represented in Indian social history a great movement of liberation from social stratification of caste. In modern times, the most widespread movement of liberation was the struggle for independence from the British colonial power. It is at this stage that Gandhi's contribution to the liberation of India becomes historical and relevant for the liberative praxis of today. Liberating ideologies and theologies, especially in India, draw from the Gandhian model. As Sebastian Kappen opines,

> In him (Gandhi) the Buddhist doctrine of nonviolence, a reinterpreted Hinduism, and the message of the gospel blended to form a powerful ideological weapon to fight colonial rule. It was the unifying power of religious symbols that enabled him to rally around him the peasant masses. He is second only to the Buddha in laying the foundation for a theology of liberation. His genius consisted in harnessing religion to liberative political praxis (Wilfred ed. 1992: 157).

In the words of Ishwar Harris,

> Gandhi gives us a theology as well as a methodology of liberation which is universal in its scope and meaning and can be applied to the theory and practice of the liberation theology movement. On the other hand, the Latin American movement can inform the *Sarvodaya* movement in India. Perhaps through a creative dialogue between the two movements, they can converse, converge, and convince each other on issues that are pertinent for human liberation. (Harris 1992: 464).

Gandhi, with his ideal of sarvodaya, sensed the inherent weakness and detected the seeds of destruction in modern society and its political and economic systems. Therefore he projected a post-modern society of small communities intended to safeguard freedom and independence. This vision of society is increasingly turning Gandhian ideals into an attractive alternative to the status quo.

Sarvodaya and Other Liberative Movements

There have always been reactions, both individual and group, to injustices and exploitations. Organized reactions often took the form of some movement. In the midst of the many ideologies and liberative movements that are at work in India, sarvodaya vision and its action programme offer a very concrete project for establishing a liberated humanity, a *Ramrajya*, the kingdom of God here and now. The emergence of many liberation movements in India indicates that Hinduism (the religion followed by the overwhelming majority of Indians) has been undergoing significant changes. The movements of the marginalized from within the Hindu fold have continued to challenge the caste system, its oppressive structures and discriminatory practices. The *bhakti* movement was one the best-known in the last few centuries. Its basic ideology is that no human group can be considered inferior or superior because of the work it does, as long as they are committed to devotion (*bhakti*) to God, before whom all are equal (O'Connell 1993). The Dalit movement is the result of searching for alternatives by the relatively powerless Untouchables, known today as *Dalits* (the oppressed). Ambedkar,[2] who dedicated his life to the liberation of the "untouchables" (Dalits i.e., oppressed) in India, focused his thrust of ideology and action on the powerless and despised castes. He advocated strongly the need on the part of the Untouchables to become politically empowered and get actively involved in exercising political power. Nationalism for Ambedkar was not simply emancipation from the external colonial power but liberation from internal oppression as well, which entailed the exorcising of the caste-spirit. This ideological orientation is continued by the Dalit Panthers, who struggle for the liberation of the Untouchables today. And then there are tribal movements.[3]

There were great religious and social reformers, like Raja Rammohan Roy (1772-1833), considered to be the father of modern India, Swami Vivekananda (1863-1902), who stressed the *karma marga*, or the way of action and gave birth to the Ramakrishna movement, M.G. Ranade (1842-1901), who gave primary importance to social reform with religious basis, Aurobindo Ghosh (1872-1950), who gave a religious legitimation to the political freedom and economic development of India.

There are other ideologies[4] and groups active in India whose goal is a liberated India. We sight a few just to highlight the place of sarvodaya as a liberating ideal and movement. But none of these systems of thought and action at work in India has proved capable of responding fully to the complexity of the Indian task of liberation. This is realized by many groups and organizations working at the grass roots. Hopes are that a distinctive vision of integral Indian humanism will slowly emerge out of the encounter of these and various other streams of thought, and above all out of the concrete praxis of liberation.

The religious pluralism, the interaction, influence and involvement between religion and politics, and the popular religiosity that are prevalent in the India of today indicate that an exclusively Christian liberation theology, for that matter any denominational theology of liberation, Hindu, Muslim or Budhist, is inadequate and that what is needed to be effective is an Indian liberation theology. It must be interreligious. As Walter Fernandes opines,

> Hindus, Sikhs, Muslims, and Christians, have to search together, each person finding inspiration in his or her own religious tradition respecting one another's expression. Together they have to search for a genuine *bhakti* in the Indian reality, knowing that every religion has a protest and a prophetic element, though it may not always be commonly expressed... To evolve a liberation theology, people of different religious traditions have to search for the prophetic elements in the context of their common option to support those who are struggling to free themselves from oppression (Wilfred ed. 1992: 62).

Liberation Theology and Sarvodaya

From among the many ideologies and liberative praxes that are at work in India toward forming a totally liberated humanity, we have selected liberation theology because it appears that sarvodaya ideals and liberation theology have a lot in common, complement one another, are mutually inspiring, and can work together for a common goal. The statement of the ninth annual meeting of the Indian Theological Association supports this claim; for it states that,"though the integral liberation which Gandhi envisaged for India is not realized, the method he evolved remains a potent and comprehensive, but unexploited resource".[5] Further support for our claim can be found in the writings of Indian liberation theologians like Ishwar Harris, S. Kappen, T. K. John, Felix Wilfred, J. Kottukapally, Samuel Rayan, George Soares Prabhu, Ignatius Jesudasan, Walter Fernandes, Michael Amaladoss, Xavier Irudayaraj, S.K. George and Subash Anand.[6]

In trying to search for some common grounds mainly from the sarvodaya perspective, we shall only be dealing with some very basic concepts. In other words, an in-depth analysis of liberation theology is not intended as part of this book. Nevertheless a few general observations about liberation theology are in order.

The genesis of liberation theology as a movement goes back to Latin America of the 1960s, where it originated as a reaction against and a Christian response to the problem of the suffering of the poor.[7] The "preferential option for the poor", echoed in the modern Church, has intensified the common struggle for liberation in the Church. This option is not an intellectual assent but a praxis.[8] As Gutierrez remarks,

> The option for the poor and the oppressed through a liberating commitment leads to the realization that this commitment cannot be isolated from the social set-up to which they belong... Solidarity with the poor implies the transformation of the existing social order. It implies a liberating praxis: the transforming activity directed toward the creation of a just, free society.[9]

What is at the centre of this movement is "liberation", and it is not the theologian but the poor and the oppressed who count in this process.

Though "liberation theology" is recent and Latin American in origin, there is something universal in the very process, namely "contextualization in theologizing". As a result, this theology has spread to many other countries, especially in the developing world, where oppression, alienation, underdevelopment and oppressive structures are more visible. The present process of Indian liberation has to be understood against the background of a complex but creative interaction between various religious and secular forces. The need of contextualizing in liberation theology, as opposed to "transplanting",[10] also has to take into serious account the socio-historical perspective in India.[11]

Gandhi and Liberation Theology

Long before the liberation theology attracted world attention, Gandhi had already given a methodology of liberation which is worth considering. Through his life and work, he laid the foundation of a theological framework that has timeless value for those concerned with the liberation of the oppressed. As "...a man who incarnates the anguish and hope of those who are struggling for national liberation and development in the Third World" (Broucker 1970:vii), Gandhi's life provides us with a good model for theologizing in the Indian context today. He was also a theologian in this sense that, "He was passionately in search of Truth and he wanted to bring all his life, private and political, under the sway of Truth. He wanted to be guided by Truth alone, to unify his whole life with Truth as its centre of gravity. Now for Gandhi, Truth is God. So we may say that the *Mahatma* was in search of God and that God was the focal point of his life and that he wanted to understand everything in relation to Truth, that is, in relation to God. In this he is a real theologian" (Anand 1979: 52).

Gandhi's life was liberative: totally committed to the cause of humanization and liberation; he believed in the coming and becoming of a liberated society; the action programme he initiated and followed was liberative, in other words, for the welfare of all—sarvodaya. Living a life that was marked by austere simplicity and bodily labour (Jesudasan 1984: 17), Gandhi gives us an illustrious example of the dynamic transition from interiority to active commitment. Gandhi was well aware of the fact that any involvement in liberative action presupposes a liberative process in the person and that only a liberated person can liberate others. This self-liberating process may be called interiority or self-realization, which in the context of total liberation becomes integral to active social involvement. Gandhi seems to evolve a new *sadhana* and thus proposes a "social spirituality for India". Realization of Truth (God) is achieved through service to humanity because Gandhi was "endeavouring to see God through service of humanity".[12] His faith in a fundamental unity in all creation made him say, "we all claim descent from the same God, and hence all life in whatever form it appears must be essentially one" (Prabhu 1955: 5). Inspired by the theology of the *Gita* and led by his instinct, Gandhi offered a unique way to salvation: Truth-realization or God-realization; and that way is service of humankind. This "way" essentially is a commitment to the removal of suffering and evil and an active and creative identification of oneself with everyone, especially with the poor, because for Gandhi to identify oneself with others and serve them is to be one with God. And to talk about this basic identity and to allow bondage, poverty, illiteracy and discrimination in any form to go on unhindered is a transgression of this truth; it is dishonour to God himself. In his own words:

> We are all...children of one and the same Creator, and as such the divine powers in us are infinite. To slight a single human being is to slight those divine powers and thus to harm not only that human being but the whole universe (*Harijan* February 1939).

Gandhi's commitment to liberative praxis and identification with the exploited stem from his basic theology. Gandhi advocated the dual paths of nonviolence and non-attachment as guidelines in the quest for God-realization. He believed that one becomes fit for God-realization particularly through self-emptying, voluntary poverty — in becoming poor with the poor (CW 33: 278). Such a way of life would also include identification with all of God's creatures and service of all. The service, especially for the poorest, the weakest and the lowliest, is a great honour rendered to God since He is found among them. Gandhi says:

> To relieve the distress of the unemployed, by providing them work, to tend the sick, to wean the people from their insanitary habits, to educate them in cleanliness and healthy living condition, should be the concern of every seeker after truth (CW 68: 43).

Self-realization, which for Gandhi is the attainment of Truth as God, is through the service of his brothers and sisters who are in need. He makes his position clear: "The whole of my activity whether it may be called social, political, humanitarian or ethical is directed to that end. And as I know that God is found more often in the lowliest of his creatures than in the high and mighty, I am struggling to reach the status of these. I cannot do so without their service. Hence my passion for the service of the suppressed classes" (*Young India* September 1924).

Thus the Gandhian action programme becomes a new kind of *sadhana* (religious self-discipline): action for social justice and participation in the national struggle for political, economic, cultural and religious freedom. His theology is praxis over theory[13] and the test of theological orthodoxy a liberating orthopraxis (Jesudasan 1984: 2). As a *karmayogi*, man of disciplined action, he tirelessly worked for the poor of South Africa and India, he gave prominence to personal example and service rather than to preaching.[14] Gandhi's efforts in the villages to rid the villages of disease, superstition and socio-economic oppression "were substantive parts of swaraj".

Liberation theology as a radical movement in the Church focuses its attention on the injustices that the poor are subjected to in the developing world. It has also challenged the Church to minister to the needs of people, especially of the poor, and for theology to become relevant and contextual to the conditions of the people. It affirms that God takes the side of the oppressed and the need of a preferential option for the poor for anyone who would be committed to the cause of liberation. It has launched a revolution against the oppressors by organizing and mobilizing the masses. Gandhi also had similar concerns. He would find the effects of capitalism alarming, as he had diagnosed the problems caused by capitalism a long time ago. He would agree that heavy industrialization, which is making the poor poorer and the rich richer, has adverse consequences all over the world. Gandhi would join hands with the liberation theologians in condemning neo-colonialism in the form of economic dependency of the poor nations on the richer nations. But, for Gandhi, liberation is never limited to the economic, political or social dimensions of human beings (as sometimes liberation theology is interpreted and understood by many); his whole focus was on the integral and total liberation of each and every person, and that was the sarvodaya of Gandhi.

The question is often asked: how far did Gandhi succeed in liberating India? Gandhi's contributions to political liberation (swaraj) are universally recognized and acclaimed. We have discussed above his contributions in the socio-economic realm. Sarvodaya was envisioned by Gandhi as a movement which would be the primary vehicle of social and economic change, especially at the grassroots level, which for India means transformation in villages. As one writer points out, "what Gandhi did accomplish in concrete terms of action was to organize a series of rehearsals for fundamental social change. Gandhianism carried to its logical conclusion would result, under the present conditions of India, in a revolution" (Lannoy 1971: 409). Lannoy's observation seems valid and relevant as he concludes that if sarvodaya is really interested in inaugurating a programme of building from below, which would mean a complete inversion of the bourgeois capitalist system of India, "it can only be accomplished by the tactics and strategy of the performance, not of the rehearsal".

Seen as a liberative praxis and viewed as a theoretical support to the active involvement of committed people to the total liberation of each and every human person, liberation theology and sarvodaya of Gandhi enhance and enrich each other.

Mutually Enriching

There are some important lessons to be learnt from liberation theology, which can be useful for the sarvodaya movement in India. The Latin American movement started as a people's movement, a cry of the oppressed against oppressive structures and oppressors themselves. Sarvodaya today does not seem to have the support of the people as the Gandhian alternative to socio-economic change. Sarvodaya needs to articulate more clearly the needs of the people and thus become the voice of the people. Gandhian institutions and sarvodaya centres should become places where people are attracted to congregate. This will happen when creative programmes at such centres are made available to the people.

A dialogue between liberation theology and Gandhian thought could be fruitful if there could be agreement on some common principles that could be used to end the suffering of humanity. Ishwar Harris suggests that Gandhi's theology of satyagraha provides us with the content where this dialogue can begin. Because "*satyagraha* is not uniquely Gandhian, it also brings into focus the life and teaching of Jesus. Together, Jesus and Gandhi give us a methodology to deal with the problem of liberation. When analyzed, it makes it clear that the answer to human suffering (due to oppression or otherwise) does not lie in short programmes, but in the total transformation of human being" (Harris 1992: 475-76). The liberated society Gandhi envisaged was an ideal one rather than one already in existence — the *Ramrajya*, a new ideal state of justice, caste reforms, and equality of all. In the words of S.K. George, Gandhi "was the greatest worker for the kingdom of God in the world of today" (George 1947: xv). This coming of the kingdom of God on earth is indeed the dream of liberation theology. This is a long journey into the future for anyone committed to the cause of liberation. Nikhil Chakravartty's description of Gandhi on August 15, 1947 (the day of independence for India) speaks the true nature of Gandhi's vision for India: "And the man who led this great nation in this final battle for freedom, that frail figure, the bald and the toothless, sitting on a plain cot in a half-dilapidated house, looking up to the wide open sky, as if telling his countrymen and women, they had many more miles to go before the last drop of tear is wiped off from the eyes of this mighty humanity that is India- the journey ahead from emancipation to empowerment" (Chakravartty 1994: 10).

Sarvodaya: A Comprehensive Concept

Sarvodaya implies an all-round — material as well as spiritual — development of each and every individual. Even more importantly, sarvodaya is concerned with a continued healthy environment so that a continued all-sided development of man may be ensured. Sarvodaya, even in its literal sense, does not exclude any created reality from its scope of development. In the light of recent scientific knowledge about the eco-system and the total inter-dependence of cosmic existence (animate and inanimate) and healthy growth, we need to extend the application of the concept of sarvodaya to other planetary and even cosmic realities. We can no longer be concerned only with the human being and its destiny, since the human is organically linked with the whole eco-system and its healthy functioning. There is need, therefore, to extend the concept of sarvodaya to the whole of sentient and non-sentient being in the universe.

Gandhi: Model for Responsible Ecological Living

Ecological issues are complex and need comprehensive understanding. What I am suggesting is that Gandhi's sarvodaya-utopian mode of holistic discourse is appropriate for a holistic-integrative approach to ecological issues, and that sarvodaya has an ecological dimension. Gandhi himself was not an ecologist in the usual sense which the word has come to mean today. He did not propound a theory of environmental protection or ethics, nor did he lead a nonviolent crusade to save rivers and forests for future generations. Gandhi never addressed global environmentalism but he did much more. He lived the life of a person who affirmed the integrity and value of life, human as well as non-human. He lived a life that was in harmony with himself as with others, with his religion as with the environment. His life, as Pearl S. Buck pointed out, passed "beyond the meaning of an individual to the meaning of a way of living in our troubled modern world" (Radhakrishnan ed. 1956: 51). For an ecologically troubled world, Gandhi might be the man of the hour. We shall therefore try to discover the ecologically pertinent insights in Gandhi's vision of future. In the observation of Rajiv Kumar Sinha, "he (Gandhi) was also a great environmentalist. The concepts of environmental conservation, sustainability, and survival, which the modern ecologists are embarking upon, are inherent in the ideology of Mahatma Gandhi who was a man far ahead of his time and all the modern environmentalists" (Sinha 1991: 209). Gandhi warned the world against large-scale industrialism and the dehumanized machine culture and emphasized small-scale industry, which promotes "production by the masses and not mass production", avoids conflicts between man and nature, is less energy-intensive and less polluting. Gandhi put great emphasis on rural development in India, advocated sustainable development and appropriate technology. Gandhi's ahimsa meant not only absence of injury to the living world but also to nature—the air, water, and the soil. The simple life-style of Gandhi had a great ecological bearing.

Ecology is rapidly becoming the central global concern of our times. As the etymology of the term indicates (*oikos* + *logos*), it is a discourse about our home, this earth. It is a question concerning what we make of this earth. This discourse (*logos*) on our home is closely linked to another discourse about our home, namely economics (*oikos* + *nomikos* = economics), the management of the household. The question is how to regulate the riches of this home, the products of this nature. Ecology thus is a human problem; it bears upon our ethical responsibilities *vis a vis* the present society and its developments.

As Philip Viegas and Geeta Menon opine, "...it is only in the context of the entire social, economic and political structure that a relatively accurate and adequate understanding of the environment can emerge" (Viegas and Menon 1988: 4). There is need for a holistic understanding of environment because of the factors involved in preserving a balanced ecological system. Gandhi's insights into eco-spirituality, sustainable development, simple living and eco-villages contribute greatly to living in harmony with nature, which is ecological balance and friendly environment.

Life-Affirming Ecology of Gandhi

The dominant Christian approach to ecology fundamentally has been based on a theology that was human-centred,[15] but Gandhi's thinking was life-centred in keeping with his Hindu beliefs. Explaining the nature of his Hindu beliefs, Gandhi said that "the chief value of Hinduism lies in holding the actual belief that ALL life (not only human, but all sentient beings) is one, i.e., all life coming from the One Universal Source, call it Allah, God, or *Parameshwara*" (Gandhi 1950: 35). Gandhi does not see nature as a separate and inferior order of existence created for the pleasure and benefit of humans. Gandhi was frequently at pains to establish his oneness with all creatures: "I want, if I don't give you a shock, to realise identity with even the crawling things upon earth, because we claim descent from the same God, and being so, all life in whatever form it appears must essentially be so".[16]

Gandhi would even go further, he would even commend reverence to trees, but would not recommend it *per se*, for fear that it would degenerate into idolatry and become "encrusted with false beliefs and doctrines". In tree worship, he saw "a thing instinct with deep pathos and poetic beauty". In addition, he argued that tree worship would serve as a symbol of "true reverence for the entire vegetable kingdom, which, with its endless panorama of beautiful shapes and forms, declares to us as it were with a million tongues the greatness and glory of God".[17] Likewise, Gandhi's cow worship and cow protection were not a mere simple-minded adoration of the so-called "sacred" cow. For him, the cow represented "the entire sub-human world". Gandhi wrote: "Man through the cow is enjoined to realize his identity with all that lives...the cow is poem of pity. One reads pity in the gentle animal. She is the mother to millions of Indian mankind." The cow was a compelling symbol that demanded compassion from humans. The idea itself of giving protection to the cow was deeply embedded in Hinduism. But Gandhi bestowed upon it a greater human significance within the context of human-animal ethical relationship. The cow pleading for all life, seemed to say to the humans, as Gandhi put it: "You are not appointed over us to kill us and eat our flesh or otherwise ill-treat us, but to be our friend and guardian" (Gandhi 1959: 105).

Gandhi's basic assumption is that a sacred duty is devolved upon humans to be friends and protectors of nature. Interestingly, the Sanskrit root underlying *dharma* (duty) means "sustain". In Hinduism, one's duty is to sustain natural harmonies and patterns. Gandhi's passion for nonviolence is the basis for this assumption. But at the same time he would place human obligation to nature not in the Christian context of love, but in the Hindu context of duty as enjoined by the *Gita*.

Viewed from Gandhi's ethical perspective, ethics involves every relationship in creation, including the tree and the cow. In his own words: "my ethics not only permits me to claim but requires me to own kinship with not merely the ape but the horse, and the sheep, the lion and the leopard, the snake and the scorpion".

For Gandhi, it was so crucial for humans to realize this interconnectedness that he asserted: "I do not want to live at the cost of the life even of a snake". It is to be, however, noted that Gandhi's adherence to ahimsa was never absolute or uncompromising when it came to non-human beings, because Gandhi said that some kind of *himsa* or violence was a fact of life. "This kind of violence is inherent in all embodied life, therefore, in man too" (Gandhi 1950: 213). Obviously, his priority was human life and its safety. For, Gandhi said: "I have no feeling to save the life of these animals who devour or cause hurt to man...Therefore, I will not feed ants, monkeys, or dogs. I will never sacrifice a man's life in order to save theirs".[18]

Sarvodaya, Ecology and Sustainable Development[19]

Gandhi's conception of what might now be called a spirituality of ecology was based on a holistic perspective derived from Indian culture, which does offer a holistic perspective to ecology.[20] Gandhi strongly felt the need of recovering the sense of the sacred in the natural world. There is an urgent need to recognise that the universe is an interdependent whole and we ourselves are parts of the cosmic whole. As Bede Griffiths puts it: "...we are members of one another and of this planetary system and we are responsible for the well being of the universe in which we live...we are the "sons of God" responsible for the "new creation", the universe which is being built up day by day into the kingdom of God" (Griffiths 1988: 26). This new sense of the sacredness of the earth and of our communion with the whole natural environment would lead to another kind of development, i.e., sustainable development, and another kind of technology, i.e., appropriate technology. An "intermediate" or "appropriate" technology, such as Schumacher envisages, would build up from the villages, as Gandhi sought to do, and develop a village economy, in which the basic needs of the people would be satisfied.

There is a close link between ecology and development. The dictionary defines development as a "gradual unfolding, fuller working out", which makes sustainable development a phrase full of insight and promise. In common usage its meaning has been altered and is now synonymous with "economic growth" which, in turn, is frequently equated with "progress". While development in the dictionary sense has endless potential, limitless growth is impossible in a finite world. It is a fact that developmental strategies based on the conventional view of development inevitably result in an elitist form of development. The rich and the super-rich are the major beneficiaries of this form of development, while the poor remain steeped in poverty and degradation. It is a development as if "people do not matter". When development is perceived purely in quantitative terms and to the neglect of quality (= the upward movement of the entire social system),[21] it would result in environmental pollution and degradation. India is a typical example of this "faulty development":[22]

> In the name of economic development, much scenic beauty is destroyed, whole tribal populations uprooted, our non-renewable resources are recklessly depleted, and our air, water, soil, and foods are polluted. Thus this conception of development causes us to ignore or undervalue the enormous ecological damage and environmental degradation that come in the wake of our mega development projects,.... Our obsession with the growth rate of national income causes us to neglect essential non-development expenditures such as health, education, housing, and social welfare. As a result, while we are in the forefront of nuclear and space research, we have high rates of illiteracy, infant mortality, and high incidence of such diseases as cholera, tuberculosis, malaria, and leprosy...and nearly fifty per cent of our population live below poverty line (Charles 1990: 181).

How does one respond to the environmental question? The environmental crisis unleashed by the over-exploitation of nature through the help of technology cannot be solved by technological solutions. There is need for a radical re-construction of the prevailing socio-political and economic order. Without the re-establishment of justice in social, economic and political realms there can be no real solutions to the environmental crisis the humanity, especially the developing countries are facing. What is behind the crisis of our environment is: 1) a dangerous belief that we have reached the final, the eschatological period of human history with the arrival of the "Messiah" of technology who will save everyone and all nations;[23] 2) and an ideology of development that places its trust in the myth of "unlimited progress".[24]

Gandhi's insights on ecological ways of living, appropriate technology, people-centred developments, and village-oriented economy stand out as realizable alternative visions of tomorrow.

Sarvodaya and Ecological Ways of Living

We need actively to envision new ways of living that reflect our understanding that the earth will be humanity's home for countless generations into the future. We need to invent new patterns of ecological living that moderate our impact on the earth—from the design of our homes and neighbourhoods to the food we eat, the clothes we wear, the transportation we use, the work we do, and much more. We could call this new way of living "voluntary simplicity" or "creative simplicity" or "ecological living" (Elgin 1993: 125). Gandhi is a source of insight and inspiration in this regard.

The ideal villages that Gandhi visualized could be termed "eco-villages", small self-sufficient communities (micro-communities). People-centred development would be the model and villages would not be exploited by towns as now, but a more wholesome balance would be established between agriculture and industry and between villages and towns. When large-scale industrialization is controlled and production is decentralized, cottage industries are promoted, especially in villages, where the majority of India's people live, then this would lead to the regeneration of rural life, and our villages would throb with new life. The Gandhian vision of regenerated rural life would then become a reality. Gandhi wrote,

> My ideal village will contain intelligent human beings. They will not live in dirt and darkness as animal. Men and women will be free and able to hold their own against anyone in the world. There will be neither plague, nor cholera, nor small- pox, no one will be idle, no one will wallow in luxury...(Nehru 1960: 50).

There are many ingredients to such eco-villages. *Swadeshi* for

Gandhi was not a narrow concept of using indigenous goods but it was (is) a constant struggle to promote genuine love and devotion for the nation and its culture. Nature cure, for instance, had been a concern of Gandhi even in South Africa. In the last years of his life, he had great interest in establishing nature cure clinics, which would be available for the poorest. Nature cure had for him a dual significance, both spiritual and utilitarian. Following its precepts for healthy living meant being in touch with and living by the laws of nature. Being healthy meant being a true servant of God; and he had always felt that sickness in himself and in others was a cause for shame because it was a sign of disorderliness of spirit, for example overwork and lack of detachment, undisciplined or ignorant consumption of too rich a diet, or an otherwise unreformed lifestyle. Further, natural medicine was cheap and readily available; if it could be actively promoted, he felt, it could solve the problems of chronic sickness which afflicted India's poor, who could never afford expensive Western style medical treatment. Though Gandhi attempted to transform the clinic into one which could serve the poor, he realized soon that an urban clinic could not teach the villagers how to lead a healthy life, so he turned instead to a village-based experiment in nature cure. He could not stay long in person, but left detailed instructions on a simple lifestyle and the type of natural treatments to be offered, including sun baths, mud packs and massage, and recitation of *Ramanama*.[25] As Judith Brown concludes, "Gandhi's experiments with simple, communal living and with health for villagers, which did not rely on expensive drugs, even led him to consideration of mankind's relations with the environment, human obligations towards animals, and use of air, water and soil...his breadth of concern again led him to ask fundamental questions about life. They make him sound distinctly modern as his ideals of simplicity and smallness of scale echo the fears of people in the later part of the century who have glimpsed some of the darker aspects and unsuspected repercussions of industrialization of the Western civilization he so condemned" (Brown 1989: 393-94).

The *Ayurveda* as a system of medicine is an impressive alternative system of medicine. Nonetheless, many Indians dismiss *Ayurveda* as a system without value and brand its practioners as quacks. If we look upon our own scientific and technological heritage with contempt, we will necessarily look to the West for every technological device. The result of this attitude is the absence of indigenous effort to develop technologies suited to our conditions and problems. Our undue technological dependence on the West has caused us to neglect local research to solve social problems with local resources. At this point *swadeshi* spirit of Gandhi serves as a basis and inspiration; it also promotes simple lifestyle i.e., a life attuned to the nature, and an environmentally friendly technology. It is true that India has not been able to use solar power and wind power on a wide scale for producing energy, or to convert human waste and animal waste for producing energy and manure on a national scale. In the words of Anil Agarwal, "Nothing could take us closer to Gandhi's concept of *gram swarajya* than striving to create village ecosystems which are biologically diverse and self-reliant in their local biomass needs to the maximum extent possible. This will clearly demand as extremely intensive use of our natural resources like land and water to create a huge and diverse growing stock of biomass. Any science which teaches how to do this will truly have the right to be called a people's science—and indeed it will have to begin with the traditional knowledge of the people. Even more so, planning for the enhancement of village ecosystem will call for village level planning with the involvement of the people..." (Agarwal 1986: 160).

Gandhi's dream to form eco-villages is being realized today. Researches done by the Centre of Science for Villages are remarkable in this context. The Centre seeks to continue the work of Gandhi by its research and action programmes in three areas: 1) rural fuel and energy, 2) rural crafts and industries, 3) rural ecology and environment.[26] There are indications in at least four areas of human endeavour that new kind of technologies (Ananthu 1990: 215) could become a possibility in the not-too-distant future. They are: farming, housing, health and energy.

Farming. The ecological ill-effects of modern farming practices are now becoming increasingly evident. The use of pesticides has resulted in damage to our health, fertilizers have led to soil erosion, use of chemicals to nitrate poisoning of drinking water, etc. Masanobu Fukuoka, a Japanese microbiologist and plant specialist, has tried out a different approach—an ecological way of farming.[27] Many are now switching over to these ecological alternatives. In the United States, the National Academy of Sciences made a study of the results obtained by eleven such farmers, and was so impressed that it has recommended to the President that the policy of providing subsidies for use of chemicals and fertilizers be reversed. In India, too, many attempts are being made to convert agricultural practices along ecologically sound lines. These new models of agriculture are being developed outside of the infrastructure of governments, universities, or other such institutions.[28] Sarvodaya centres and Gandhian institutes need to give more efficient leadership in this regard and become centres of ecological farming. "Farmers are the very heart of rural life and without them we wouldn't have countryside". There is hope and optimism when Charles, Prince of Wales, says that "a consensus is emerging today for farming which is economically viable, responsive to the needs of consumers, socially acceptable, environmentally friendly and moving towards genuine sustainability."[29]

Housing. Both bricks and cement are extremely energy-intensive materials and demand mining of the land. Moreover, the bulk of India's urban population cannot afford even the cheapest low-cost brick and cement building. Anil Agarwal suggests the possibility of mud building, and he is of the view that science and technology should be used to improve mud building. CSV has made conical tiles, which are economically viable and environmentally friendly; CSV has built more than 300 of such arch roof house in various villages.[30] Low-cost housing pioneered by Laurie Baker is an ecologically sound, relatively inexpensive approach to housing and is certain to catch up in the years to come.

Health. A holistic, ecological approach is surfacing in the field of medicine and health. Gandhi emphasized the balanced diet to be provided to each, which should be within the means of the villagers. He also advocated use of green leaves. To produce enough vegetables, fruits, and milk in the villages is an essential part of the nature cure scheme. Village sanitation (e.g., tanks and wells to be cleaned and used as such; lanes and streets to be cleaned of all the rubbish; manure pits to bury all the refuse for the double purpose of promoting the villagers' health and their material conditions) was of high priority in Gandhi's eco-village programme. Investigation has to be made to find out what the villages can supply in the shape of drugs. There is need for research in this area and also there is need to educate people about the potential of indigenous systems, such as nature cure, the richness and curative power of herbs and trees,[31] *ayurveda, yoga* etc.[32]

Energy. Gandhi insisted on local generation and control of electrical power. When G.D. Birla offered to electrify Sevagram, Gandhi's reply was: "You want to give us electricity here at Sevagram by bringing it from a distance of 500 miles. I do not want to consider such an offer of electrical power. I will accept electricity only if it can be produced and controlled within Sevagram itself" (Ananthu 1989: 340). Energy-supplying technologies like bio-gas plants, solar cookers, and fuel briquetting plants have great scope for local generation and control of energy. Davidson in his book chronicles the story of about a dozen devices in operation today to meet the requirement that Gandhi placed before Birla, i.e., they are all devices for generating electrically powered devices in a decentralized, user-controlled setting. Davidson proposes an ecological lifestyle as did Gandhi, "...a move away from commercial centres, such as towns, to a more rural existence. Man needs to live with nature to maintain his sense of harmony with her or else he destroys his environment and himself to boot..." (Ananthu 1989: 346).

Sarvodaya: An "Ultimate" Response

Holistic environmental concern demands a holistic response, a holistic approach to life. Gandhi believed in a holistic view of life. It would seem that Gandhi offers a well-thought-out and tested strategy for action to halt the massive destruction that is being inflicted on the planet. Gandhi's nonviolence puts in the hands of every single human being a potent and intensely active weapon of mass use that can turn the devastation of the earth around. The Chipko Movement[33] is a clear illustration of employing Gandhi's nonviolence in protecting nature from exploitation. As Anil Agarwal remarks, "Somehow it looked as if it was Gandhi's ghost had come alive to lead the movement. The spirit of nonviolent protest, the spirit of caring and sharing, the spirit of self-reliance, and so many other things that Gandhi had talked about were all there in this movement. As the years have gone by, the movement has grown to envelop the consciousness of entire India..." (Agarwal 1987: 649).

Besides such protests against anti-ecological practices and policies, the people's movements direct their attention towards the use of alternative renewable sources of energy and devising of appropriate technology. What humans need to do is more than hug trees in a Gandhian fashion—they need to embrace a philosophy of action and thought that will save the planet. Gandhi's life and example provide affirmations of ecological integrity and stability. Gandhi's "people-centred", "need-oriented" economy, as opposed to "machine-centred", "greed-oriented" economy, promotes appropriate technology and advocates sustainable developments. Gandhi's "voluntary simplicity",[34] holistic approach to life, love for everything that is indigenous, vision of eco-villages and ecological living, "represent an invisible tide, a surge of new ideas and actions that might herald a truly Gandhian revolution in the new century" (Ananthu 1991: 491).

If we should confess deep inside our souls that the environmental problem is fundamentally one of greed, egoism, materialism and anthropocentrism, then we may state that the environment will be sustained only to the extent that we truly love one another, only to the extent that we love all of the earth in its diversity and sacrifice our selfish interests on its behalf. Gandhi's ahimsa is nothing but an affirmation of this universal love. Ahimsa—love in action—necessarily promotes the welfare of all in the last analysis. The welfare of all, sarvodaya, can be attained only through a harmony in the universe. Natural harmony—global equilibrium, human harmony, and peace—is being disturbed and destroyed by the egoistic and greedy intervention of humans. There is a moral imperative or social responsibility to limit needs and to be trustees of nature. Viewed from such moral imperative and sense of social responsibility, Gandhi's sarvodaya vision has deep environmental implications. In self-sufficient villages, simplicity of living, people oriented economy, promotion of swaraj and protection of swadeshi Gandhi envisioned a realistic and realizable utopia: welfare of all, sarvodaya.

References

1. Ishwar Harris gives a good insight as he searches for a relation of liberation theology to Gandhi. In his own words, "Was it not Jesus of Nazareth who gave humankind the insight that where a segment of humanity is oppressed, God is oppressed also? Did he not preach that when the poor suffer, God suffers also? In the Twentieth century it took a man like Gandhi, who made the teachings of Jesus come alive, not only by his beliefs but by his actions." Ishwar Harris, "Gandhi and Liberation Theology," *Gandhi Marg* 14 (October-December 1992): 463.
2. Ambedkar (Dr. Bhimrao Ambedkar, 1891-1956), born one of India's socially despised Untouchables, became a powerful voice calling for a radically new society. During a lifetime of teaching India's oppressed how to work toward their own liberation, Ambedkar campaigned for democratic government and the rights of workers and women, formed political parties and reform societies, founded night schools and colleges. Near the end of a life of exploring the meaning of religion and philosophy, Ambedkar became a Buddhist and was joined in this by hundreds of thousands of his supporters. *One Hundred Years For Freedom 1891-1991*, edited by Members and Friends of the Ambedkar Mission of Canada (Toronto: Ambedkar Mission, Inc., 1991), 3.
3. As for the tribals, their independence, self-respect and human dignity were closely linked with their forests and land. Consequently, loss of these resources jeopardized their family, cultural, religious and social life. Their very identity was under attack. Their protest in the beginning took a violent form: major rebellions in Chotanagpur in 1820; the Santal Rebellion of 1855-57. Similar movements arose among the Warlis of Maharshtra, the Bhils of Rajasthan and other tribes of western India. See Walter Fernandes, "A Socio-historic perspective," 16-17.
4. The Marxist analysis of Indian socio-economic life and the root causes of poverty has found much response among the downtrodden and those who support them in the struggle, especially wherever this analysis is coupled with the commitment of the Marxist to the task of liberation. Marxism has introduced a new and complementary dimension of the historical, social and collective to traditional Indian thinking and culture; it has infused

into Indian thinking the importance of human responsibility in shaping the world, history and the future. But the limitation and inadequacies of Marxian ideology, especially its failure to take adequate account of the role of culture and the subjective dimension of life and history and its devaluation of religion, have kept this ideology from having a mass appeal.

5. Statement of the Indian Theological Association, 9th Annual Meeting (Bangalore: Dharmaram College, 1985), 11.
6. For this section of the book we shall be giving frequent references to the authors cited. They are pioneers as well as advocates of a theology that is Indian in its content and method giving primacy to the present socio-political and religio-cultural milieux for the praxis of theology.
7. Roger Haight, *An Alternative Vision: An Interpretation of Latin American Liberation Theology,* (New York: Paulist Press, 1985), 27, 41. Some see it as a consequence of the collapse of the post-World War II optimism regarding economic development. Others link it to the student unrest and mass demonstrations in the United States, Mexico and France in 1968.(See Michael Novak, "Liberation Theology and the Pope", in James V. Schall, *Liberation Theology in Latin America* (San Francisco: Ignatius Press, 1982), 278-290.
8. Gustavo Gutierrez defines the method of liberation theology as "critical reflection on christian praxis in the light of the world", G. Gutierrez, *A Theology of Liberation* (New York: Orbis Books, 1973), 13. Praxis in liberation theology is a dialectical process of learning from the world, acting on the world, and reshaping theory in the light of action taken. Gutierrez makes a distinction between "historical praxis" and "liberating praxis", the first being the activity by which men and women continually transform the natural and social conditions of their lives, while the second is what historical praxis does or should become. He understands that the conditions in which we live today are so profoundly unjust that our historical praxis certainly ought to be a liberating praxis, even to the point of immersing us in "the political process of revolution".
9. Gustavo Gutierrez, "Liberation, Theology and Proclamation," *Concilium* 10 (1974): 60. The poor here includes the economically poor, the oppressed, those who are politically marginalized, a race which is discriminated against, a social class subtly or openly exploited by another class. Opting for them obviously is entering into the universe of their values and cultural categories. This also means solidarity with their interests and their struggles.
10. That one cannot transfer Latin American liberation theology to

India is clear from the very nature of liberation theology. Instead, one must reinvent liberation theology in India according to the local situation and the conditions of the exploited.

11. Class and caste inequalities, population explosion, malnutrition, illiteracy, ill health, cultural dominance, political powerlessness, cultural marginalization and religious dogmas and beliefs at work in India are just some of the issues that are to become key to Indian liberation theology. Alfred de Souza, *Relevance of Religion and Inter-Religious Dialogue in Modern Society* (New Delhi: Indian Social Institute, 1986), 35-36; Walter Fernandes, "A Socio-Historic Perspective of Liberation Theology in India", in *Leave the Temple*, 9.
12. R.K. Prabhu, ed., *Truth is God* (Ahmedabad: Navajivan Publishing House, 1955), 5.
13. Ishwar Harris, "Gandhi and Liberation Theology", 468 ff. While comparing the four axioms of liberation theology (1. praxis over theory, 2.action over reflection, 3.people's exegesis over academic exegesis, 4. political struggle over solitary contemplation) with Gandhi's theology of liberation, the author is of the view that Gandhi must have taken the command of Jesus, "therefore go and do likewise" (Luke: 10: 37), to heart.
14. *CW*, 63: 347, 417. In 1936 Gandhi settled in Sevagram village, to live among the poor and "show them how to live".
15. See, for example, Christopher Derrick, *The Delicate Creation: Towards a Theology of Environment* (London: Tom Stacey Ltd., 1972); Robert Faricy, *Wind and Sea Obey Him: Approaches to a Theology of Nature* (London: SCM Press, 1982); John Carmody, *Ecology and Religion: Towards a New Christian Theology of Nature* (New York: Paulist Press, 1983); Matthew Fox, *Original Blessing* (New Mexico: Bear and Company fourth printing 1984); J. Moltmann, *God in Creation: An Ecological Doctrine of Creation* (London: SCM Press, 1989); *Jeevadhara* 18 (January 1988); *Vidyajyoti* 56 (August-September 1992).
16. M. K. Gandhi, *Truth is God* (Ahmedabad: Navajivan Publishing House, 1959), 50.
17. Cited by Candadai Seshachari, "Towards a Life-affirming Ecology: A Gandhian Approach," *Gandhi Marg* 12 (October-December 1990): 287. Gandhi's praises of God seeing the beauty and wonders of the world, remind one of the Psalm 8: "O Lord, our Sovereign, how majestic is your name in all the earth!...When I look at your heavens, the work of your fingers,...", or Psalm 19 which says: "The heavens are telling the glory of God; and the firmament proclaims His handiwork." *The Holy Bible*, New Revised Standard Version (New York: Collins Publishers, 1989).

18. Gandhi 1950: 216. It is worth noting that a position akin to Gandhi's has found favour with the "deep ecologists" ("Deep Ecology" movement was founded by Norwegian Arne Naess, in 1972.) Their central intuition is that there is "no firm ontological divide in the field of existence.... Rather all entities are constituted by their relationship." The mystical resonance here can hardly be surprising, especially when even the "new physics"— Fritjof Capra, *The Tao of Physics*—seems to echo the same theme. The Special "Deep Ecology" Issue of *The Ecologist* 18/4-5 (1988) carries several articles on "Deep Ecology": Arne Naess, "Deep Ecology and Ultimate Premises", Grover Foley, "Deep Ecology and Subjectivity", Henryk Skolimowski, "Eco-philosophy and Deep Ecology", Brian Tokar, "Social Ecology, Deep Ecology and the Future of Green Political Thought", and Richard Sylvan & David Bennett, "Taoism and Deep Ecology". See also Rudolf C. Heredia, S.J., "Towards an Ecological Consciousness: Religious, Ethical and Spiritual Perspectives," *Vidyajyoti* (September 1991): 489-586. They argue that killing is ethically justifiable if it meets the "vital" needs of the people. For instance, they saw no difficulty at all in people in advanced technological societies using appropriate technology that is vital to their living. They would, however, expect the people to gradually "reduce their excessive interference with the non-human world." See also, Candadai Seshachari, "Towards a Life-affirming Ecology: A Gandhian Approach", 290.
19. In 1987, after years of work, a United Nations Committee headed by Norway's prime minister, Gro Harlem Brundtland, completed its report on environment and development. Published as *Our Common Future* (New York: Oxford University Press, 1987), it described in bleak detail the assault by our species on the planet's life support systems. The report urged that the earth and its productivity must be protected and nurtured for all future generations. Henceforth, economics and the environment must be linked inseparably. Brundtland's major contribution was the phrase "sustainable" development, which has been adopted and repeated like a mantra ever since.
20. Such a perspective is fostered by the following principle of Brahminic Hindu life: 1. man's attitude to nature is neither one of subjugation, nor one of domination and exploitation, but one of harmony. This sense of harmony is based on concern, respect and nonviolence. 2. *Dharma* provides a holistic framework to life in many ways. The *purusharthas* (righteousness, wealth, pleasure and liberation) and four *ashramas* (student, householder, forest-dweller,

and *sannyasi*), indicate an awareness that does not cut life off from the world and community. 3. The ideal of *lokasamgraha* (world-maintenance), in which each has a role and to which each makes his contribution, as expounded by texts like the *Bhagavadgita* underlines a sense of social responsibility. 4. The practice of *panchayajna* (five sacrifices) in which the householder is expected to make daily food offerings to the gods, to the ancestors, to guests, to the animal world and to the self manifests a universal concern. 5. The practice of *yoga* promotes integration, not only of the body and spirit in man but also of man and the universe.

21. Gunnar Myrdal, *Asian Drama* (New York, 1968), 1869. "Upward movement refers to the transition both in the inner and outer form of the human collectivity or society. So the change would be reflected in material, moral, cultural, and spiritual life of the people, since the transformation of society would be beneficial and advantageous only when the internal and external stimuli work harmoniously... Thus development as a by-product of the synthesis of external and internal stimuli would bring peace, prosperity, and a new way of life in each age..." G. Palanithrai, "Understanding the Process of Development through Natural Theory of Nationalism," *Gandhi Marg* 14 (October-December 1992): 480.
22. Felix Wilfred, "Nature and Human Survival," *Jeevdhara* 18 (January 1988): 60-63. The author is of the view that "The present ecological crisis brought forth by a RUINOUS MODEL OF DEVELOPMENT appropriating science and technology to its ends cannot be solved by minor technical solutions. It cannot be solved by simply reducing the rate of growth, by anti-pollution legislation etc.... What is required is a basic re-orientation in understanding human progress and in defining human needs. There should be a break from the understanding of human progress in terms of quantity to quality of life..."
23. This is a kind of technological *chiliasm*. See J. Moltmann, *Man, Christian Anthropology in the Conflicts of the Present* (Philadelphia: Fortress Press, 1974); see also H. Marcuse, *One-Dimensional Man* (Boston: Beacon Press, 1966).
24. The myth of endless progress is today being exploded. Such reports like that of the Club of Rome in 1972 have brought about a sense of sober realism upon enthusiasts who had pinned their hope on ever greater human conquests. It has brought about the realization that there are "limits to human growth", that it is not possible to go on the same path without seriously endangering human life on earth.
25. Gandhi's instructions for the new village clinic at Uruli-Kanchan,

March 1946, *CW*, 83, 336-7; further observations on the experiment, *Harijan* (26 May and 2 June 1946); *CW*, 84, 179-80; see also Judith M. Brown, *Gandhi: Prisoner of Hope*, 361-62.

26. Centre of Science for Villages was started in 1976 by Devendra Kumar, an associate of J. C. Kumarappa (who was Gandhi's right hand in his village industries movement and principal spokesman of his economic philosophy). CSV has a full time staff of more than fifty, which consists of scientists/technologists, artisans/craftsman and knowledgeable rural youth. CSV has evolved more than 15 techniques which are novel in character and have wide applicability, such as: scientific handling of rock bee; utilization of the trunk of banana plant for making into pulp, paper boards and other products; steam cooker using only one handful of charcoal for cooking a full meal for one family; parabole solar reflector, made of pulp pasted with metallized plastic for reflection which can be easily fabricated by the villager...etc. See the mimeographed paper "Important Researches done by CSV", Wardha, India 1986.
27. Masanobu Fukuoka, *The One Straw Revolution* (Mapusa, Goa, India: The Other Indian Press, 1992). Fukuoka describes his natural farming method as do-nothing farming. This approach stems from a world-view that promotes protection of nature, limiting of needs and sustainable future. For him, "the ultimate goal of farming is not the growing of crops but the cultivation and perfection of human being". See A. Y. Joshi, "Masanobu Fukuoka's Timely Message," *Gandhi Marg* 10 (August 1988): 311-14; and T. S. Ananthu, "Technology and Ecology: Some Examples of Confluence", 215.
28. T. S. Ananthu gives extracts from a report by Dr. Pratap Agarwal for evaluation among farmers engaged in sustainable agricultural practices. The case study is a small seven-acre farmer near Bangalore, India, Narayana Reddy: "No chemical fertilizers have been used on Narayan's farm for six years...Narayan also does not use any pesticides or "westicides"- no poisons whatsoever. He is a great believer of soil building with the assistance of earthworms and various other insects...Many farmers approach him and ask for advice. His dream is someday to see an organic farmer every 20 kilometre distance. They can provide a model and then all farmers might change..." T. S. Ananthu, "Technology and Ecology", 216-18.
29. Extract from *Resurgence* (July and August 1991), the annual lecture given by HRH the Prince of Wales, to the Royal Agricultural Society of England; see *Science for Villages* 149/152 (November/December/January/february 1992): 12-13. [sic]

30. "Editorial," *Science for Villages* 149/152 (Nov./Dec./Jan./Feb. 1992): 2.
31. The deeply held view that all things are useful for humans and, therefore, that they should learn to live in harmony with non-human nature is well illustrated by a *jataka* tale. On completing his studies in *ayurveda*, Jivaka was asked by his teacher to search in the nearby forest for and bring back a plant of no use to humans. When, after an intensive search, Jivaka returned empty-handed and reported to the teacher that he was not able to find such a plant, the teacher patted him on the back and declared that, having accomplished this, his final examination, his education was now complete. See Moonis Raza, "The Gandhian Paradigm and the Emerging World-View of the Twenty-First Century," *Gandhi Marg* 13 (April-June 1991): 16-17.
R. Ashok Kumar examines nine commonly known trees for their usefulness to us, for our health: "The nine trees are Sesban, Neem, Karanj, Palmyra, Moring Oleifera, Tamarind, Mango, Jackfruit and Fig. Each tree has certain unique health functions, which are peculiar to that species only. Thus Sesban for anaemia, Neem for consumption, and as an insecticide; ...Tamarind for inflammatory swellings, vertigo, sprains, gastritis,..." R. Ashok Kumar, "Modern Civilization and Normal Civilization: The Need for Small Self-sufficient Communities," *Gandhi Marg* 8 (May 1986): 86-87.
See also, S. N. Chaturvedi, "The Relevance of the Gandhian concept of Rural Development," *Gandhi Marg* 12 (July-September 1990): 208-13.
32. In India, a new hospital is being set up near Dehra Dun, which will specialize in holistic medicine. Ayurveda colleges and hospitals, nature cure centres, yoga classes established in different parts of India and even other countries, are more welcome signs that people look for alternatives to healthy and harmonious living.
33. The Chipko Movement was totally indigenous, a kind of grassroots movement launched by the people who lived on the slopes of the Himalayas to protect their forests from destruction at the hands of forest contractors who bid for the right to cut ash trees to be sold as lumber in the plains. (*Chipko* is a native word of command meaning "go hug", thereby giving the movement its name. Women would literally hug a tree to prevent its being cut). Anil Agarwal, "Gandhi, Ecology and the Last Person," 649; see also Candadai Seshachari, "Towards a Life-affirming Ecology: A Gandhian Approach", 292-93; Felix Wilfred, "Nature and Human Survival," 68; Mark Shepard, *Gandhi Today*, 63-80.

34. Efforts are being made all over the world by individuals, small groups and communities to simplify their lives along Gandhian lines. Richard Gregg had termed this effort, "voluntary simplicity". A research study made by the prestigious Stanford Research Institute has estimated the number of people who have introduced voluntary simplicity into their lives during the last two decades is several millions—a very significant development, even though it does not result in screaming headlines. See T.S. Ananthu, "New Trends Around the World," *Gandhi Marg* 12 (January-March 1991): 484-86.

Glossary

Acharya	Teacher
Acharyakul	Association or family of teachers.
Adivasis	Tribal people
Advaita	Non-dualism of God and the world, of God and human being
Ahimsa	Nonviolence; non injury; This is an ancient Hindu precept, proclaimed by Buddha, by devotees of Vishnu, Mahavira, founder of Jainism
Akhil Bharat Sarva Seva Sangh	All India Association for the Welfare of All.
Akhil Bharatiya Vidyarthi Parishad	An All India Student's Association
Anasakti	Spiritual detachment; non-attachment; spiritual freedom
Anasaktiyoga	Unselfish action
Anekantavada	Jain epistemology bearing on the many-sidedness of truth and the consequent value affirmation
Ashram	Religiously-oriented community; a monastery or hermitage.
Avarnas	Those without category (*varna*), hence casteless
Ayurveda	Ancient and traditional herbal medicine in India.

Bania	Person of commercial caste (e.g., *Modh Bania*: Gandhi's own sub-caste)
Bapu	Affectionate name for Gandhi; 'Father'
Bhagavad-Gita (often shortened to *Gita*)	A section of the *Mahabharata* (a sacred text of Hinduism). The *Gita* had a profound influence on Gandhi.
Bhakti	Devotion to God as a way of salvation.
Bharat	The name of an ancient king in India, now used as the official, indigenous-language name of independent India. As used by Hindu nationalists, the term or its adjectival form, "*bharatiya*," refers to an India whose essential character derives from Hindu tradition.
Bhoktas	A sub-caste in Bihar, India.
Bhoodan	"Gift of land", the basis of Vinoba Bhave's "mild experiment" with sarvodaya; voluntary gift of land by landowners to the landless
Blockdan	Extension of the *gramdan* idea to block, an administrative unit in the Community Development Programme.
Brahmacharya	Literally, cult of *Brahman* (sacred essence); a vow of celibacy. Taken by Gandhi in 1906 to signify devotion to God, self discipline, and dedication to public service.
Buddhidan	Gift of mental abilities.
Champaran	Name of a village area in Bihar, India.
Charkha	Spinning wheel; a symbol of the Gandhian khadi programme.
Chhatra Sangharsh Samiti	Students Struggle Committee.
Dan	Gift, donation.

Daridranarayan	"Divinity of the poor," a term used by Gandhi and others to support social change.
Devanagari	The Hindi script which Vinoba Bhave advocated as the common script for all Indian languages.
Dharma	Adherence to the Hindu code of morality and duty. Its opposite is *adharma* or immorality.
Dharmashala	Resting place for pilgrims at a sacred site.
Gandhi Samadhi	Place of Gandhi's cremation in Delhi.
Goseva	Cow-service.
Gramdan	Gift of village.
Gramsabha	Village assembly.
Gramsevak	Village worker (often salaried).
Gramswarajya	System of village self-government envisaged by Gandhi.
Gujarat	The province of India where Gandhi was born.
Guru	Spiritual leader or teacher.
Harijan	"People of God (Hari)", name given by Gandhi to people formerly considered untouchable; also the title of his weekly journal after 1933.
Hind Swaraj	*Indian Home Rule*, the title of Gandhi's first book, published in 1909 in South Africa and setting forth the basis of his political thought, especially the connection between Swaraj and satyagraha.
Hindustani Talimi Sangh	All-India Board of Education.
Hindutvavada	Doctrine that India belongs to Hindus.

Jan Sangharsh Samitis	People's struggle committees.
Janata Sarkar	People's government.
Jati	The term used to refer to the highly localized and differentiated endogamous groups within caste system, in India.
Jiva	Individual life; soul.
Jivan-mukta	One who attains liberation or salvation while yet alive on earth.
Karma	The force generated by a person's actions, the ethical consequences of which determine one's destiny in one's next existence.
Karmayoga	"Discipline (*yoga*) of action" set forth in *Gita*. Gandhi interpreted it as a gospel of political and social action, performed in a selfless manner without desire for personal rewards.
Khadi (or *Khaddar*)	Homespun cotton cloth. Gandhi promoted its production (by the spinning wheel) and use as the dress of nationalist movement to symbolize identification with the masses and practice of *swadeshi*.
Kisan	Peasant.
Kushta seva	Service of lepers.
Lok nayak	Leader of the people.
Lok niti	Politics of the people, Vinoba's term for the new politics of truth and love.
Lok Sangharsh Samiti	People's Struggle Committee.
Lok sevak	Servant of the people, sarvodaya worker.
Lok Sevak Sangh	Association of Servants of the People.
Lok shakti	People's power.

Mahatma — "Great (Maha) soul (Atma)." An honorific title bestowed on Gandhi by Rabindranath Tagore.

Maun — Silence.

Moksha — Spiritual liberation in Hindu thought. Gandhi sometimes interpreted it as synonymous with *swaraj* though *moksha* usually did not connote political independence.

Musahar — A sub-caste in Bihar, India.

Nai Talim — Basic education.

Nishkama karma — Selfless, unattached action.

Panchayat — Village council (of five persons); local organ of political administration advocated by Gandhi to form the basic unit of a decentralized system of democracy in an independent India

Panchayat raj — System of rural self-government in India.

Phoenix — The name Gandhi gave to his ashram in Durban.

Purna swaraj — Complete independence.

Ram(a) — Character in Hindu mythology seen as an incarnation of Vishnu; hence also a name of God.

Ramrajya — "Rule of Ram," the Hindu ideal of ancient India's golden age, evoked by Gandhi to mean an ideal society of harmony and justice for all; the rule of God; the kingdom of God.

Rishi — Sage.

Sadhana — Religious self-discipline.

Samaj — Fellowship.

Samanvaya (ashram) — Synthesis (ashram); name given to an ashram in Bihar, India.

Sampattidan — Donation of money, income or wealth.

Sampurna kranti — Total revolution.

Sanatana — Universal, (universalist).

Sarva Seva Sangh — Association for the Service of All.

Sarvodaya Samaj — Society for the Welfare of all.

Sat — Truth, being.

Satya — Truth or truthfulness. Gandhi combined the word with "agraha," thus coining the key word "satyagraha," to mean literally "clinging to the truth".

Satyagraha — Gandhi's method of civil disobedience based on nonviolence. Sometimes translated as "truth force" or "soul force". It includes various forms of political action: individual or mass civil disobedience or fasting for communal harmony, or campaigns for social reform.

Satyagrahi — One who practices the method of satyagraha.

Sevamandir — "Temple of service".

Seva Sangh — Service Society.

Shambhoomela — Gathering of curious and abnormal people.

Shanti Sena — Peace Army.

Statedan — Extension of the gramdan idea to one of the Indian states.

Stri Shakti — Women's power.

Sulabh gramdan — Simplified donation of a village.

Swadeshi — Of the soil; indigenous; name of a movement to promote Indian products and national pride and dignity.

Swadharma	One's own dharma; one's law of being.
Swaraj	Self-determination; self-rule; Gandhi enlarged its meaning to emphasize personal as well as political liberation.
Varna	Social rank or classification, of which there were four in traditional Hindu social theory. Each varna had a specific social function. *Varna* is sometimes translated as "caste," but Gandhi tried to distinguish them arguing that while caste should be abolished, the system of *varna* was in theory consistent with democratic values of freedom and equality and should be preserved as a model of social harmony and cooperation.
Varnashramadharma	Duties of caste and stage in life; used by Gandhi to denote his ideal of a society, with groups having their own occupations but without any sense of rank.
Vaishnava	Hindus giving particular veneration to Vishnu rather than Shiva
Vidyapith	University.
Vishnu	Major Hindu god.
Viswa Hindu Parishad	Worldwide Hindu Organization.
Yajna	Sacrifice. Gandhi used this in a political sense, i.e., *satyagraha* should be offered as a *yajna* in a spirit of sacrifice.
Zamindar	Landlord in the system of land tenure in India under which the landlord was regarded as proprietor on condition of payment of revenue to the state.

Select Bibliography

Books in English

Adams, Robert M., trans. and ed. *Sir Thomas More Utopia: A New Translation Background Criticism*. New York: W.W. Norton & Company Inc. 1975.

Adiseshiah, Malcom S., ed. *Sustainable Development: Its Content, Scope and Prices*. New Delhi: Lancer International, 1990.

Agarwal, S. N., ed. *Sarvodaya: Its Principles And Program*. Ahmedabad: Navajivan Publishing House, 1951.

———. *Relevance of Gandhian Economics*. Ahmedabad: Navajivan Publishing House, 1970.

Alexander, Horace. *India Since Cripps*. Harmondsworth, Middlesex, Eng. Penguin Books, 1944.

———. *Gandhi Through Western Eyes*. Bombay: Asia Publishing House, 1969.

Alves, Rubem A. *Tomorrow's Child; Imagination, Creativity and the Rebirth of Culture*. New York: Harper & Row, 1972.

Ambedkar, B. R. *Mr. Gandhi and the Emancipation of the Untouchables*. Bombay: Thacker & Co., 1943.

Andrews, C. F. *Mahatma Gandhi's Ideas*. London: Allen and Unwin, 1929.

Anjaria, J.J. *An Essay on Gandhian Economics*. Bombay: Vora & Co., 1945.

Appadorai, A. *Indian Political Thinking in the Twentieth Century: An Introductory Survey*. 2nd ed. New Delhi: South Asian Publishing Pvt. Ltd., 1987.

Apter, David E. and James Joll, eds. *Anarchism Today*. New York: Macmillan Press, 1971.

Arokiasamy, S., S.J., and G. Gispert-Sauch, S.J., eds. *Liberation in Asia: Theological Perspectives*. Anand, Gujarat: Gujarat Sahitya Prakash, 1987.

Arora, V. K. *Rammanohar Lohia and Socialism in India*. New Delhi: Deep and Deep Publications, 1984.

Arunachalam, K. *Khadi Economics: A Few Facts*. Madurai: Koodal Publishers, 1974.

Arunachalam, K. *Integrated Rural Development: Rev. Dr. R.K. Keathalm Felicitation Volume*. Madurai: Kodal Publishers, 1977.

———. *On the Frontiers: Strategy for a New Social Order; Essays in Honour of Rev. Dr. Keathalhm*. Madurai: Kodal Publishers, 1977.

Arunachalam, K. and S. Jayapragasam, eds., *The Gandhian Techniques for the Liberation of the Weaker Sections*. Madurai: Sarvodaya Ilakkiya Pannai, 1987.

Ashe, Geoffrey. *Gandhi: A Study in Revolution*. Bombay: Asia Publishing House, 1968.

Asthana, Vandana. *The Politics of Environment: A Profile*. New Delhi: Ashish Publishing House, 1992.

Bahuguna, Sunderlal. *Towards Basic Changes in Land Use*. New Delhi: INTACH, 1989.

Bakker, J. I. (Hans). *Toward a Just Civilization: A Gandhian Perspective on Human Rights and Development*. Toronto: Canadian Scholars' Press Inc, 1993.

Bakshi. S. R. *Gandhi and the Mass Movements*. New Delhi: Atlantic Publishers, 1988.

———. *Jayaprakash Narayan: His Socialistic Ideology*. New Delhi: Anmol Publications, 1992.

Bandyopadhyaya, J. *Gandhi: Theory and Practice: Social Impact and Contemporary Relevance*. Shimla: Indian Institute of Advanced Study, 1969.

Banerjee, Hiranmay. *Experiments in Rural Re-construction*. Calcutta: Visva-Bharati, 1966.

Barik, R. *Politics of the JP Movement*. New Delhi: Radiant Publishers, 1977.

Basham, A. L. *The Wonder That Was India*. London: Fontana Collins, 1971.

Basu, S. K. *Foundations of the Political Philosophy of Sarvodaya*. Delhi: Bliss and Light Publishers, 1984.

Baum, Gregory. *Religion and Alienation: A Theological Reading of Sociology*. New York: Paulist Press, 1975.

———. and Andrew Greely, eds. *The Church as Institution*. New York: Herder and Herder, 1974

Bentley, James. *Between Marx and Christ: the Dialogue in German-Speaking Europe*. London: Verso, 1982.

Bepin Behari. *Gandhian Economic Philosophy*. Bombay: Vora & Co., 1963.

Bergmann, Theodor. *The Development Models of India, the Soviet Union and China: A Comparative Analysis*. Assen, the Netherlands: Van Gorcum & Comp., 1977.

Besant, Annie. *For India's Uplift: Collection of Speeches and Writings on Indian Questions*. 2nd ed. Madras: G.A. Nateson and Co. 1917.

Bharathi, K. S. *The Social Philosophy of Mahatma Gandhi*. New Delhi: Concept Publishing Company, 1991.

Bhargava, B. S., C. R. Bada and V. N. Torgal. *Panchayati Raj System*. New Delhi: Jackson, 1982.

Bhattacharya, Buddhadeva. *The Evolution of the Political Philosophy of Mahatma Gandhi*. Calcutta: Calcutta Book House, 1969.

Bhave, Vinoba, and Jayaprakash Narayan, *Gramadan for Gramswaraj*. Varanasi: Sarva Seva Sangh Prakashan, 1967.

Bhave, Vinoba. *The Intimate and The Ultimate*. Longmead, Shaftesbury, Dorset: Element Books, 1986.

———. *Bhoodan Yajna: Land-gifts Mission*. Ahmedabad: Navajivan Publishing House, 1957.

———. *Random Reflections by Vinoba*. Translated by V. Nargolkar. Varanasi: Sarva Seva Sangh Prakashan, 1971.

———. *Gramdan: Why and How*. Tanjore: Sarvodaya Prachuralaya, 1957.

———. *Democratic Values*. Varanasi: Sarva Seva Sangh Publication, 1962.

Bilpodiwala, Noshir. *The Social Order and Sarvodaya*. Varanasi: Sarva Seva Sangh Prakashan, 1961.

Biswas, S. C., ed. *Gandhi: Theory and Practice, Social Impact and Contemporary Relevance*. Shimla: Indian Institute of Advanced Study, 1969.

Bloch, Ernst. *The Philosophy of the Future*. New York: Herder and Herder, 1970.

———. *The Principle of Hope*. Oxford: Basil Blackwell, 1986.

Bloomfield, Paul. *Imaginary Worlds or the Evolution of Utopia*. London: H. Hamilton, 1932.

Bokare, M. G. *Economic Theory of Sarvodaya*. Varanasi: Sarva Seva Sangh Prakashan, 1985.

Boudurant, Joan V. Conquest of Violence, Princeton: Princeton University Press, 1958.

Bondurant, Joan V. and Margaret W. Fisher. *Indian Approaches to a Socialist Society*. Berkeley: Indian Press Digest, 1956.

Bonino, Jose Miguez. *Doing Theology in a Revolutionary Situation*. Philadelphia: Fortress Press, 1983.

———. *Towards a Christian Political Ethics*. London: SCM, 1983.

Bookchin, Murray. *Toward an Ecological Society*. Montreal: Black Rose Books, 1980.

Breman, J., and Sudipto Mundle, eds. *Rural Transformation in Asia*. New Delhi: Oxford University Press, 1991.

Breton, Denise, and Christopher Largent. *The Soul of Economies: Spiritual Evolution Goes to the Market Place*. Wilmington, Delaware: Idea House Publishing Company, 1991.

Broucker, Jose De. *Don Helder Camara; the Violence of a Peacemaker*. Maryknoll, NY: Orbis Books, 1970.

Brown, Judith M. *Gandhi's Rise to Power*. Cambridge: University Press, 1972.

———. *Gandhi and Civil Disobedience*. London: Cambridge University Press, 1977.

———. *Modern India: The Origins of An Asian Democracy*. Oxford: University Press, 1985.

———. *Gandhi: Prisoner of Hope*. New Haven and London: Yale University Press, 1989.

Buber, M. *Paths in Utopia*. London: Routledge & Kegan Paul, 1949.

Cameron, Kenneth. *Humanity and Society: A World History*. Bloomington, Ind: Indiana University Press, 1973.

Capra, Fritjof. *The Tao of Physics*. Boulder, Colo: Shambhala, 1975.

———. *The Turning Point*. New York: Simon & Schuster, 1982.

Carmody, John. *Ecology and Religion: Towards a New Christian Theology of Nature*. New York: Paulist Press, 1983.

Chakravartty, Gargi. *Gandhi, a Challenge to Communalism: A Study of Gandhi and Hindu-Muslim Problem*. New Delhi: Eastern Books, 1991.

Chanter, A. P., ed. *Tagore and Gandhi Argue*. Lahore: Indian Printing Works, 1945.

Chaudhary, Ramanarayan. *Bapu as I Saw Him*. Ahmedabad: Navajivan Publishing House, 1959.

Chavan, Sheshrao. *India after Mahatma Gandhi*. Aurangabad: Mahatma Gandhi Mission Trust, 1993.

Chopra, Deepak. *Perfect Health*. New York: Harmony Books, 1991.

Chouduri, Manmohan. *Exploring Gandhi*. New Delhi: The Gandhi Peace Foundation, 1989.

Cole, H. S. D., ed. *Thinking about the Future: A Critique of the Limits to Growth*. London: Chatto & Windus for the Sussex University Press, 1973.

Copley, Antony. *Gandhi: Against the Tide*. Oxford and New York: Basil Blackwell Ltd., 1987.

Cox, Harvey. *The Secular City*. New York: Macmillan, 1966.

Dagli, Vadilal, ed. *Khadi and Village Industries in the Indian Economy*. Bombay: Commerce Publications, 1976.

Dalton, Dennis. *Mahatma Gandhi: Nonviolent Power in Action*. New York: Columbia University Press, 1993.

Dantwala, M.L. Gandhism Reconsidered. Bombay, Padma Publications, 1945.

Das, Amritananda. *Foundations of Gandhian Economics*. Bombay: Allied, 1979.

Das Gupta, S. compiled and edited. *Total Revolution: A Symposium*. Calcutta: Naya Prokash, 1978.

Das, Kumar B. *Rural Development through Decentralisation*. New Delhi: Discovery Publishing House, 1990.

Datta, Dhirendra. *The Philosophy of Mahatma Gandhi*. Madison: University of Wisconsin Press, 1961.

Davis, J. C. *Utopia and the Ideal Society*. Cambridge: Cambridge University Press, 1981.

Derrick, Christopher. *The Delicate Creation: Towards a Theology of Environment*. London: Tom Stacey Ltd., 1972.

Desai, Mahadev. *Gandhji in Indian Villages*. Madras: S. Ganesan Press, 1927.

———. *Diary of Mahadev Desai*. Translated from the Gujarati and edited by Valji Govindji Desai. Ahmedabad: Navajivan Publishing House, 1953.

———. *Gospel of Selfless Action* or *The Gita According to Gandhi*. Ahmedabad: Navajivan Publishing House, 1956.

Desai, A. R. *Rural Sociology in India*. Bombay: Popular Prakashan, 1978.

Desai, Chitra. *Sage of Sevagram*. Bombay: Bharat Prakashan, 1952.

Desai, Dinkar. *Primary Education in India*. Bombay: Servants of India Society, 1938.

Deshpande, P. G. *Gandhiana: A Bibliography of Gandhian Literature*. Ahmedabad: Navajivan Publishing House, 1948.

Devadoss, T. S. *Sarvodaya and the Problem of Political Sovereignty*. Madras: University of Madras, 1974.

———. *Mahatma Gandhi*. Madras: University of Madras, 1983.

Devanesan, Chandran. *The Making of the Mahatma*. Bombay: Orient Longmans, 1969.

Dharmadhikari, Dada. *Philosophy of Total Revolution*. Varanasi: Sarva Seva Sangh Prakashan, 1982.

Dhawan, Gopinath. *The Political Philosophy of Mahatma Gandhi*. New Delhi: The Gandhi Peace Foundation, 1990.

Dhiman, O. P. *Gandhian Philosophy: A Critical and Comparative Study*. Ambala Cantt: Indian Publications, 1972.

Diwakar, R. R. *Gandhi, The Spiritual Seeker*. Bombay: Bharatiya Vidya Bhavan, 1964.

———. *Social Virtues in Gandhian Concept of Ahimsa*. Ahmedabad: Gujarat Vidyapith, 1984.

———. *Gandhi is Spirituality in Action*. New Delhi: Gandhi Peace Foundation, 1985.

———. and Mahendra Agrawal, eds. *Vinoba: The Spiritual Revolutionary*. New Delhi: Gandhi Peace Foundation, 1984.

Diwan, Romesh, and Mark Lutz, eds. *Essays in Gandhian Economics*. New Delhi: Gandhi Peace Foundation, 1985.

Doctor, Adi H. *Sarvodaya: A Political and Economic Study*. Bombay: Asia Publishing House, 1967.

———. *Gandhi, India and the World*. Philadelphia: Temple University Press, 1970.

Dogra, Bharat. *Forest, Dams and Survival in Tehri Garhwal*. New Delhi: Avon Printofast, 1992.

Donner, H. W. *Introduction to Utopia*. London: Sidgwick & Jackson, 1945.

Dorr, Donal. *Option for the Poor: A Hundred Years of Vatican Social Teachings*. Maryknoll, New York: Orbis Books, 1983.

Dumont, Louis. *Religion, Politics and History in India: Collected Papers in Indian Sociology*. Paris and the Hague: Mouton Publishers, 1970.

———. *Homo Hierarchicus: An Essay on the Caste System*. Chicago: The University of Chicago Press, 1970.

Dutt, Vishnu. *Gandhi, Nehru and the Challenge*. New Delhi: Abhinav Publications, 1979.

Dutta, D. K. *Social, Moral and Religious Philosophy of Mahatma Gandhi: A Critical Analysis*. New Delhi: Intellectual Book Corner, 1980.

Easwaran, Eknath. *Gandhi the Man*. Petaluma, California: Nilgiri Press, 1978.

———. *The Compassionate Universe: The Power of the Individual to Heal the Environment*. Petaluma, California: Nilgiri Press, 1989.

Elgin, Duane. *Voluntary Simplicity: Toward a Way of Life that is Outwardly Simple, Inwardly Rich*. New York: William Morrow and Company Inc., 1981 (rev. ed., 1993)

———. *Awakening Earth: Exploring the Evolution of Human Culture and Consciousness*. New York: William Morrow and Company Inc., 1993.

Eliav-Feldon, Miriam. *Realistic Utopias: The Ideal Imaginary Societies of the Renaissance, 1516-1630*. Oxford: Clarendon Press, 1982.

Elliot, R. C. *The Shape of Utopia: Studies in a Literary Genre*. Chicago and London: 1970.

Embree, Ainslie T. *Imagining India: Essays on Indian History*. Delhi: Oxford University Press, 1989.

Erikson, Erik H. *Gandhi's Truth: On the Origins of Militant Non-Violence*. London: Faber and Faber, 1970.

Etienne, Gilbert. *India's Changing Rural Scene, 1963-1979*. Delhi: Oxford University Press, 1982.

Eurich, N. *Science in Utopia: A Mighty Design*. Cambridge, Mass.: Harvard University Press, 1967.

Fabella, V., and others, eds. *Asian Christian Spirituality: Reclaiming Traditions*. New York: Orbis Books, 1992.

Faricy, Robert. *Wind and Sea Obey Him: Approaches to a Theology of Nature*. London: SCM Press, 1982.

Feuer, Lewis S. *Ideology and the Ideologists*. New York: Harper & Row, Publishers, 1975.

Fischer, Louis. *The Life of Mahatma Gandhi*. New York: Harper & Brothers, 1950.

———. *Gandhi: His Life and Message for The World*. New York: New American Library, 1954.

———. ed. *The Essential Gandhi: An Anthology: His Life, Work and Ideas*. New York: Random House, 1962.

Fourier, Charles. *Design for Utopia*. New York: Schocken Books, 1971.

Fox, Matthew. Original Blessing, Santa FE, New Mexico: Bear and Company, 1983.

———. *Creation Spirituality*. San Francisco: Harper, 1991.

———. and Brian Swimme. *Manifesto for a Global Civilization*. Santa Fe, N.M: Bear & Co., 1982.

Fox, Richard. G. *Gandhian Utopia: Experiments with Culture*. Boston: Beacon Press, 1989.

Frankel, Boris. *The Post-Industrial Utopians*. Madison: University of Wisconsin Press, 1987.

Freeman, J. B. *Gandhiji in South Africa*. Madras: S. Viswanathan, 1950.

Fromm, Erich. *The Sane Society*. London: Routledge & Kegan Paul, 1963.

———. *The Revolution of Hope*. New York: Harper & Row, 1968.

Galtung, Johan. *The Way is the Goal: Gandhi Today*. Ahmedabad: Gujarat Vidyapith Peace Research Centre, 1992.

Gandhi, Kanakmal. *Sevagram Ashram Pratishthan: Progress Report 1978-83*. Wardha: Samyayoga Mudranalaya Maganwadi, 1983.

Gandhi, M. K. *An Autobiography: The Story of My Experiments with Truth*. Ahmedabad: Navajivan Publishing House, 1983. (First edition 1927).

———. *Hind Swaraj or Indian Home Rule*. Ahmedabad: Navajivan Publishing House, 1938.

———. *Constructive Programme: Its Meaning and Place*. Ahmedabad: Navajivan Publishing House, 1941.

———. *India of My Dreams*. Ahmedabad: Navajivan Publishing House, 1947.

———. *Hindu Dharma*. Ahmedabad: Navajivan Publishing House, 1950.

———. *Sarvodaya: Its Principles and Programme.* Ahmedabad: Navajivan Publishing House, 1951.

———. *Non-Violent Resistance.* Ahmedabad: Navajivan Trust, 1951.

———. *Khadi (Hand-Spun Cloth) Why and How.* Edited by Bharatan Kumarappa. Ahmedabad: Navajivan Publishing House, 1955.

———. *Ashram Observances in Action.* Ahmedabad: Navajivan Publishing House, 1959.

———. *Truth is God.* Ahmedabad: Navajivan Publishing House, 1959.

———. *Birth-Control: The Right Way and The Wrong Way.* Compiled by R. K. Prabhu. Ahmedabad: Navajivan Publishing House, 1959.

———. *The Removal of Untouchability.* Compiled and edited by B. Kumarappa. Ahmedabad: Navajivan Publishing House, 1959.

———. *Discourses on the Gita.* Ahmedabad: Navajivan Publishing House, 1960.

———. *Congress and Its Future.* Compiled by R.K. Prabhu. Ahmedabad: Navajivan Publishing House, 1960.

———. *Village Industries.* Compiled by R.K. Prabhu. Ahmedabad: Navajivan Publishing House, 1960.

———. *My Philosophy of Life.* Bombay: Pearl Publications, 1961.

———. *Village Swaraj.* Compiled by H.M. Vyas. Ahmedabad: Navajivan Publishing House, 1962.

———. *My Picture of Free India.* Compiled and Edited by Anand T. Hingorani. Bombay:Bharatiya Vidya Bhavan, 1965.

———. Socialism of my Conception. Bombay: Bharatiya Vidya Bhavan, 1966.

———. *The Gospel of Swadeshi.* Edited by Anand T. Hingorani. Bombay: Bharatiya Vidya Bhavan, 1967.

———. *Political and National Life and Affairs.* Compiled and edited by V.B. Kher. Ahmedabad: Navajivan Publishing House, 1967.

———. *The Collected Works of Mahatma Gandhi.* Vols. 1-90 to date. New Delhi: Publications Division of the Ministry of Information and Broadcasting, Government of India, 1958-1990.

Gandhi, Rajmohan. *The Good Boatman: A Portrait of Gandhi.* New Delhi: Viking, 1995.

Gangal, Anurag. *New International Economic Order: A Gandhian Perspective.* Delhi: Chanakya Publications, 1985.

Gangrade, K. D. *Gandhian Ideal Development and Social Change*. New Delhi: Northern Book Centre, 1991.

Ganguli, B. *Gandhi's Vision of The Ideal Social Order*. Hyderabad: Andhra Mahila Sabha, 1972.

———. *Gandhi's Social Philosophy*. Delhi: Vikas Publishers, 1973.

Geoghegan, V. *Reason and Eros: The Social Theory of Herbert Marcuse*. London: Pluto Press, 1981.

George, S. K. *Gandhi's Challenge to Christianity*. Ahmedabad: Navajivan Publishing House, 1947.

George, S. K., and G. Ramachandran, eds. *The Economics of Peace: The Cause and the Man*. New Delhi: Peace Publishers, 1992.

Ghose, Sankar. *Political Ideas and Movements in India.* Bombay: Allied Publishers, 1975.

Goodman, Paul. *Utopian Essays and Practical Proposals*. New York: Vintage Books, 1962.

Goodwin, Barbara, and Keith Taylor. *The Politics of Utopia: A Study in Theory and Practice*. London: Hutchinson, 1982.

Gore, Al. *Earth in the Balance: Ecology and the Human Spirit*. Boston: Houghton Mifflin Co., 1992.

Goyal, O. P. *Studies in Modern Indian Political Thought: Gandhi, an Interpretation*. Allahabad: Kitab Mahal Press, 1964.

Green, Martin. *Tolstoy and Gandhi: Men of Peace*. New York: Basic Books, 1983.

Griffiths, Bede. *Return to the Centre.* London: Fount Paperbacks, 1981.

———. *Marriage of East and West*. Glasgow: William Collins and Co. Ltd., 1982.

Gupta, K. M., ed. *Himalaya: Man and Nature*. New Delhi: Lancers Books, 1990.

Haight, Roger. *An Alternative Vision: An Interpretation of Latin American Liberation Theology*. New York: Paulist Press, 1985.

Haring, Bernard. *The Healing Power of Peace and Nonviolence*. England: St. Paul Publications, 1986.

Hirsch, F. *Social Limits of Growth*. Cambridge, Mass: Harvard University Press, 1976.

Holloway, Mark. *Heavens on Earth: Utopian Communities in America, 1680-1880*. London: Turnstile Press, 1951.

Hombergh, Heleen Van Den. *Gender, Environment and Development: A Guide to the Literature*. Utrecht: International Books, 1993.

Horsburgh, H. J. N. *Non-Violence and Aggression: A Study of Gandhi's Moral Equivalent of War*. New York: Oxford University Press, 1968.

Husain, S. Abid. *Gandhiji and Communal Unity*. New Delhi: Orient Longmans, 1969.

———. *The Way of Gandhi and Nehru*. Bombay: Asia Publishing House, 1959.

Indira, Surineni. *Gandhian Doctrine of Trusteeship*. New Delhi: Discovery Publishing House, 1991.

Iswaran, K. *Tradition and Economy in Village India*. London: Routledge & Kegan Paul, 1966.

Iyer, Raghavan N. *The Moral and Political Thought of Mahatma Gandhi*. New York: Oxford University Press, 1973.

———. ed. *The Essential Writings of Mahatma Gandhi*. New Delhi: Oxford University Press, 1991.

Jack, Homer A., ed. *The Gandhi Reader: A Source Book of His Life and Writings*. New York: Grove Press, 1956 (reprint 1989).

Jain, Jagdish Chandra. *Gandhi, the Forgotten Mahatma*. Delhi: Mittal Publications, 1987.

Jain, Pratibha. *Gandhian Ideas, Social Movements and Creativity*. Jaipur: Rawat Publications, 1985.

Jaju, Srikrishnadas. *The Ideology of the Charkha*. Varanasi: Akil Bharat Sarva Seva Sangh Prakashan, 1951.

Jathar, R. V. *Evolution of Panchayat Raj in India*. Dharwar: Institute of Economic Research Publication No.2, 1964.

Jesudasan, Ignatius, S.J. *A Gandhian Theology of Liberation*. Maryknoll, New York: Orbis Books, 1984.

Jha, Shiva Chandra. *Indian Economic Thought: Mahatma Gandhi to Indira Gandhi*. New Delhi: Deep & Deep Publications, 1988.

Jose, P. K. *Foundations of Gandhian Thought*. Calicut: Gandhi Peace Foundation Trust, 1985.

Joshi, Nandini. *Development without Destruction*. Ahmedabad: Navajivan ublishing House, 1992.

Juergensmeyer, Mark. *Fighting Fair: A Nonviolent Strategy for Resolving Everyday Conflicts*. San Francisco: Harper & Row, Publishers, 1986.

Kanter, Rosabeth Moss. *Commitment and Community: Communes and Utopias in Sociological Perspective*. Cambridge, Mass.: Harvard University Press, 1972.

Kantowsky, Detlef. *Sarvodaya, the Other Development*. New Delhi: Vikas, 1980.

Kapur, J.C. *India in the Year 2000*. New Delhi: Publications Division, India International Centre, 1975.

———. *India: an Uncommitted Society*. New Delhi: Vikas Publishing House Pvt. Ltd., 1982.

Karunakaran, K. P. *New Perspectives on Gandhi*. Shimla: Indian Institute of Advanced Study, 1969.

Kateb, George. *Utopia*. New York: Atherton Press, 1971.

———. *Utopia and Its Enemies*. New York: Schocken Books, 1972.

Kaufmann, M. *Utopias*. London: Kegan Paul, 1879.

Kellner, D. *Herbert Marcuse and the Crisis of Marxism*. London: Macmillan, 1984.

Kihlberg, Mats. *The Panchayati Raj of India: Debate in a Developing Country*. New Delhi: Young Asia, 1976.

Koestler, A. *The Lotus and the Robot*. London: Hutchinson, 1966.

Kohler, Anton. *Indian Villages between Traditions and Transformation*. Bern: Peter Lang, 1981.

Korten, David C. *Getting to the 21st Century: Voluntary Action and the Global Agenda*. Connecticut: Kumarian Press, 1990.

Kozhuvanal, Antony. "The Emerging Roman Catholic Theology in India: The Significance of Mahatma Gandhi". Ph.D. diss., Toronto: Toronto School of Theology, 1987.

Kripalani, Jiwantram. *Gandhian Thought*. New Delhi: Gandhi Smarak Nidhi, 1961.

Kumar, Devendra. *Four Faces of Human Progress*. Gandhigram India: Gandhigram Rural Institute, 1985.

———. *Universities and the Community: Outline of a New Response*. Gandhigram, India: Gandhigram Rural Institute, 1989.

———. and J. C. Kumarappa. *Whither Science: Pause and Think*. Wardha, India: Centre of Science for Villages, n.d.

Kumar, Krishan. *Prophecy and Progress: The Sociology of Industrial and Post-Industrial Society*. Harmondsworth: Penguin Books, 1978.

———. *Religion and Utopia*. Canterbury: Centre for the Study of Religion and Society, 1985.

———. *Utopia and Anti-Utopia in Modern Times*. Oxford: Basil Blackwell, 1987.

Kumar, R., ed. *Essays in Gandhian Politics: the Rowalt Satyagraha of 1919*. Oxford: Clarendon Press, 1971.

Kumarappa, J. C. *Public Finance and Our Poverty*. Ahmedabad: Navajivan Publishing House, 1930.

———. *Europe through Gandhian Eye*. Wardha: The All India Village Industries Association, 1948.

———. *The Gandhian Economy and Other Essays*. Wardha: The All India Village Association, 1949.

———. *The Cow in Our Economy*. Varanasi: Akil Bharat Sarva Seva Sangh Prakashan, 1957.

———. *Why the Village Movement?* Kashi: Akhil Bharat Sarva Seva Sangh, 1960.

———. *Economy of Permanence*. Varanasi: Sarva Seva Sangh Prakashan, 1984.

———. *Peace and Prosperity*. Wardha: The All India Village Industries Association, n.d.

———. *Present Economic Situation*. Wardha: The All India Village Industries Association, n.d.

Kuppuswamy, Bangalore. *Population and Society in India*. Bombay: Popular Prakashan, 1975.

———. *Dharma and Society: A Study in Social Values*. Delhi: Macmillan Press, 1977.

Kurien, C. T. *Poverty and Development*. Madras: The Christian Literature Society, 1974.

———. E. R. Prabhakar and S. Gopal, eds. *Economy Society and Development: Essays and Reflections in Honour of Malcom S. Adiseshiah*. New Delhi: Sage Publications, 1991.

Lal, Kumar Sheo, ed. *Gandhiji and Village*. New Delhi: Agricole Publishing Academy 1981.

Lannoy, Richard. The Speaking Tree: A Study of Indian Culture and Society. London: Oxford University Press, 1971.

Lappe, F. M. *Diet for a Small Planet*. Rev. edition, 9th printing. New York: Ballantine Books, 1978.

Larrain, Jorge. *The Concept of Ideology*. Athens: The University of Georgia Press, 1979.

Lasky, M. *Utopia and Revolution*. London: Macmillan, 1976.

Levitas, Ruth. *The Concept of Utopia*. New York: Philip Allan, 1990.

Lewis, M. D., ed. *Gandhi: Maker of Modern India*. Boston: D.C. Heath and Co., 1965.

Linton, Erica. *Fragments of a Vision: A Journey through India's Gramdan Villages*. Varanasi: Sarva Seva Sangh Prakashan, 1971.

Lohia, R. *Marx, Gandhi, and Socialism*. Hyderabad: Nava Hind Publications, 1963.

Luckmann, Thomas. *The Invisible Religion: The Problem of Religion in Modern Society*. New York: The Macmillan Company, 1967.

Macy, Joanna. *Dharma and Development*. West Hardford Conn: Kumarian Press, 1983.

Madan, Gurmukh Ram. *Western Sociologists on Indian Society*. London: Routledge & Kegan Paul, 1979.

———. *India's Social Transformation*. New Delhi: Allied Publishers, 1979.

———. *India's Developing Villages*. Lucknow: Print House, 1983.

———. *Village Development in India: A Sociological Approach*. New Delhi: Allied Publishers, 1983.

Mahadevan. T. K., ed. *Jayaprakash Narayan and the Future of Indian Democracy*. New Delhi: Affiliated East-West Press Pvt. Ltd. 1975.

Mahajan, P. Mani, and K. S. Bharathi. *Foundations of Gandhian Thought*. Nagpur: Dattsons, 1987.

Maine, Henry Sumner. *Village Communities in the East and West*. London: John Murray, 1881.

Majumdar, Haridas. *Mahatma Gandhi: A Peaceful Revolutionary*. London: Charles Scriber's Sons Ltd., 1952.

Mallac, Guy de. *Seven Steps to Global Change: Gandhi's Message for Today*. Madurai: Sarvodaya Ilakkiya Pannai, 1987.

Mallik, Guardial. *Gandhi And Tagore*. Ahmedabad: Navajivan Publishing House, 1961.

Mammen, P. M. *Gandhian Utopia: Its Relevance and Justification*. Calcutta: Minerva Publications, 1988.

Mannheim, K. *Ideology and Utopia: An Introduction to the Sociology of Knowledge*. New York: Harvest Books, 1936.

Mansata, Bharat and Prabhat Menon, eds. *Ecological Visions: Exploring Alternatives for Co-evolution*. Calcutta: Classic Books, 1989.

Manuel, Frank E., ed. *Utopias and Utopian Thought*. London: Souvenir Press, 1973.

Manuel, Frank E. and Fritzie, P. Manuel. *Utopian Thought in the Western World*. Oxford: Basil Blackwell, 1979.

Marcuse, Herbert. *Five Lectures: Psychoanalysis, Politics and Utopia*. Boston: Beacon Press, 1970.

———. *One Dimensional Man: Studies in the Ideology of Advanced Industrial Society*. Boston: Beacon Press, 1972.

Martin, David, ed. *Sociology and Theology: Alliance and Conflict*. Brighton, Sussex: The Harvester Press, 1980.

Masani, Minoo. *JP Mission Partly Accomplished*. Delhi: The Macmillan Company of India Limited, 1977.

Mathur, J. S. *Industrial Civilization and Gandhian Economics*. Allahabad: Pustakayan, 1971.

———. ed. *Non-violence and Social Change*. Ahmedabad: Navajivan Publishing House, 1977.

Mathur, P. N. *Socio-Economic Schism of Indian Polity and Gandhi*. Shillong: North- Eastern Hill University, 1985.

Maureen, Swan. *Gandhi: The South African Experience*. Johannesburg: Raven Press, 1985.

McLaughlin, E. *Ruskin and Gandhi*. Lewisburg, PA: Bucknell University Press, 1974.

McRobie, G. *Small is Possible*. San Francisco: Harper & Row, 1981.

Meadows, Donella, et al. *The Limits to Growth*. New York: Universe Books, 1972.

———. *Beyond the Limits*. Post Mills, Vt.: Chelsea Green Publishing Co., 1992.

Mehta, Vaikunth L. *Decentralised Economic Development*. Bombay: Khadi and Village Industries Commission, 1964.

Mehta, Ved. *Mahatma Gandhi and His Apostles*. London: Andre Deutsch Limited, 1977.

Merton, Thomas. *Gandhi on Non-Violence*. New York: New Directions Publishing Corporation, 1964.

Metz, B. Jahannes. *Theology of the World*. New York: Herder, 1969.

Milbrath, Lester W. *Envisioning a Sustainable Society: Learning our Way out*. Albany, NY: State University of New York Press, 1989.

Misra, D.K., ed. *Gandhi and Social Order*. Delhi: Research Publications in Social Sciences, 1972.

Misra, K.P. and S.C. Gangal, eds. *Gandhi and the Contemporary World: Studies in Peace and War*. New Delhi: Chanakya Publications, 1981.

Misra, R.P., ed. *Gandhian Model of Development and World Peace*. New Delhi: Concept Publishing Company, 1989.

Mittal, Surendra Kumar. *Peasant Uprising and Mahatma Gandhi in North Bihar: a Politico-Economic Study*. Meerut: Anu Prakashan, 1978.

Molnar, Thomas. *Utopia: The Perennial Heresy*. New York: Sheed and Ward, 1972.

Moltmann, J. *Theology of Hope*. London: SCM Press, 1967.

———. *Theology Today*. London: SCM Press, 1988.

———. *God in Creation: An Ecological Doctrine of Creation*. London: SCM Press, 1989.

———. *Man, Christian Anthropology in the Conflicts of the Present*. Philadelphia: Fortress Press, 1974.

Moment, Gairdner B., and Otto F. Kraushaar, eds. *Utopias: The American Experience*. Metuchen, N. J., & London: The Scarecrow Press, Inc. 1980.

More, Thomas. *Utopia*. Harmondsworth: Penguin Books, 1965.

Mudiraj, C. E. *Revive Gandhism and Save Democracy*. Hyderabad: Aurora Printers, 1969.

Mukherjee, Subrata. *Gandhian Thought: Marxist Interpretation*. New Delhi: Deep & Deep Publications, 1991.

Mumford, Lewis. *The Story of Utopia*. New York: The Viking Press, 1968.

———. *The Myth of the Machine: Technique of Human Development*. New York: Harcourt Brace Jovanovich Inc., 1967.

Murphy, Stephen. *Why Gandhi is Relevant in Modern India: A Western Gandhian's Personal Discovery*. New Delhi: The Gandhi Peace Foundation, 1990.

Myrdal, Gunnar. *Asian Drama: An Inquiry into The Poverty of Nations*. 3 vols. New York: Twentieth Century Fund, 1968.

———. *Against The Stream: Critical Essays on Economics*. New York: Pantheon Books, 1973.

Nag, Kalidas. *Tolstoy And Gandhi*. Patna: Pustak Bhandar, 1950.

Nagchaudhuri, B. D., and S. Bhatt. *The Global Environment Movement: A New Hope for Mankind*. New Delhi: Sterling Publishers Private Ltd. 1987.

Naipaul, V. S. *India: A Wounded Civilisation*. New York: Alfred A. Knopf, 1977.

Nair, Kusum. *Blossoms in the Dust: The Human Element in Indian Development*. London: G. Duckworth and Co, 1962.

Namboodiripad, E. M. S. *The Mahatma and the Ism*. New Delhi: People's Publishing House, 1958.

Nanda, B. R. *Mahatma Gandhi: A Biography*. London: Union Books, 1965.

———. *Gandhi and His Critics*. New Delhi: Oxford University Press, 1985.

Narain, Iqbal, and M. V. Mathur, eds. *Seminar on Panchayati Raj, Planning and Democracy, Jaipur, 1964*. London: Asia Publishing House, 1969.

Narain, Jai. *Economic Thought of Mahatma Gandhi*. New Delhi: Sehgal Publishers Service, 1991.

Narayan, Jayaprakash. *Towards a New Society*. New Delhi: The Office for Asian Affairs, 1958.

———. *Socialism, Sarvodaya and Democracy*. London: Asia Publishing House, 1964.

———. *Swaraj for the People*. Varanasi: Sarva Seva Sangh Prakashan, 1977.

———. *Prison Diary 1975*. Bombay: Popular Prakashan, 1977.

———. *Towards Total Revolution*. 4 vols. Bombay: Popular Prakashan, 1978.

Narayan, Shriman. *India Needs Gandhi*. New Delhi: S. Chand & Co. Pvt. Ltd, 1976.

———. *Gandhi The Man and His Thought*. New Delhi: Publications Divisions, Ministry of Information and Broadcasting. Government of India, 1969.

Nargolkar, Vasant. *J P's Crusade for Revolution*. New Delhi: S. Chand, 1975.

Nayar, Kuldip. *India: The Critical Years*. Delhi: Vikas Publishing House, 1971.

Neale, W. C. *Economic Change in Rural India: Land Tenure and Reform in Uttar Pradesh, 1800-1955*. New Haven and London: Yale University Press, 1962.

Negley, G., and J. M. Patrick. *The Quest for Utopias: An Anthology of Imaginary Societies*. Garden City, NY: Doubleday, 1962.

Nehru, Jawaharlal. *Nehru on Gandhi*. New York: John Day Co., 1948.

———. *A Bunch of Old Letters*. Bombay: Asia Publishing House, 1960.

———. *Mahatma Gandhi*. Bombay: Asia Publishing House, 1966.

———. An Autobiography. New Delhi: Oxford University Press, 1982.

Nelson, William, ed. *Twentieth Century Interpretations of Utopia: A Collection of Critical Essays*. New Jersey: Prentice-Hall Inc., 1968.

Nikam, N. A. *Gandhi's Discovery of Religion*. Bombay: Bharatiya Vidya Bhavan, 1963.

Oommen, T.K. *Charisma, Stability and Change: An Analysis of Bhoodan-Gramdan Movement in India*. New Delhi: Thomson Press, 1972.

Orwell, G. *Nineteen Eighty-Four*. Harmondsworth: Penguin, 1954.

Ostergaard, Geoffrey. *Nonviolent Revolution in India*. New Delhi: Gandhi Peace Foundation, 1985.

———. and Melville Currell. *The Gentle Anarchists*. Oxford: Clarendon,1971.

Pandey, B.P. *Gandhi, Sarvodaya and Organisations*. Allahabad, India: Chugh Publications, 1988.

———. ed. *Gandhi and Economic Development*. New Delhi: Radiant Publishers, 1991.

Pantham, Thomas, and Kenneth L. Deutsch. *Political Thought in Modern India*. New Delhi: Sage, 1986.

Parvate, T. V. *Jamnalal Bajaj: A Brief Study of His Life and Character*. Ahmedabad: Navajivan Publishing House, 1962.

Patel, P. Jehangir, and Marjorie Sykes. *Gandhi: His Gift of the Fight*. Rasulia: Friends Rural Centre, 1987.

Patil, V. T., ed. *Studies on Gandhi*. New Delhi: Sterling Publishers, 1983.

———. *New Dimensions and Perspectives in Gandhism*. New Delhi: Inter-India Publications, 1989.

Patwardhan, Appa. *Towards a New Society*. Kashi: Akhil Bharat Sarva Seva Sangh Prakashan, 1959.

———. *Chalanashuddhi or Nature Forging towards Sarvodaya*. Ahmedabad: Navajivan Publishing House, 1967.

Payne, Robert. *Life and Death of Mahatma Gandhi*. London: The Bodley Head, 1969.

Perkins, William L. "*Hind Swaraj: An Analysis of Gandhi's Early Ethical Thought*". M.Th. Thesis., Toronto: Regis College, Toronto School of Theology, 1979.

Pieper, Josef. *Hope and History*. Translated by Richard and Clara Winston. London: Burns & Oats Limited, 1969.

Plath, David W., ed. *Aware of Utopia*. Urbana: University of Illinois Press, 1971.

Plattel, Martin G. *Utopian and Critical Thinking*. Pittsburgh: Duquesne University Press, 1972.

Power, F. Paul. *Gandhi on World Affairs*. London: George Allen & Unwin Ltd., 1961.

Prabhu, R. K. *Truth is God*. Ahmedabad: Navajivan Publishing House, 1955.

———. and U. R. Rao. Compiled and edited. *The Mind of Mahatma Gandhi*, Rev. edition. Ahmedabad: Navajivan Publishing House, 1968.

Pradhan, Benudhar. *The Socialist Thought of Mahatma Gandhi*. Vols. I & II. New Delhi: GDK Publications, 1980.

Prasad, Bimal. *Gandhi, Nehru and JP: Studies in Leadership*. Delhi: Chanakya Publications, 1985.

Prasad K. M. *Sarvodaya of Gandhi*. New Delhi: Raj Hans Publications, 1971.

Prasad, L. G. *Religion, Morality and Politics According to Mahatma Gandhi*. New Delhi: Classical Publishing Company, 1991.

Prasad, Mahadev. *Social Philosophy of Mahatma Gandhi*. Gorakhpur: Vishwavidyalaya Prakashan, 1958.

Prasad, Nageshwar, ed. *Hind Swaraj: A Fresh Look*. New Delhi: Gandhi Peace Foundation, 1985.

———. *JP and Social Change*. New Delhi: Radiant Publishers, 1992.

Prasad, Rajendra. *Constructive Programme: Some Suggestions*. Ahmedabad: Navajivan Publishing House, 1948.

Pyarelal. *Mahatma Gandhi: The Last Phase*, 2 Vols. Ahmedabad: Navajivan Publishing House, 1956, 1958.

———. *Towards New Horizons*. Ahmedabad: Navajivan Publishing House,1959.

———. *Gandhian Techniques in the Modern World*. Ahmedabad: Navajivan Publishing House, 1959.

Radhakrishnan, S. *Mahatma Gandhi: Essays and Reflections on His Life and Work*. Bombay: Jaico Publishing House, 1956.

———. ed. *Mahatma Gandhi: 100 Years*. New Delhi: Gandhi Peace Foundation, 1968.

———. *The Hindu Way of Life*. London: Allen and Unwin, 1961.

Radhakrishnan, N. *Gandhian Perspective of Nation Building for World Peace*. New Delhi: Konark Publishers Pvt. Ltd, 1992.

Raghava Rao, D. V. *Panchayats and Rural Development*. New Delhi: Ashis, 1980.

Raj, Sebasti L. *Total Revolution: The Final Phase of Jayaprakash Narayan's Political Philosophy*. Madras: Satya Nilayam Publications, 1986.

Ram, Suresh. *Vinoba and His Mission*. Kashi: Akhil Bharat Sarva Seva Sangh, 1954.

Ramachandran, G., and T. K. Mahadevan, eds. *Gandhi: His Relevance for Our Times*. New Delhi: Gandhi Peace Foundation, 1967.

———. *Quest For Gandhi*. New Delhi: Gandhi Peace Foundation, 1970.

Raman, T. A. *What Does Gandhi Want*? New York: Oxford University Press, 1942.

Ramana Murti, V. V., ed. *Gandhi: Essential Writings*, New Delhi: Gandhi Peace Foundation, 1970.

Rao, V. K. R. V. *Gandhian Alternative to Western Socialism*. Bombay: Bharatiya Vidya Bhavan, 1970.

Ray, Amitava. *Political Utopianism: Some Philosophical Problems*. Calcutta: Minerva Associates Pvt. Ltd., 1979.

Ray, Ritendra K., ed. *Gandhi and King: Dialogue on Non-Violence*. Toronto: Gandhi and King Conference Committee, 1993.

Ray, Sibnarayan, ed. *Gandhi, India And The World*. Philadelphia: Temple University Press, 1970.

Reynolds, Reginald. *A Quest For Gandhi*. Garden City, N.Y: Doubleday, 1952.

Richter, Peyton E., ed. *Utopias: Social Ideals and Communal Experiments*. Boston: Holbrook Press, 1971.

———. *Utopia/Dystopia?* Cambridge, Mass: Schenkman, 1975.

Ricoeur, Paul. *Lectures on Ideology and Utopia*. New York: Columbia University Press, 1986.

Roberts, Ron E. *The Communes Coming Together in America*. Engelwood Cliffs, N.J.: Prentice-Hall Inc. 1971.

Roszak, Theodore. *The Voice of the Earth: An Exploration of Ecopsychology*. New York: A Touchstone Book published by Simon & Schuster, 1993.

Rothermund, Indira. *The Philosophy of Restraint*. Bombay: Popular Prakashan, 1963.

Roy Choudhary, Pranab Chandra. *Gandhi, The Man*. Mysore: Geetha Book House, 1974.

Roy, Ramashray. *Self and Society: A Study in Gandhian Thought*. New Delhi: Sage Publications, 1985.

Rudolph, Lloyd I., and Suzanne Hoeber Rudolph. *The Modernity of Tradition: Political Development in India*. Chicago: University of Chicago Press, 1967.

———. *Gandhi: The Traditional Roots of Charisma*. Delhi: Orient Longmans, 1987.

Ruskin, John. *Unto This Last*. London: J.M. Dent & Sons Ltd., 1907.

Sacks, Wolfgang, ed. *Global Ecology: A New Arena of Political Conflicts*. Halifax, Nova Scotia: Fernwood Publishing, 1993.

Saiyidain, K.G. *Problems of Educational Reconstruction*. Bombay: Asia Publishing House, 1950

Sarva Seva Sangh. *The Ashram at Sevagram: A Guide for Visitors*. Sevagram: Sarva Seva Sangh, 1968.

———. *Challenge of Poverty: And the Gandhian Answer*. Varanasi: Sarva Seva Sangh Prakashan, 1973.

———. *Industrialisation Through Poverty* or *Poverty Through Industrialisation?* Wardha, Maharashtra: Paramdham Mudranalaya, 1989.

———. *New Economic Relations: The Gandhian Alternative*. Sevagram: Sarva Seva Sangh, 1991.

Saxena, K. S., ed. *Gandhi Centenary Papers*. Bhopal: Council of Oriental Research, 1971.

Schall, V. James. *Liberation Theology in Latin America*. San Francisco: Ignatius Press, 1982.

Schumacher, E. F. *Small is Beautiful, a Study of Economics as if People Mattered*. Great Britain: Blond and Briggs Ltd., 1973.

———. *A Guide for the Perplexed*. San Francisco: Harper & Row, 1977.

Selbourne, David, ed. *In Theory and in Practice: Essays on the Politics of Jayaprakash Narayan*. Delhi: Oxford University Press, 1985.

Sen, Amartya. *On Ethics and Economics*. New York: Basil Blackwell, 1987.

Sen, Mankumar. *Gandhian Way and the Bhoodan Movement*. Varanasi: Sarva Seva Sangh Prakashan, 1964.

Sethi, J.D. *Gandhi Today*. Sahibabad: Vikas Publishing House, 1978.

———. ed. *Trusteeship: The Gandhian Alternative*. New Delhi: Gandhi Peace Foundation, 1986.

Shah, Ghanshyam. *Gandhian Approach to Rural Development: The Valod Experiment*. Delhi: Ajanta Publications, 1983.

Shah, Ghanshyam S. *Protest Movement in two Indian States: A Study of the Gujarat and Bihar Movements*. Delhi: Ajanta Publications, 1977.

Shah, Kantibhai. *Vinoba, Life and Mission: An Introductory Study*. Varanasi: Sarva Seva Sangh Prakashan, 1979.

Shah, Kantilal, ed. *Vinoba on Gandhi*. Translated by J.P. Uniyal. Varanasi: Sarva Seva Sangh Prakashan, 1973.

Sharma, Jagdish Sharan. *Mahatma Gandhi: A Descriptive Bibliography*. Delhi: S.Chand, 1955.

Sharma, S. L., ed. *At the Feet of Mahatma Gandhi*. (n.d). New Delhi: Centenary Souvenir.

Sharp, Gene. *The Politics of Non-Violent Action*. Boston: Porter Sargent Publishers, 1973.

———. *Gandhi as a Political Strategist*. Boston: Porter Sargent Publishers, 1979.

Shepard, Mark. *Gandhi Today: The Story of Mahatma Gandhi's Successors*. Washington: Seven Locks Press Publishers, 1987.

Shi, David. *The Simple Life*. New York: Oxford University Press, 1985.

Shiva, Vandana. *Ecology and the Politics of Survival*. New Delhi: Sage Publications, 1991.

Shiviah, M., et al., *Panchayati Raj: An Analytic Survey*. Hyderabad: National Institute of Community Development, 1976.

Shriman, Narayan. *Principles of Gandhian Planning*. Allahabad: Kitab Mahal, 1960.

———. *Letters from Gandhi, Nehru, Vinoba*. London: Asia Publishing House, 1968.

———. *Relevance of Gandhian Economics*. Ahmedabad: Navajivan Publishing House, 1970.

———. *Towards the Gandhian Plan*. New Delhi: S. Chand, 1978.

———. ed. *Selected Works of Mahatma Gandhi*, Six Volumes. Ahmedabad: Navajivan Publishing House, 1968.

Singh, Avtar. *Leadership Patterns and Village Structure: A Study of Six Indian Villages*. New Delhi: Sterling Publishers, 1973.

Singh, Charan. *India's Economic Policy: The Gandhian Blueprint.* New Delhi: Vikas, 1978.

Singh, Vijai Bahadur. *Development and Social Change in Rural India.* New Delhi: National Book Organisation, 1989.

Singh, Yogendra. *The Panchayati Raj of India.* New Delhi: Young Asia, 1969.

———. *Images of Man: Ideology and Theory in Indian Sociology.* Delhi: Chanakya Publications, 1984.

Sinha, A. *The Social and Political Philosophy of Sarvodaya.* Patna: Janaki Prakashan, 1978.

Sinha, Durganand. *Indian Villages in Transition: a Motivational Analysis.* New Delhi: Associated Publishing House, 1969.

Sinha, M. P., ed. *The Contemporary Relevance of Gandhi.* Bombay: Nachiketa Publishers, 1970.

Sinha, Sasadhar. *Social Thinking of Rabindranath Tagore.* London: Asia Publishing House, 1962.

Sinha, S. N. *Gandhian Philosophy of Sarvodya.* New Delhi: Classical Publishing Company, 1990.

Slater, Gilbert. *Some South Indian Villages.* London: Oxford University Press, 1918.

Sondhi, Madhuri, and Mary M. Walker, eds. *Ecology, Culture and Philosophy: Metaphysical Perspectives from Bausanta Kumar Mallik.* New Delhi: Abhinav Publications, 1988.

Sorel, Georges. *The Illusions of Progress.* Berkeley: University of California Press, 1972.

Spiro, M. E. *Kibbutz: Venture in Utopia.* New York: Schocken Books, 1970.

Spratt, P. *Gandhism: An Analysis.* Madras: The Huxley Press, 1939.

Springs, Eileen, and David, eds. *Ecology and Religion in History.* New York: Harper Torch Books, 1974.

Srinivasa, Inguva. *Gandhi and Development Theory: An Inquiry into the Economic Philosophy of Mahatma Gandhi.* Machilipatnam: I.S. Publishers, 1971.

Srinivas, M. N. *India's Villages.* 2nd rev. ed. Bombay: Asia Publishing House, 1963.

———. *Caste in Modern India and Other Essays.* Bombay: Asia Publishing House, 1964

———. *The Remembered Village.* California: University of California Press, 1976.

———. *The Dominant Caste and Other Essays*. Delhi: Oxford University Press, 1987.

Tagore, Rabindranath. *Mahatma Gandhi*. Calcutta: Visva-Bharati, 1963.

Tandon, Vishwanath. *The Social and Political Philosophy of Sarvodaya after Gandhi*. Varanasi: Sarva Seva Sangh Prakashan, 1965.

———. *Selections From Vinoba*. Varanasi: Sarva Seva Sangh Prakashan, 1981.

Tendulkar, D.G. *Mahatma*. 8 Vols. New Delhi: Publications Division, Ministry of Information and Broadcasting, Revised ed., 1960-1963.

Teselle, Sallie, ed. *The Family, Communes, and Utopian Societies*. New York: Harper Torchbooks, 1972.

Tirtha, N.V. and L.K. Oad. *Philosophy of Sarvodaya and its Educational Implications*. Chandigarh: Mohindra Capital Publishers, 1969.

Thomson, Mark. *Gandhi and His Ashrams*. Bombay: Popular Prakashan, 1993.

Thoreau, D. Henry. *Walden and Civil Disobedience*, New York: Penguin Books, 1968.

Tikekar, Indu. *Integral Revolution: An Analytical Study of Gandian Thought*. Varanasi: Sarva Seva Sangh Prakashan, 1970.

Toffler, Alvin. *Future Shock*. New York: Bantam Books,1971.

———. *The Third Wave*. New York: Bantam Books, 1981.

Tolstoy, Leo. *Tolstoy's Writings on Civil Disobedience and Non-Violence*. New York: Bergman Publishers, 1968.

———. *The Kingdom of God Is within You*. New York: Farrar, Straus & Cudahy, 1961.

Toynbee, Arnold. *Surviving the Future*. New York: Oxford University Press, 1971.

Unnithan, T. K. N. *Gandhi and Free India: A Socio-Economic Study*. Bombay: Vora & Co., 1956.

———. *Tradition of Non-Violence*. New Delhi: Arnold Heineman, India, 1973.

———. *Change Without Violence: Gandhian Theory of Social Change*. Ahmedabad: Gujarat Vidyapith, 1987.

Vakil, A. K. *Gandhi-Ambedkar Dispute*. New Delhi: Ashish Publishing House, 1991.

Varma, V. P. *The Political Philosophy of Mahatma Gandhi and Sarvodaya*. Agra: Lakshmi Narain Agarwal, 1959.

Venkatarangaiya, M. *Gandhiji's Gospel of Satyagraha*. Bombay: Bharatiya Vidya Bhavan, 1966.

Vepa, Ram K. *New Technology: A Gandhian Concept*. New Delhi: Gandhi Book House, 1975.

Verma, Surendra. *Metaphysical Foundation of Mahatma Gandhi's Thought*. New Delhi: Orient Longmans on behalf of Gandhi Peace Foundation, 1970.

Vidyarthi, L.P., et al. *Gandhi And Social Sciences*. New Delhi: Bookhive, 1970.

Viegas, Philip, and Geeta Menon. *The Impact of Environmental Degradation on People*. New Delhi: Indian Social Institute, 1988.

Wadhwa, Madhuri. *Gandhi Between Tradition and Modernity*. New Delhi: Deep & Deep Publications, 1991.

Wagar, Warren. *A Short History of the Future*. Chicago: University of Chicago Press, 1989.

Walsh, Chad. *From Utopia to Nightmares*. London: Geoffrey Bles, 1962.

Webber, Everett. *Escape to Utopia: The Communal Movement in America*. New York: Hastings House, 1959.

Weber, Max. *The Religion of India: The Sociology of Hinduism and Buddhism*. Translated and edited by H.H. Gerth and D. Martindale. Glencoe: The Free Press, 1952.

Weber, Thomas. *Conflict Resolution and Gandhian Ethics*. New Delhi: The Gandhi Peace Foundation, 1991.

Wells, H. G. *A Modern Utopia*. London: Chapman & Hall, Ltd., 1905.

Whitworth, John M. *God's Blueprints: A Sociological Study of Three Utopian Sects*. London: Routledge & Kegan Paul, 1975.

Wilfred, Felix, ed. *Leave the Temple: Indian Paths to Human Liberation*. Maryknoll, New York: Orbis Books, 1992.

Williams, R. *Towards 2000*. London: Chatto & Windus, 1983.

Wilson, Bryan. *Religion in Sociological Perspective*. New York: Oxford University Press, 1982.

Wiser, Charlotte Melina. *Behind Mud Walls*. Berkeley: University of California Press, 1967.

Woodcock, George. *Gandhi.* London: Fontana / Collins, 1972.

Worster, Donald. *Nature's Economy: A History of Ecological Ideas.* Cambridge: Cambridge University Press, 1985.

Young, John. *Post-Environmentalism.* London: Belhaven Press, 1990.

Younger, Paul. *From Ashoka to Rajiv: An Analysis of Indian Political Culture.* Bombay: Popular Prakashan, 1987.

Articles in English

Adiseshiah, Malcolm S. "Gandhi and the Indian Economy Today." *Gandhi Marg* 13 (January-March 1992): 389-403.

Agarwal, Anil. "Politics of Environment." *Gandhi Marg* 8 (June 1986): 137-162.

———. "Gandhi, Ecology, and the Last Person." *Gandhi Marg* 8 (February 1987): 648-664.

Ali, Sadiq. "A Gandhian Approach to Current Problems." *Gandhi Marg* 14 (January-March 1993): 549-558.

Allen, Douglas. "Philosophical Foundations of Gandhi's Legacy, Utopian Experiments, and Peace Struggles." *Gandhi Marg* 16 (July-September 1994): 133-160.

Amaladoss, M. "Ecology and Culture—Some Indian Perspectives." *Jeevadhara* 18 (January 1988): 40-54.

Ambroise, Yvon. "The Ecological Problem in India and its Consequences." *Jeevdhara* 18 (January 1988): 5-22.

Anand, Subhash. "A Prolegomenon to Theologizing in India Today." *Vidyajyoti* 43 (February 1979): 50-58.

Ananthu, T. S. "Gandhi's 'Hind Swaraj': Its Appeal to Me." A document prepared for seminar being organized by Kerala Gandhi Smarak Nidhi, Trivandrum, (August 11 and 12, 1982). (photocopy).

———. "New Trends Around the World." *Gandhi Marg* 11 (October-December 1989): 340-348.

———. "Technology and Ecology: Some Examples of Confluence." *Gandhi Marg* 12 (July-September 1990): 214-222.

———. "The Invisible Tide." *Gandhi Marg* 11 (January-March 1991): 483-491.

Arokiasamy, Soosai. "Sarvodaya through Antyodaya—The liberation of the Poor in the Contextualisation of Morals." *Vidyajyoti* 51 (November 1987): 545-564.

———. "Liberation Ethics of Ecology." *Jeevadhara* 18 (January 1988): 32-39.

———. "Ecological Ethics in a Divided World." *Jeevadhara* 21 (November 1991): 484-498.

Avinashilingam, T. S. "Vivekananda and Gandhi." *Gandhi Marg* 6 (October 1962): 351- 359.

Bahuguna, Sundarlal. "Environment and Development." *Gandhi Marg* 7 (June 1985): 182-185.

Bawa, Vasant K. "Environment and Development—A Gandhian Approach." *The Asian Economic Review* 36 (August 1994): 145-160.

Bhushan, Rama. "Philosophy and Content of Constructive Work in India." *Gandhi Marg* 7 (September 1985): 347-363.

Bilimoria, Purusottama. "Gandhi's Thoughts on Education in the Context of Religion." *Journal of Dharma* 9 (October-November 1984): 353-373.

Chakravartty, Nikhil. "Memories of the First Day of Freedom." *India Abroad* (August 12, 1994): 10.

Charles, K. J. "What is Development?" *Gandhi Marg* 12 (July-September 1990): 177-191.

Charles, Prince of Wales. "Culture and Agriculture." *Science For Villages*, (Nov./Dec./Jan./Feb. 1992): 12-13. (extracted from *Resurgence* (July-August 1991). The annual lecture given by HRH The Prince of Wales, to the Royal Agricultural Society of England).

Chaturvedi, S. N. "The Relevance of the Gandhian Concept of Rural Development." *Gandhi Marg* 12 (July-September 1990): 208-213.

Chauduri, Alok Narayan. "Jayaprakash Narayan: In Quest of Gandhian values." *Gandhi Marg* 7 (June 1985): 156-167.

Chowdhuri, Kunal Roy. "Gandhi's Theory of Sarvodaya Socialism." *Gandhi Marg* (April-June 1993): 62-77.

Coward, Harold. "New Theology on Population, Consumption, and Ecology." *Journal of the American Academy of Religion* 65 (Summer 1997): 259-273.

Dasgupta, Sugata. "Gandhian Constructs for a New Society." *Gandhi Marg* 14 (October 1970): 333-343.

Deshpande, A. S. "Gandhian Social Philosophy." *Gandhi Marg* 14 (January 1970): 25-41.

Dhar, P. L. "Holistic Technology—A Conceptual Framework." *Gandhi Marg* 9 (March 1988): 755-763.

———. "The Gandhian Vision of Technology." *Gandhi Marg* 10 (January 1989): 648-655.

Diwakar, R. R. "Sarvodaya: A Comprehensive Concept." *Gandhi Marg* 8 (June 1986): 173-176.

———. "Gandhi's Spiritual Quest." *Gandhi Marg* 7 (April 1963): 107-112.

———. "A Journey to Sarvodaya." *Gandhi Marg* 7 (July 1985): 197-208.

———. "Gandhian Studies in the Universities." *Gandhi Marg* 11 (October-December 1989): 372-379.

Diwan, Romesh. "Minorities, Development, and Communalism." *Gandhi Marg* 15 (April-June 1993): 5-23.

Fernandes, George. "Ideal Man, Ideal Society." *Gandhi Marg* 13 (October-December 1991): 337-341.

Foley, Grover. "Deep Ecology and Subjectivity." *The Ecologist* 18, 4/5 (1988): 119-124.

Gandhi, Arun. "Gandhi Ashrams - No Gandhian Spirit." *The Illustrated Weekly of India* 97 (1 February 1976): 17-18.

Gangal, Anurag. "Gandhi and the Third World: Quest for Development." *Gandhi Marg* 8 (May 1986): 111-116.

Gangal, S. C. "Mankind and the Environment." *Gandhi Marg* 6 (June 1984): 131-134.

Ghai, S. K. "Gandhi and his Vision of Indian Villages." *Gandhi Marg* 13 (October- December 1991): 357-361.

Goldie, Fay. "Last of the Gandhis in South Africa." *The Illustrated Weekly of India* 92 (3 October 1971): 20-21.

Griffiths, Bede. "Nature, Technology and the New Society." *Jeevadhara* 18 (January 1988): 23-31.

Gupta, Naresh Kumar. "Gandhi and the North-South Confrontation." *Gandhi Marg* 8 (May 1986): 117-127.

Harris, C. Ishwar. "Vinoba Bhave: A Model and Teacher of Renunciation." *Journal of Dharma* 5 (July-September 1980): 291-309.

———. "Sarvodaya in Crisis." *Asian Survey* 27 (September 1987): 1036-1052.

———. "Gandhi and Liberation Theology." *Gandhi Marg* 14 (October-December 1992): 463-476.

Hay, N. Stephen. "Jain Influences on Gandhi's Early Thought." South Asia Series. Centre for South and Southeast Asia Studies, Institute of International Studies, University of California, Berkeley, Reprint No. 959; 29-38.

Hendrick, G. "Gandhi, Indian Opinion and Freedom." *Gandhi Marg* 2 (April 1958): 153- 159.

Heredia, Rudolf C. "Towards an Ecological Consciousness: Religious, Ethical and Spiritual Perspectives." *Vidyajyoti* 55 (September 1991): 489-587.

Hunt, Susan. "The Alternative Economics Movement," *Inter Culture* 22 (Winter 1989): 1-26.

Iyer, Raghavan. "Gandhi on Socialism and Communism." *Gandhi Marg* 7 (October 1985): 393-412.

Janata, Renu. "Environmental Aspects of the Ancient and Modern Indian Culture." *The Asian Economic Review* (August 1994): 276-282.

Jesudasan, I. "Sarvodaya—Gandhi's Critique of the Old Ideas of Economics." *Gandhi Marg* 8 (April 1986): 9-22.

Jeyaraj, Xavier, et al. "Ethical Perspectives on Theology and Ecology." *Vidyajyoti* 57 (April 1993): 222-230.

Joshi, A.Y. "Masanobu Fukuoka's Timely Message." *Gandhi Marg* 10 (August 1988): 311-314.

Kalelkar, S.D. "Thoreau and Gandhi." *Gandhi Marg* 8 (January 1964): 56-61.

Kapur, Sudarshan. "Satygraha and Sarvodaya after Gandhi." *Gandhi Marg* 16 (January-March 1995): 409- 425.

Kateb, George. "Utopias and Utopianism." *International Encyclopedia of the Social Sciences*. The Macmillan Company & The Free Press, 1968, Vol. 16: 267-274.

Kulandai, John. "Basics in Eco-Spirituality." *Vidyajyoti* 56 (September1992): 488-501.

Kumar, Ashok R. "Modern Civilization and Normal Civilization: The Need for Small Self-Sufficient Communities." *Gandhi Marg* 8 (May 1986): 70-92.

Kumar, Devendra. "Labs and Villages—Three Fallacies." *Science For Villages* 70 (July 1983): 1.

———. "Sarvodaya." *Science For Villages* 82 (July 1984):, 1, 12.

———. "Remembering Gandhi." *Science For Villages* 97-98 (October-November 1985): 1, 28.

Lal, Vinay. "Book Reviews." *Gandhi Marg* 17 (July-September 1990): 239.

Mahadevan, T. K. "A Forgotten Alternative." *Gandhi Marg*, 15 (January 1967): 1-5.

Mathai, M. P. "Christian Attitudes and Responses to Ecology." *Gandhi Marg* 17 (July-September 1995): 163-174.

Matthew, K. M. "In Search of Theology of the Environment." *Vidyajyoti* 57 (April 1993): 215-222.

Mehta, Geeta. "Gandhi's Contribution to Indian Culture With Special Reference to Liberation." *Gandhi Marg* 6 (January 1985): 721-729.

Mehta, V. L. "Gandhian Concept of Modern Society." *Gandhi Marg* 7 (January 1963): 26-31.

Metz, J. B. "Creative Hope." *New Theology* No. 5, edited by Martin Marty and Dean Peerman. (London: Macmillan 1969): 130-141.

Mishra, P. N., and Pandit Shailendra. "Environmental Concern: The Missed Issue." *Gandhi Marg* 16 (January-March 1995): 487-490.

Mukalel, Joseph. "Vision of the Future: The Outlook." *Gandhi Marg* 12 (October- December 1990): 336-342.

Mukherji, Partha. "*Gramdan* in Village Berain: Sociological Analysis." *Human Organization* 25 (Spring 1966): 33-41.

Naess, Arne. "Deep Ecology and Ultimate Premises." *The Ecologist* 18, 4/5 (1988): 128-132.

Narayan, Jayaprakash. "Gandhi, Vinoba and The Bhudan Movement." *Gandhi Marg* 4 (January 1960): 28-38.

———. "Gandhi and Social Revolution." *Gandhi Marg* 13 (October 1969): 5-15.

Narayanaswamy, K. S. "Lokaniti or Peoples Polity." *Gandhi Marg* 2 (June 1980): 121-131.

Narayanan, Vasudha. "'One Tree Is Equal to Ten Sons': Hindu Response to the Problems of Ecology, Population, and Consumption." *Journal of the American Academy of Religion* 65 (Summer 1997):291-332.

Natesan, B. "Gandhi and Thoreau." *Gandhi Marg* 2 (July 1958): 218- 222.

Nayar, Kuldip. "Many Questions Still Needing Answers." *India Abroad* (18 December, 1992).

———. "Can Seculaism be Reused in India?". *India Abroad* (1 January 1993).

Nelson, S. "Caste and Untouchability—and Gandhi." *Gandhi Marg* 13 (April 1969): 150-169.

O'Connell, Jospeh T. "Religious Movements and Social Structure: The Case of Chaitanya's Vaisnavas in Bengal". Occasional Paper 4. Shimla: Indian Institute of Advanced Study, 1993.

O'Leary, Basil. "An Approach to the Gandhian Economics." *Gandhi Marg* 2 (June 1980): 132-152.

Palanithurai, G. "Understanding the Process of Development through Natural Theory of Nationalism." *Gandhi Marg* 14 (October-December 1992): 478-488.

Pandey, S. "J.P. Movement in Retrospect." *Gandhi Marg* 17 (January-March 1996): 456-463.

Patil, V. T. "Gandhian Technique for Liberation of the Weaker Sections." *Gandhi Marg* 7 (September 1985): 340-363.

Peritore, Patrick N. "Environmental Attitudes of Indian Elites: Challenging Western Post-modernist Models." *Asian Survey* 33 (August 1993): 804-818.

Pillai, Mary. "Grassroot Movements: Utopian or a Sign of Hope for the 1990s?" *Jeevadhara* 20 (January 1990): 29-41.

Prasad, Nageshwar. "The Meaning of Total Revolution." *Gandhi Marg* 1 (November 1979): 490-505.

Prasad, Siddheshwar. "Towards a Perfect Society." *Gandhi Marg* 14 (July 1970): 289-299.

Pushparajan, A. "Eco-Harmony and Economic Equity: A Vindication of Gandhian Economics." *Journal of Dharma* 18 (October-December 1993): 340-363.

———. "Gandhi's Approach to Women's Liberation." *Journal of Dharma* 13 (January-March 1988): 39-63.

Rai, M. K. "Global Environmental Issues: Three Major Challenges." *Gandhi Marg* 12 (July-September 1992): 387-392.

Raja, R. J. "As It was in the Beginning...: Eco-Spirituality in the Book of Revelation." *Vidyajyoti* 55 (December 1991): 681-697.

———. "Wisdom, Psalms and Environmental Concerns." *Vidyajyoti* 57 (April 1993): 201-214.

Ramachandran, G. "The Gandhian Contribution to Education." *Gandhi Marg* 4 (April 1960): 162-170.

———. "The Slow Rising Tide of Sarvodaya." *Gandhi Marg* 5 (July 1961): 189-192.

Ratna, Anurag. "Relevance of the Gandhian Model of Democracy." *Gandhi Marg* 10 (April 1988): 28-42.

Raza, Moonis. "The Gandhian Paradigm and the Emerging World-View of the Twenty-First Century." *Gandhi Marg* 13 (April-June 1991): 12-24.

Rivett, K. "The Economic Thought of Mahatma Gandhi." *The British Journal of Sociology*, 10 (March-December 1959): 1-13.

Sandhu, Amardeep S. "Gandhi's Mahatmahood in the Context of an Evolutionary and Ecological Ethic. *Gandhi Marg* 13 (January-March 1992): 484-487.

Saran, A.K. "Gandhi and the Concept of Politics: Towards a Normal Civilization." *Gandhi Marg* 1 (February 1980): 675-726.

Schumacher, E.F. "Notes on Indian Development Problems." *Gandhi Marg* 5 (July 1961): 249-253.

Seshachari, Candadai. "Towards Life-Affirming Ecology: Gandhian Approach." *Gandhi Marg* 12 (October-December 1990): 284-294.

Sethi, J.D. "Gandhian Critique of Modern Economic Theory." *Gandhi Marg* 7 (September 1985): 327-339.

Sharma, Mamta. "The Gandhian Approach to India's Development." *Gandhi Marg* 10 (February 1989): 732-736.

Singh, Ram Bhushan. "Economic Thought of Gandhi and Its Relevance." *Gandhi Marg* 9 (November 1987): 477-490.

Singh, Tarlok. "Sarvodaya and Antyodaya as Social Concepts: Implications for India's Future." *Gandhi Marg* 8 (October 1986): 407-414.

Sinha, Rajiv Kumar. "Mahatma Gandhi: The Great Environmentalist and Human Ecologist." *Gandhi Marg* 13 (July-September 1991): 207-209.

Sivaraksa, Sulak. "Buddhism and Development—Is Small Beautiful?" *Gandhi Marg* 2 (June 1980): 765-779.

Skolimowski, Henryk. "Eco-philosophy and Deep Ecology". *The Ecologist* 18, 4/5 (1988): 124-128.

Sohoni, Shrinivasrao S. "Rural Industrialization: The Ideological Background." *Gandhi Marg* 13 (April-June 1991): 61-74.

Sundrani, Dwarko, ed. *Bulletin*, Nos. 39, 40, 41 and 42. Samanway Ashram, Bodhgaya, (May 1989-November 1990).

Suzuki, David. "Re-thinking Sustainable Development." *Toronto Star* (September 17, 1994): E 5.

Sylvan, Richard & David Bennett. "Taoism and Deep Ecology." *The Ecologist* 18, 4/5 (1988): 148-160.

Tandon, Vishwanath. "Present-day Sarvodaya Thinkers and War." *Gandhi Marg* 15 (January 1971): 64-72.

———. "Vinoba as a Child of Indian Renaissance." *Gandhi Marg* 17 (January-March 1996): 423-440.

Tiwari, S. M. "Four Questions on Gandhi's Philosophy: An Attempt to Their Answer." *Gandhi Marg* 13 (July 1969): 205-242.

Tokar, Brian. "Social Ecology, Deep Ecology and the Future of Green Political Thought." *The Ecologist* 18, 4/5 (1988): 132-142.

Tripathi, S. D. "Gandhian Perspectives on Socialism and Social Transformation." *Gandhi Marg* 19 (April 1975): 168-177.

Veeraraj, Anand. "Eco-Spirituality and the Religious Community." *Indian Theological Studies* 28 (June 1991): 132-147.

Verma, S. "The Four Noble Truths of Gandhi's Social Philosophy." *Gandhi Marg* 13 (January 1969): 65 -71.

Wilfred, Felix. "Nature and Human Survival." *Jeevadhara* 18 (January 1988): 54-75.

Wood, Evelyn. "Communications by Neo-Gandhians." *Gandhi Marg* 4 (April 1960): 113-122.

Yamunacharaya, M. "Some Fresh Perspectives on Gandhi." *Gandhi Marg* 2 (April 1967): 261-265.

Books in Malayalam

Bheeman Nair, K. *Marditharkuvendi* (For the Oppressed). Trivandrum: Kerala Gandhi Smaraka Nidhi, 1979.

Damodaran, K. *Indiyaude Atmavu* (The Soul of India). Kumaranalloor: Current Books, 1987.

Deekshith, Gopinadh. *Gandhism Communism*. Translated by N.P. Sukumaran. Trivandrum: Current Books, 1987.

Janardhanan Pillai, K. *Samoohya Viplavam: Sankalpavum Yadhardhyavum* (Social Revolution: Reality and Illusion). Trivandrum: Kerala Gandhi Smaraka Nidhi, 1989.

Krinshnan Nair, K. *Gandhijiyum Aadhunika Dharsanikarum* (Gandhiji and Contemporary Philosophers). Trivandrum: Kerala Gandhi Smaraka Nidhi, 1979.

Kumara Pillai, G., ed. *Saamoohyajeevitham* (Social Life). Gandhian Literature Series, Vol. II. Trivandrum: Kerala Gandhi Smaraka Nidi, 1983.

Kumara Pillai, M. Kainikkara, ed. *Tattvachintayum Matavum* (Philosophy and Religion). Gandhian Literature Series, Vol.VI. Trivandrum: Kerala Gandhi Smaraka Nidhi, 1983.

Lakshamana Panicker, K.S., ed. *Arthasaastram* (Science of Economics). Gandhian Literature Series, Vol.IV. Trivandrum: Kerala Gandhi Smaraka Nidhi, 1983.

Mazundar, Dheerendra. *Bharanamukthamaya Samudayathilekku* (Anarchic Society). Trivandrum: Kerala Gandhi Smaraka Nidhi, 1983.

Shrini, Dr. *Bhaviyude Pratyayasaastram* (The Philosophy of Future). Trivandrum: Kerala Gandhi Smaraka Nidhi, 1983.

Sukumaran Nair, V.K., ed. *Rashtratantram* (Political Life). Gandhian Literature Series, Vol. III. Trivandrum: Kerala Gandhi Smaraka Nidhi, 1983.

Udayabhanu, A.P. *Ramarajyamevide?* (Whither Ramarajya?). Trivandrum: Prabhath Book House, 1989.

Velayudhan Nair, K. *Gandhidarsanam* (Gandhian Vision). Trivandrum: Current Books, 1987.

Name Index

P

R

S

T

U

V

W

Subject Index

R

S